The
International
Golf
Almanack
1995

The
International
Golf
Almanack
1995

Edited by
Ben Clingain

BLANDFORD

A BLANDFORD BOOK

First published in the UK 1994 by Blandford
A Cassell imprint
Cassell plc, Villiers House, 41-47 Strand, London WC2N 5JE

Distributed in Australia by Capricorn Link (Australia) Pty Ltd
2/13 Carrington Road, Castle Hill, NSW 2154

British Library Cataloguing-in-Publication Data.
A catalogue record for this title is available
from the British Library.

ISBN 0 7137 2505 2

Typeset by Midlands Mac
Northampton NN1 1JF
(0604) 232262

Printed and bound in Great Britain

CONTENTS

THE WORLD OF GOLF
News Round up. 7
Cheat.Fact/Fiction? 21
New Courses 27
Women Golfers
and the Voice of Reason 39
The Golf Foundation 42

THE INTERNATIONAL GOLF
ALMANACK AWARDS
A Fantasy Golfing Tour
featuring Lake Nona 46
Colour Gallery of Stars 49
Gary Player. The First Hero 65
Two Men and a Dream 71
Owen McKenna 74

CELEBRITY GOLF
Connery Bonds with Golf 76
From Tee to Jelly 79
Celebrity Golf Handicaps 83
Celebrity Stories 85
Speaker's Corner 87

GOLFING MISCELLANY
Songs For Swinging Golfers 89
Golf at the Movies 91
George Houghton,
a Golf Legend 97
The Rise and Rise of the Golf
Society 101
Royal Golf 107
Just Once in your Life.
A Golfer's Fantasy 109
What's in a Name? 111

Hooked on Golf 115
Golf with a Gallic Flavour 119
Poles Apart 123
Golfing Doctor 124
Golf Women 125
Skegness Mon Amour 127
The Nostalgia Trail 135
A Question of Ethics 137
Parliamentary Golf 141
Golf, the Yankee Clipper and
Marilyn Monroe 143

THE PROFESSIONALS
Year in Review 149
The Masters 152
The US Open 154
British Open 154
The Return of Saint Jude 157
The Ryder Cup 159
The Solheim Cup 179
The Women's Game 181
Renton Laidlaw.
Around the World in 260 days 183
The Clown Prince of Golf,
Noel Hunt 185
A 'Beta' Deal for Golfers 187
Professional Standings 188

WORLDWIDE RESULTS
Professional Results 190
PGA European Qual. School 233
USPGA Qual. School 234
Selected Amateur Results 235

AWARDS NOMINATIONS 1996 240

Acknowledgements.

The Editor wishes to thank the Kent Messenger, the Milton Keynes Citizen and National Golfer for the use of their copyright photographs.
The following contributors have also played a vital role in assembling this first International Golf Almanack:
Chris Plumridge, Richard Baker, John Cook, Malcolm Campbell, Bob Warters, Greg Garber, Glen Greenspan, Kay Houghton, Gary Norman, Jerry Stevens, Eddie McGraw, Paul Instrall, Patrick Armstrong and Alex Morris.

THE WORLD OF GOLF

IT'S BEEN ANOTHER WONDERFUL YEAR FOR THE GAME OF GOLF. The US ended 1993 by keeping the Ryder Cup, brilliantly (some say luckily!) won at Kiawah Island, and retained, under the inspirational leadership of Tom Watson, at the Belfry. There followed a purple patch for the Americans in team golf with the winning of the Dunhill Cup, and the World Cup at Lake Nona. Corey Pavin won the Toyota, but, for all their brilliant team displays, there were only two Americans in the Top Ten of the Sony Rankings by the middle of 1994.

When Greg Norman won the Players Championship early in 1994 in awesome style, the world waited for more of his magic. But it was not to be. Jose-Maria Olazabal won the Masters, and the young South African Ernie Els captured the US Open. For Spain especially it was good news. Seve Ballesteros had his first win in over two years at St. Mellion, and they became the only country outside the United States to provide two winners of the Masters. Colin Montgomerie returned to the top of the European Order of Merit in June and made a brave effort in the heat of Oakmont to force a playoff with Els and American Loren Roberts. But Nick Faldo and Ian Woosnam continued to struggle with their swings and consistency. For women golfers, Laura Davies dominated the Ping Leaderboard and Catrin Nilsmark won her first Major.

Some of the old names continued to play well, despite their years. Jack Nicklaus led the US Open for a while before fading, Tom Watson kept up the challenge till the last day, and the amazing 64-year old Arnold Palmer retired from the US Open on an emotional 18th green at the end of the second day at Oakmont.

But the game belongs to everyone, and it's also been a wonderful year for other golfers throughout the world, young and old. Joe Busse, taking part in the Lawrence Batley over-80's competition, summed up the great game: "Being old has great advantages. If you have a bad round, your memory is so bad you've forgotten all about it before you get to the locker room." So here we summarise some of the other topics in the World of Golf, from records to quirky facts, from amateurs to seniors :

** How wet was it in the winter of 93/94? Some kind of record must have been set by Torquay G.C. which had to be closed for some five weeks due to being waterlogged. Secretary Barry Long measured the rainfall at the course and found a total of 63.8 MILLION GALLONS had fallen from September to January.

** How wet was it in the Peugeot Spanish Open in May? Torrential rain, bunkers flooded and a few short hours play on the second day left only

22 players with complete rounds. Many players quit for medical reasons after the second day and eventually an official amnesty was declared. Anyone who wanted to go home for any reason was excused. The rain in Spain falls mainly anywhere in May, and the 1993 Catalan Open in Barcelona was cut to 54 holes by rain, hail, sleet and even snow.

** Is this a record? Henbury Golf Club, Bristol, has five golfers aged 80 plus, who play three times a week on average. Donald MacBeth (87), Harry Wylie (83), George Prescott (83), Bill Rangecroft (81), and Peter Kirk (81) are the active octogenarians. Can any club beat that?

** This IS a record. Gary Harris broke the Little Aston course record with a sizzling 64 on his way to winning the 1994 Brabazon Trophy. He also collected the Philip Scrutton Jug, the Georges Henriques Salver for the best under-20 player, and a memento for his course record.

** This IS a record. The largest margin of victory in the British Open was 13 strokes, set by Old Tom Morris in 1862.

** This IS a record. The lowest score ever recorded for a round in the British Open is 63. The score is shared by seven players, Mark Hayes (1977), Isao Aoki (1980), Greg Norman (1986), Paul Broadhurst (1990), Jodie Mudd (1991), Nick Faldo (1993) and Payne Stewart (1993).

** Can you believe it? The Lawrence Batley Over-80's competition at Royal Mid-Surrey in June was covered by Sky TV. Amongst the field were two octogenarians holding single-figure handicaps, Tom Galloway (84) from Dunfermline who plays off nine, and Dale Ward from Wildernesse who is 80 and plays off eight. Other over-80's tournaments in the year included Moortown on September 5 and Pannal, near Harrogate, on September 12. Lawrence Batley, himself 82 and still a keen golfer, is a cash and carry magnate who gave his name to the competition and is a member of Fixby, near Huddersfield.

** Can you believe it? Golf buggies are now allowed on the hallowed turf at St Andrews. Shock, horror, disbelief. But rest easy, they won't be allowed on the Old Course. And they're available on only two of the five courses at the home of golf, in an attempt to bring golf to a wider range of players who need to use carts.

** Is this for real? Members of the Rovaniemi Arctic Golf Club in Lapland have turned a frozen river into an 18-hole golf course. Players can now tee off outside their igloo clubhouse, and use fluorescent balls. Temperatures can fall as low as minus 30 degrees Centigrade.

** Is this a record? Husband and wife John and Carolyn Robinson, of the Northumberland Club in High Gosforth Park, had holes in one five days apart at different holes. Not long before, another husband and wife team, George and Joyce Cutting, holed out at the 175 yard 5th a week apart at the same club.

** Is this a record? Paul Morris, a 12-handicapper and captain of Isle of Man club Ramsey, recorded his FOURTH hole in one, all in the space of two years. This time it was at the short third.

** This IS a record! On Friday, May 27, 1994, three golfers made a little piece of golfing history when they all scored holes in one on the same day on the same course, a British record. The Rochford Hundred Golf Club in Essex is entering the feat of Paul Cairns, Paul Francis and Jim Crabb for the Guinness Book of Records. Cairns holed out at the 205 yard 15th, then Francis did the same at the156 yard 7th, followed by Crabb at the 136 yard 11th. The club presented them with a bottle of bubbly each. It is not recorded which one bought the traditional round of drinks afterwards.

** Is this a good idea? The National Hole-In-One Association will provide insurance cover against the cost of someone winning a prize, say a car, offered for a hole in one. If someone gets an ace at the named hole, the company pays for the prize. Minimum premium is £149 and you can contact them on 071-353-4212.

** Is this a good idea? Bill Brampton has opened his own High Street video golf school in Bournemouth. For £15 you can just pop in, have a lesson and take it home on video. Just don't try to watch when Coronation Street is on. Or Eastenders. Or Neighbours. Or Home and Away.

** This IS a record. Ryder Cup player Paul Broadhurst broke the course record with a 66 at the Midlands PGA Pro-Am at Moor Hall in June, 1994

** Is this a coincidence? In May the London Golf Club, the prestigious new course designed by Jack Nicklaus, announced the identity of its new honorary member... Sean Connery. His membership number? HN007. He is, they say, the seventh honorary member, and his number is a pure coincidence. Ha ha.

** Is this a coincidence? The fictional James Bond was a member at Huntercombe, near Henley on Thames. So is the new head of MI6, David Spedding, who plays off 20. Not as much time for golf as they had in the old days, it seems, as Bond played off nine.

** Is this a record? Roy Gregory retired in June after organising Pro-ams for 20 years at Werneth Low. Gregory, 64, is a past captain and president of the Hyde club, and Andrew Murray, Derrick Cooper and Mark Roe were scheduled to turn out for his last event. Noel Hunt also offered to put on a free show at the event where, years ago, he tried out some of his original trick shots.

** Is this a dream? Donald Steel has designed a course for a private client on his own land, exclusively for the use of the owner and his guests. Rumours that he is building the course for Nigel Mansell were denied.

** Is this a tall story? Seve Ballesteros confessed on BBC Radio that the only reason he took up golf was that his home was next to a golf course. "If it had been a bull ring, or a football pitch, things would have been different," he claims. Yes, Seve, if you say so.

** Is this a betting coup? Bookmakers William Hill paid out almost £36000 to an expert sporting punter for a stake of £455, and Ian Woosnam played a crucial role. The guesswork started in August 1993 and the winner picked seven winners from four sports. He bet on Sally Gunnell to win the World Championship women's 400 metres hurdles (9/2 on); Kevin Young to win the men's hurdles at 6/4 on; America to win the Ryder Cup at 5/4 on; Dallas Cowboys to win the Superbowl at 100/30; Glasgow Rangers and Manchester United to win their respective leagues at 5/1 on and 7/4; and Woosnam to win the English Murphy's Open at 10/1. He must have breathed a heavy sigh of relief when Woosnam came through against the odds and provided him with his first winner.

** Was this an omen? Beeline Golf presented the entire Chelsea football team with sets of golf clubs BEFORE the F.A Cup Final in May. They lost 4-0, and we understand they made a "beeline" for the Algarve after the game to lick their wounds.

** Is this a temper? Well-known actor and golf nut Jack Nicholson escaped a heavy fine and a possible six months in gaol after settling out of court with a salesman in Los Angeles in June. Nicholson exploded with rage after he was cut up in traffic, went to the boot of his car where he always keeps his golf clubs, and smashed the windscreen of the salesman's 1969 black Mercedes with a driver. " I never normally use my driver," he told newsman. " I prefer a three-wood, but I was so mad I just lost my head, I was in such a rage." Assault and vandalism charges were dropped after Nicholson apologised and settled out of court. Informed sources in Los Angeles are claiming that the actor has been signed up for a series of commercials by Wilson Firestick, despite heavy competition from Ping Zing and Mizuno. Bob Warters of Fore! Magazine has denied that Nicholson will be writing a column next year. There is strong speculation in the motor trade that Mercedes are now ready to produce a limited edition of head covers, especially for motorists in the L.A area.

** How deep is your pocket? An auction in June at Christies raised almost half a million pounds for the Samaritans. The "Auction of Promises" featured a round with Ryder Cup captain, Bernard Gallacher, two nights at Turnberry with a round of golf as well as a tour of the Prince of Wales' gardens at Highgrove and other prizes.

** How expensive was this round? A party of White House golfers hitched a ride to Holly Hills Country Club in Frederick, Maryland in May. Unfortunately for them, the ride was in President Clinton's helicopter, which costs over $2000 an hour to maintain, and the story of their unauthorised jaunt was broken by the Frederick News-Echo. One of them, David Watkins, the President's Director of Administration, claimed that they were merely scouting out the club, where Clinton had been invited to play. The President, clearly embarrassed, denied the culprits story and promised that they would all pay their own travel costs. Watkins resigned, as did Dick Cellon, the Camp David commanding officer. President Clinton is a self-confessed golf nut, but prefers cars to copters for his jaunts to the golf course.

** How rich is this? Business Age in May revealed its rankings of the 100 richest and the 100 biggest annual earners in British sport. After leader in the counting house, Nigel Mansell, came Nick Faldo with £35 million in overall wealth, Ian Woosnam in fifth place with £14 million, and Sandy Lyle in twelfth with £7 million. Sam Torrance has £4.5 million, Tony Jacklin £4.25 million, Colin Montgomerie £3.6 million and Peter Alliss a paltry £3.5 million. The list of 1993 annual earnings placed Faldo third behind Lennox Lewis and Mansell with £7 million, Woosnam in seventh with £2.2 million and Montgomerie in ninth with £1.9 million.

Ian Woosnam, 7th

Woosnam's wallet was swelled by the announcement in July of a four-year sponsorship deal with Hippo, said to be worth £6 million. Many of those on the list dismissed it as trivial and wildly inaccurate. Alliss was the most forthright. In typical fashion he referred to it as "total bollocks." We can't wait for a repeat next May.

** How far-fetched is this? A woman doctor from Texas is credited with a sizeable role in the US team winning the Ryder Cup at Kiawah Island! Her method was to put the American players in a mental state to fight tension and pressure. United States captain Dave Stockton called in Deborah Graham, a clinical psychologist, and none of the team was spared. Bernhard Langer just missed the historic putt, the rest is history, and Dr Graham's list of clients includes over 100 US Tour golfers.

** How exclusive is this? The Player Club is looking for worldwide membership of over 1000 by the end of 1994. Inspired by Gary Player, this exciting concept offers the opportunity to rub shoulders with the mega rich and famous and play at your own network of exclusive clubs scattered throughout the world. In return for £25000 plus annual subs of £1700 you can play a selection of courses like St Andrews, Valderrama, site of the 1997 Ryder Cup, and championship courses in Mexico, Hawaii, Bali, Japan, Thailand, Malaysia, Ireland and New Zealand. At each location, accommodation and a clubroom is provided without any extra payment. For the U.K. the "home" Player club is Gosford Park, near Edinburgh, where Player is designing a new course within the 2500 acres of woodland. Response so far has been encouraging.

11

** How welcome was this win? Seve Ballesteros ended 26 months in the tournament wilderness when he won the Benson & Hedges International Open at St. Mellion. The flamboyant Ryder Cup star ended over two years of winless self-doubt, heading off Nick Faldo's challenge to claim his 69th professional title. His win astonished the pundits who had written him off after his next-to-last finish in the previous event, the Balearic Open in Majorca. Ballesteros, much relieved after over two years of agony and self-criticism, gave much of the credit to his coach, American Mac O'Grady.

** Is this a hint? Sunningdale teenager Anthony Wall hit his mother on the cheek with a drive at Porters Park, then whacked his father on the elbow at Little Aston. Despite this they think a lot of their son. "He keeps us in stitches," says his mum. Insurance companies, please note.

** Is this a gas? A golf club in Sweden is being sued by a local farmer over the death of a cow. It was grazing near a hole where the out of bounds area was pretty tight. (You all know those holes where you're not allowed to climb over the fence, and the farmer won't throw your ball back, and then supplements his set aside with a tax free windfall of golf balls.) The cow swallowed the balls, died and the vet diagnosed "blocked gaseous transfer", i.e it couldn't pass wind. So now you know the remedy for that little affliction, don't you?

** Is this a statement? John Daly shaved off all his hair after a bad round at the Greater Greensboro Open in April. He then shot an 84 to miss the cut. He then won the Bell South Classic in Atlanta, Georgia, thanks to a second round 64 and a last hole birdie. It was his third US tour championship and, according to him, his first while sober!

** Is this long overdue? Rule changes by the R & A and the USGA will mean more places at the US and British Opens for top European golfers. Automatic places will be offered to the top 15 on the previous year's European Tour. And 15 new exemptions will be introduced, beginning with the 1994 British Open, spread equally between the tours in Europe, USA and Japan.

** The rage of 1993/94, Fantasy Football, Cricket etc, finally came to golf. Golf World and Golf Weekly announced Golf Gold in their July issue. Readers were asked to choose a team of ten professionals from five groups of twenty. If your team won the most money overall, you'll be on your way to Oak Hill in New York for the next Ryder Cup. The only catch? To enter you had to buy a copy of Golf Weekly.

** His Royal Highness the Duke of York has pledged his support to junior golf by agreeing to be the official Patron of the Golf Foundation. At a special charity dinner held in his honour in April, Prince Andrew was presented with a cheque for £15000, donated to the Golf Foundation by Alan Goodenough, Chief Executive of London Clubs International.

** Gary Orr was the Sir Henry Cotton Rookie of the Year for 1993, following in the footsteps of Tony Jacklin, Sandy Lyle, Peter Baker and Nick Faldo. He had six top ten finishes, including third in the BMW and also the Bell's Scottish Open.

** England Boys captain Gary Harris claimed the Brabazon Trophy - the English strokeplay championship - at Little Aston. The 18-year old from Broome Manor, Wiltshire destroyed the rest of the field with a record breaking third round 64, knocking two strokes off the course amateur record set by Paul Downes, and left runner up Warren Bennett six shots behind.

** Leicestershire won the Midlands Schools Championship in June at Sherwood Forest Golf Club. Star performer was talented teenager Robert Duck, a pupil at Oakham School, and a member of Northamptonshire County Golf Club, who shot 148 over two rounds to qualify for the English Schools Championship in the summer at Beau Desert.

** A significant centenary was celebrated in June. J.H.Taylor became the first English professional to win the Open Championship at Royal St. Georges in 1894, the first time the Open had been held outside Scotland. Taylor was a member of the Royal Winchester Club and the club held a week's celebration at the end of June, including a five-club championship - JHT won his first Open using only five clubs -and a match involving all the clubs he was associated with, including Royal North Devon, Royal Wimbledon, Burnham and Berrow and the home club. Taylor was only 23 when he picked up the famous claret jug, and went on to win a further four times and finished second on six occasions.

** Gordon Jeffrey (59) from Southport is the new captain of the Royal & Ancient Golf Club of St. Andrews. The Liverpool solicitor is a six-handicap member of Royal Birkdale, and an ex-captain of the club. He joined the R &A in 1974.

** Catrin Nilsmark isn't superstitious. The Swedish girl, who sank the putt that won the Solheim Cup, got her first title win after six years on the tour and after three second place finishes. The welcome win came at the 13th Ford Ladies Classic at Woburn in April.

Catrin Nilsmark

** Jerry Barber (77) became the first man on the US Tour since Sam Snead in 1979 to shoot his age when he scored 77-71 in the Buick Invitational. He claims to keep fit by walking five miles every morning.

** A new charity golf championship was launched in September. The 105-year-old Macclesfield Golf Club has teamed up with the Rotary Club to launch the first North West Golf Society Championship. Societies were invited to enter a team of four and the success of the competition will be monitored by the organisers with a view to the creation in 1995 of a National Championship for Golf Societies. If you are a golf society secretary interested in competing next year, call Bill Milligan on 0625-427943.

** The Senior Golfers Association was launched in early 1994, to provide golfers over 50 with a package of golfing, insurance and leisure benefits designed especially for them. These include winter golf tours, reduced rates for UK hotel golf and leisure breaks. Further info from SGA on 081-563-7981. At press time, there are 300 members and growing.

John Garner

** Former Ryder Cup player John Garner has been appointed as director of teaching at St Mellion, the venue for the Benson & Hedges International Open. Garner, a professional for 31 years, won the European Matchplay championship in 1972, and is the national coach to Iceland, Wales and the English Ladies European Team championships.

** Ryder Cup player Paul Broadhurst signed to represent the Stratford Oaks Golf Club worldwide in a two year deal. He will be available for six days a year for clinics and games with members.

** Golfers worldwide - and golf clubs too - have been shaken by a lawsuit in the US, especially those who have ever accidentally hit a spectator or fellow player. And all because James Henn was allegedly struck by a colleague in a company golf day at the Rockaway Hunting Club in New York. He sued the club, the head professional and his colleague for damages because of the pain, shock and mental anguish caused by the blow. This shock etc left him unable to carry out his normal duties and pursuits. The club, he claimed, were negligent because they failed to monitor the abilities and actions of those playing the course they are supposed to control. The Manhattan Supreme Court has yet to set a date, but the news of the action has led to ripples of fear throughout the golf world, and is sure to lead to a rash of lawsuits from those struck by fellow golfers as well as closer monitoring of the handicaps of societies and companies.

** A unique training facility is scheduled to open at The Belfry in October 1995. The £5.5 million plan is to build a National Training Academy, enabling the PGA to centralise their training operation, at present split between LIlleshall, Bisham Abbey and Inverclyde. Included is a lecture theatre, seminar rooms, indoor teaching rooms, plus accommodation for up to 72 students.

** Zara Bolton, the former Curtis Cup player, died at the age of 79 at her home in County Antrim. She was the captain of the Great Britain & Ireland team that was victorious in 1956, and played in the 1948 Curtis Cup as well as representing England in 1939, 1949, 1950, 1951, 1955 and 1956. She has been Ladies President of the Royal Portrush Club since 1961 and Life Vice President of the Irish Golfing Union. She had four sons and six grandchildren.

** Ada O'Sullivan of Monkstown won the European Amateur Masters Strokeplay Championship at Sotogrande in style with a come-from-behind win over Marie-Jose Pons. The match went to sudden death, where, amid unbearable tension, Ada won, and is now the proud owner of a yellow Masters jacket.

** Arnold Palmer, who retired from the US Open at Oakmont in June, was awarded the PGA of America's Distinguished Service Award. Palmer missed the cut at Oakmont and retired amid emotional scenes at the eighteenth green at the end of the second day.

** Elaine Bruce won the Midlothian Women's County Championship for the third time in four years, after being down by 4 to Valerie Atchinson after eleven holes in the semi final. She staged a dramatic comeback to win by a hole, then defeated Marion Stavert by the same margin in the final.

** Six time Curtis Cup player Vicki Thomas, now playing in the USA, has been doing well on the American amateur circuit. At the time of writing, Vicki was in 13th place in the rankings. Vicki recently won the Glamorgan Championship in her native Wales, and the South Atlantic Amateur in America, as well as her eighthWelsh Women's Championship in May at Porthcawl. Despite this, the 39-year old was left out of the Curtis Cup team for Chattanooga at the end of July.

** Curtis Cup star Nicola Buxton claimed her fifth consecutive Yorkshire Ladies title at Lindrick, beating 14-year old opponent Rebecca Hudson 4 &3 in the final, and equalled the county record.

** Slaley Hall, the North-East course which went into receivership with debts of over £27 million, has been put on the market at a sale

Nicola Buxton

price of £4 million. For that price, the buyer would get the course, which staged the Northern Electric Seniors event in June, the 140-bed hotel and nine timeshare lodges. The only snag is that the buyer will have to find another £5 million to finish the hotel and other facilities.

** A Bridge Too Far? Hessle Golf Club in Yorkshire celebrates the 20th anniversary of its new site at Raywell in 1995. The club was forced to move in 1971 because its site would have to accommodate the staunchions for the new Humber Bridge. The 6600 yard par 72 course with its tight fairways and guarded greens was designed by Peter Alliss and Dave Thomas.

** English golf began 1994 on a high with many fine individual performances during the closed season. The leading amateur players held national titles on three continents, with David Fisher the Hong Kong Amateur champion, Gary Wolstenholme the Chinese amateur champion, James Healey and Warren Bennett the Spanish and Australian champions respectively. In addition Warren Bennett and Colin Edwards won the Nations Cup, held in conjunction with the Centenary Australian Amateur Championship.

** The R & A Golfers' Handbook, "Five Golfers of the Year" has chosen Greg Norman, Nick Faldo, Nick Price, Bernhard Langer and Trish Johnson as the five best golfers of 1993. The choices were made by Michael Williams of the Daily Telegraph and the editor of the handbook, Ken Schofield, Executive Director of the PGA European Tour, and the Secretary of the R & A, Michael Bonallack.

** Bill Light, the long serving professional at Whitley Bay, retired early in 1994. He was replaced by Gary Shipley, whose father, Newton, is the secretary and treasurer of the Society of Northumberland Golf Captains. Gary was the professional at Rochford Hundred, Essex since 1984.

** Iain Pyman, who so impressed the world of golf with his showing at Sandwich in the 1993 Open, ended his days as an amateur in mid-1994 with victory in the prestigious Hawksworth trophy at Bradford. The 22-year old, enjoying his final competitive play before joining the professional ranks, needed all his talent to hold off the challenge from Gary Harland to win at the second hole of a sudden death play-off. Pyman's pro debut was at the Memorial Tournament at Muirfield Village, Ohio, courtesy of an invite from the great Jack Nicklaus himself.

** Jay Sigel, the American career amateur, turned professional at the age of 50 and joined the US Seniors tour. He won his first ever event as a pro, beating veteran Jim Colbert in a sudden death playoff at the GTE West Classic, picking up his first paycheck of $82,500. Not bad for a first few days at work. He then eased up, winning $25000 in his next two competitions.

** There seems to be some kind of competition going on for the longest hole in Britain. The 17th at Knaresborough is 627 yards, Hever Castle in Kent has one of 644 yards, and Gedney Hill, between Spalding and Wisbech, boasts a 671 yard 2nd, to make it the longest in Europe. Any others?

** Holland has introduced a "Green Card" to prevent congestion on the country's limited number of courses. To get one you have to undergo a three part test, one on written etiquette, a golf technique test and finally a skill test, where you have to play four holes with an examiner. Sound easy? Beware. Over 4000 tried it in 1993 and 78% passed. There's still 22% out there in Holland trying to get ready for a re-test.

** No M'Alliss intended? The unseemly row between Peter Alliss and Nick Faldo, which has simmered for a couple of years, reared its head again in May when Alliss accused Faldo of being boring and unloved. "He's admired, rather like Lester Piggott, but he would like to be loved. He's a hero, but he doesn't fully understand it," Alliss was quoted as telling Fore! Magazine in an interview with Ian Stafford. Ever since Alliss criticised Faldo's swing, and the then World number one sarcastically retorted,"What does he know? He climbs 14 steps to the commentary box and suddenly he's an expert," relations between the two have been slightly "iffy." Alliss resented the implied insult, denying there was any jealousy involved.

Faldo. Unloved?

Alliss' pedigree as a golfer is unquestioned, as is his popularity with the older listeners and watchers of golf. He played in every Ryder Cup competition between 1953 and 1969, except 1955, winning ten, halving five of thirty matches. "I never set out to be hurtful," he claims. "I try to be constructive." But there is an obvious gap between the 63 year old Alliss and superstars like Faldo. The forthright Alliss has been there, done it and he doesn't suffer fools lightly. His comments have not endeared him to some, but he freely admits you can't mix old with young. He cites Faldo's view of older players as those who would "hit half a dozen practice balls, go out and hit a 72, then go back to the bar and hope the next day they'd play better" as ignorant and stupid. At press time there was no obvious healing of the rift, with the generation gap still evident in golf.

** The English Golf Union have issued a new booklet free to all golf society secretaries. Entitled GOLF ETIQUETTE, it has the Tony Jacklin stamp of approval and covers such topics as care of the course, courtesy, dress and general behaviour. It is a very useful quick guide in colour, priced at from 50p per copy for orders of 251 upwards to 90p for orders up to 50. "With 200 new clubs opening in the past three years, and many new converts to the game, it is important for new members to be advised about the rules of etiquette," says Paul Baxter, EGU

Secretary. The main points in the booklet are: DON'T lose your temper, verbally abuse players or officials, or deliberately distract opponents, but DO play without delay, and consider the enjoyment of others. Details from EGU, 1-3 Upper King Street, Leicester LE1 6XF, tel: 0533-553042

** The Royal and Ancient Golf Club of St Andrews has issued a new publication, "The Rules of Amateur Status," designed to help amateur golfers and administrators. It is available for £6 from The R & A, St Andrews, Fife KY16 9JD (£8 outside Europe).

** Geoff Nicholas failed by two strokes in July to qualify for the next elimination stage in his bid to play in the British Open. So did scores of others. But what makes the 32-year old Australian different is that he has only one leg. He was a Thalidomide victim, born with his right leg six inches shorter than his left. At the age of 13, his right leg was amputated below the knee, and he was fitted with an artificial limb. Despite this, he gained his Australian Tour card early in 1994. His ambition is to finish in the Top 100 on the Australasian Tour, which will give him an exemption from the pre-qualifying tournaments, and a better chance of making history and playing in The Open.

** Since 1990, VAT has been charged on golf club subscriptions. Now, according to EU law, such subs should be exempt from tax, and a £50 million windfall for clubs is in the offing, due to the blunder.
This about turn benefits the members of non-profit-making sports clubs registered for VAT, and the refund claims started going in on April 1st, when the new rules came into force. Because golf club subscriptions are so high - average £500 - members in theory are due a refund of over £250 for the past three years. So the average club with 500 members could have a windfall of over £130,000. But it is not clear just where the refunded money will go. Some clubs might spend it on improvements or reduce future subs, rather than give it back to the members.
But some golfers see the issue as crystal clear. "We paid the VAT, therefore the clubs have no legal right to hold on to it," said one irate member from Northamptonshire. That view is shared by many golfers across the country, although some see the compromise view, i.e. a reduction of future subs, as only practical answer to the clubs' dilemma.
The real problem lies in the attitude of the VATman. They say they will refund the money to the body which makes the claim, i.e the golf club. What the club does is a matter for the parties to resolve between themselves. Any golfer who does want a refund is advised to examine his club's constitution. And there's another twist in the tale. Many lady members cannot vote at their club's AGM, so men are deciding what to do with money paid by ladies, and owed to ladies. Rachael Heyhoe Flint, former England women's cricket captain, is a member at South Staffs Golf Club, and intends to take up legal cudgels on her own behalf, and women generally. Expect the row to brew on and on.....

** Joanne Morley, the former Curtis Cup player who had a distinguished amateur career, turned professional this year at the age of 27. She's not superstitious at all. Her first professional appearance in the Ford Ladies Classic at Woburn was marked by an ace at the 13th hole. Presently at number 13 On the Solheim Cup standings, she revealed that she helped finance her career by stacking shelves in Woolworths in her native Manchester. Now that she's a pro, she often models clothes for the Marks and Spencer range.

Joanne Morley

** Sir Bobby Charlton headed a star-studded cast at Mottram Hall for Sir Matt Busby's Charity Golf Day on August 1st. The event, organised by Sandy Busby, son of the late Manchester United supremo, and the Christie Hospital, aimed to raise over £20,000 for cancer research. Ian Botham, Mike Atherton, Jonathan Davies and Dennis Taylor joined many of the Busby Babes who won the 1968 European Cup, including Pat Crerand and Bill Foulkes. Other stars from the entertainment world, including Michael Parkinson and Robert Powell, attended the event.
Mottram Hall also hosted the Norman Wisdom Classic on August 14th, which similarly raised money for the Christie Hospital Appeal.

** Lee James booked his place in the British Open and the 1995 US Masters by winning the Amateur Championship at Nairn with a sizzling victory over Scottish giant Gordon Sherry. The 21-year old from Dorset beat his opponent by 2 &1 over a gruelling 36 hole final.

** Darren Prosser is thinking about heading West to try his luck in America. The 25-year old from the West Midlands has had a career dogged by illness, but is now returning to his best form. He has played in several events in Dallas and Florida and may move there permanently.

** It's official. Joe Higgins IS accident prone. First he mislaid his £3000 winnings at Milan Airport. After the carabinieri had spent three hours searching for the money, Higgins remembered he'd tucked it away in a suitcase. Then a large rat jumped into his car at Turnberry and hid behind the radio. Luckily he found a friendly Jack Russell to sort it out. And just recently at Slaley Hall, he was bending down to put his ball on the tee when a ball struck from 200 yards away by Wayne Stephens hit him on the head. The Canadian-born pro at Pattshull Park now wears a rabbit's foot around his neck!

** Ernest Tupling had never won the Captain's Prize before. But he did it this year at Davyhulme Park at the tender age of 81. Playing off 20, he returned an impressive nett score of 66 and had been trying to win the prize for over 45 years. Another octogenarian, Alan Robinson, 84, took the Captain's Prize at North Shore with a gross 84, nett 66, beating over 100 members in the process. And the much younger Albert Magson, 72, recorded his first ace at the first hole at Sutton Park, Hull, after trying for over 35 years.

** Plans are afoot to bring the Sarazen World Open Championship to Europe. The event, which takes place this year at The Legends course in Atlanta, Georgia in the first week of November, is planned to be held in Europe in 1996, back to the US in 1997, then Japan in 1998. It is open to the past two winners of all national Open championships, as well as the Masters and USPGA.

** Manchester's Heaton Park municipal course is to get a face-lift, thanks to newspaper tycoon and best-selling author Eddie Shah. In a £2 milion deal, Shah's company will improve and operate the course.

** Bill Giles has bagged a few birdies in his life. Now he's got a squirrel to his credit! On the 18th hole at Honiton Golf Club in Devon, he hooked his tee shot into the trees. When he went to look for his ball, out fell a dead squirrel.

** David Bray, vice-captain of Upchurch River Golf Club in Rainham, Kent, had a narrow escape from death recently. During a flash storm, a bolt of lightning leapt from the shaft of his umbrella onto his putter, and he was flung ten feet away. Doctors said later that if his hands hadn't been wet from the rain, the lightning would have gone straight through his heart.

"CHEAT"
SLUR DRIVES GOLFER TO COURT

A comment on one of golf's burning issues by Alex Morris, who has strong views on "Car Heaters" and "Handicap Mechanics".

A piece of legal history was made in April 1994 when a golfer accused of cheating took his accusers to Court. John Buckingham, 57, was accused of cheating during a medal competition at the Sherwood Forest Golf Club in August 1990. Two other members alleged that he kicked his ball into a better lie and twice dropped a ball out of his pocket when in the woods. It was also alleged that he moved his ball after hitting it into a bunker during another game.

Both his accusers wrote letters to the club committee, the charges were considered by the club, and Buckingham, a ten handicapper, was cleared. When the two refused to apologise, the accused sued them. Legal experts are still at a loss to find any legal parallel.

The matter was finally resolved at Nottingham County Court at the end of April after a ten-day trial, when Buckingham lost his libel action against his accusers and faced a legal bill of £250,000. He was comforted somewhat when the jury forewoman said that the outcome could not be interpreted as proof that Buckingham had cheated. The jury, however, did not feel that his accusers had acted maliciously.

David Robertson: Banned

One of his accusers, Reginald Dove said afterwards that the verdicts reaffirmed golf as a game of honesty and integrity. But the reverse is actually true. Recent years have uncovered some fairly spectacular attempts to cheat at the famous old game, the most notorious being Charles Carey of Hanging Tree, Indiana, who regularly chased - and won - prizes in competitions all over the United States. When his clumsy efforts- including kicking the ball on to the green - were uncovered, he was jailed for three months for theft! Johan Tumba, the Swedish professional, altered his card during a qualifying competition for the PGA European Tour and was banned for ten years. This was later reduced to three. The heaviest punishment meted out to a golfer was a £5000 fine and a 20 year ban to David Robertson for alleged "putting irregularities" during qualifying for the 1985 British Open.

There have been four celebrated cases since 1986 of professionals caught "cheating". Sandy Lyle put a piece of sticking plaster over his shiny putter to stop the sun's reflection at a tournament in Morocco, Nick Faldo reported him, although he said nothing to Lyle at the time, and the Scot was disqualified for "changing the character of a club in the middle of a round". Two Spaniards were disqualified in 1986. Manuel Pinero was also fined £1000 for adopting an illegal stance and Antonio Garrido disqualified for incorrectly marking his ball on the greens.

Every golfer knows the story of poor Craig Stadler, who, with his ball in a virtually impossible lie, was forced to play his shot on his knees. As the grass was wet, he put a towel under his knees. A viewer on TV complained, and he was disqualified for "building an illegal stance". Had Stadler merely slipped on his wet suit bottoms he would have had no problem. There is also the classic story of the British professional who was disqualified in a tournament for having fifteen clubs in his bag. The fifteenth club was his son's toy putter that had accidentally slipped down out of sight. No matter about the lack of intent or the perfect innocence of the toy club, he was disqualified. David Feherty escaped the ultimate penalty in Houston recently, but was penalised one stroke for using his hotel room key as a ball marker!

But does cheating really go on? One book, "How to Cheat at Golf" and two videos, one by Canadian actor, Leslie Nielsen of "Airplane" fame, entitled "Bad Golf Made Better", all on sale worldwide, would make you think that the practice is widespread. After all, do you ever see a book on how to cheat at cards, or bowls or cricket? It's hardly possible, although Allan Lamb's accusations of cheating by Pakistan's bowlers were greeted with astonishment at the time, later admitted by no less a person than the ex-captain, Imran Khan. But in golf, some say that the handicap system is continually abused by players who don't play in medals, or hand in their cards. Everyone will also recognise the golfer at his club who plays off 16 or 17, and maintains that handicap religiously, even though in tournaments with prizes at stake he will miraculously score well over forty Stableford points! Yet the same golfer plays in club medals and takes great care to keep his handicap exactly where he wants it. Handicap engineering rules O.K.

I know two such cheats at my club. They always play together like Siamese twins in local tournaments, society days, company days and the like where the prizes are not great, but usually worth winning. Off respective handicaps of 16 and 14, I've seen them score over 40 points every single time in Stableford competitions. Now that's difficult to do consistently, but they do it time after time. And they always do it away from their home course. Yet in their own club medals they shoot around ninety! Unfortunately very few of the members will do other than groan, "Oh no, not those two again!" when they inevitably walk off with the prizes. Challenge them about it and they quote their handicaps. Ask them if they hand in their cards for the tournament they've just won to their home club, and they look at you in disbelief. "If I do that, they'll cut me on general play," they say brazenly. I'm quite sure they don't even feel a twinge of guilt, but they're probably the worst examples of "engineering" that I can relate. They're now well known in local circles, and they're even being referred to as the "handicap mechanics". If only I could persuade them to play in Hanging Tree, Indiana!

And every single reader of this Almanack will know a golfer who finds it impossible to count past six. Some of these are excellent business-men who can read a balance sheet, but have dire memories when it comes to counting golf shots. Many golfers undeniably do cheat even when there are only a few pounds at stake. Others do cheat through sheer ignorance of the rules. Michael Williams, one of the most respected writ-ers on golf in the world, says that there is proba-bly not a single golf club in the world that doesn't have suspicions that their membership includes at least one cheat, maybe more. "Malpractice is so easy, deep in the rough, with

CHECK HIS POCKETS
FOR HOLES

your partners far away on the other side of the fairway. Some cheat because they can't help it, the temptation is irre-sistible." One would like to think that these are swiftly weeded out by the clubs and the word soon gets around. But does it? If you see your opponent drop a ball out of the proverbial hole in his pocket in the rough or the woods, would you challenge him? Would you report him? And once a golfer gets a reputation for cheating, it usually stays with him for the rest of his life. He soon runs out of partners, or one would like to think so. Fore! Magazine recently examined the subject of cheating and broke the "car-heaters" - cheaters - down into six main cate-

WATCH HIM IN
THE WOODS

gories. Dropping an extra ball seems to be the most common method of cheating, so always ask your opponent before you start which ball he's playing. It helps if you also pick his ball out of the hole, or mark it for him on the green now and again, and look to see if he's still playing the same ball. Don't be surprised if it's a different ball, and watch his face when you mention that it's not the same ball he started with! A friend who plays in the Cinncinnati, Ohio, area has a perfect solution when he plays with someone he suspects of cheating. He owns a novelties compa-ny and has a constant supply of PINK golf balls. He offers a free pink ball to the suspect at the

DON'T LET HIM STEAL
A YARD ON THE GREEN

start of the match, knowing it's virtually impossible he'll have another of the same colour in his bag. It works every time, for what golfer can resist a free ball, even a pink one?

Moving the ball in the rough with the toe or a club is another trick exposed by Fore! editor Bob Warters, as is tramping down the rough with the foot to give yourself a better lie. Some golfers caught doing this claim

they thought it was winter rules! So it's a good idea in these wet British Isles, where so many clubs play winter rules from October to June, to state before you play exactly what you're allowed to move and where. Usually you may move a ball under these rules on the fairway only.

As Leslie Nielsen showed in a recent golf video, the fourth method is to replace the ball on the green several inches ahead of the marker. The most outrageous cheat will toss a coin onto the green as he approaches the ball, then pretend to mark the original ball, but picking up the marker and ball in the same motion. The final two ways are by playing to a false handicap - the "handi-

WATCH THE 'VELCRO'
TRICK ON THE TEE

cap mechanics" referred to above and, most obvious of all, altering the scorecard. According to Bob Warters, you can spot the former because they all have high handicaps, ranging from 16-21, carry both a one and two-iron, have three wedges and play only for high stakes and in big prize-money events! They usually play as regular partners and always finish in the top three, except on their own course. The latter shouldn't be a problem if the marker gets the scores hole by hole and doesn't leave it three or four holes before asking for scores, as even the best memory can be faulty.

There are other ways of cheating not spotted by Fore! magazine. These

WATCH OUT FOR THAT
'FOUND' BALL

are the psychological methods practiced by only the most experienced, and ex-cricketers. Sledging is accepted by cricketers as pretty normal, and it can be effective on the golf course too. "Watch the trees on the left and the lake on the right" may be totally innocent, or an attempt to put you off. If you're on a strange course and your opponent is above suspicion, it's an attempt to help. If you know the course well, it's cricket's version of sledging. Swing your driver close to his nose a few times and he'll get the message. If he carries on, here's how to get your own back, using innocent Velcro as a weapon. He's on the tee. As he starts his backswing, remove your

DON'T LET HIM TRAMP
DOWN THE ROUGH

glove. Velcro is loud, very noisy indeed. Apologise profusely if his drive goes into the trees he's just mentioned. Then show him you're on his case. As he starts that crucial six foot putt, take off your glove again. At the next tee, make a big show of putting ON your glove. This time, as he starts his backswing, do nothing. He'll be a psychological wreck by the time you finish. But more importantly, he'll have stopped sledging and you can get on with your game in peace. But beware, only do this to known cheats.

And yet it is staggering just how totally honest golfers can be, although Bobby Jones, on being praised for not cheating, said, "You might as well praise a man for not robbing a bank". A few months ago I was playing in the summer league against a golfer of slightly better standard. It was a close game, a see-saw affair and level at the second-last. We came to the par five green, both in three, I thought. His tee shot had been long, but had gone to the left, over the dunes onto an adjoining fairway, and out of sight.

"I've had four," he muttered gloomily, "bad lie, tried to dig it out and ballooned it." He had been totally out of my sight, there was nobody on the other fairway and I hadn't seen his duffed shot. One would optimistically like to think the vast majority of golfers would make the same admission. But would they? In the 1971 British Open at Birkdale, Arnold Palmer was addressing the ball in a bunker when it moved. He immediately called a penalty on himself even though the thousands watching could not possibly have seen. He still won, but a man like that had to own up, he couldn't have lived with himself if he hadn't admitted the stroke.

Today cynics say that even golf reflects the kind of society we live in, so there must be a certain amount of lying, cheating and deception. A few months ago, David Watkins, a White House staffer and a lifelong friend of US President Bill Clinton, borrowed the Presidential helicopter to take some friends to a nearby golf course. When he was challenged about misuse of official transport, he claimed that he was only using it to scout a new course for the President. The White House denied that story and Watkins resigned. As Jaime Diaz of the New York Times said, "If he lies about how he got to the course, how could you believe him when he said he shot 80?"

Lying, sadly, pervades our whole society, as shown by recent examples of the 14-year old cricketer who picked at the seam of a cricket ball to make it swing, and the 24 Annapolis naval cadets who were accused of cheating in their final exams, so we shouldn't be surprised to find it on the increase in the world of golf. Most golfers would rightly say that cheats are only cheating themselves. For writers as respected as Williams and Warters to concede that every club has at least one car-heater is extremely disturbing. But it is also a deeply sensitive issue and John Buckingham was quite willing to spend £250,000 in an attempt to clear his name, so serious did he regard the slur on his character. What is truly astonishing is that the whole sick affair took four years to sort out, made a tidy little fortune for lawyers, and did little for the good name of golf.

"I SUPPOSE IT'S NO USE EXPECTING
YOU CHAPS TO KEEP YOUR MOUTHS SHUT"

NEW COURSES
AND DEVELOPMENTS

Since the spring of 1993, there are an astonishing 272 new golf courses, or extensions to existing ones, which have opened, or are planned to open, with more in the pipeline as you read this. Of these, 239 are in England, Wales and Scotland, 33 in Ireland. By far the greater proportion are in England (215), and of the total, 8 are in Scotland, 11 in Wales.

The most active area for new development is Kent, with 20, including the Faldo-designed Chart Hills at Biddenden which opened last autumn and three by the Barrelfield Golf Network at Maidstone, Ashford and Malling Heath. The opening dates of the Neil Coles development at Cowden and the Peter McEvoy design at Rotherfield have still to be decided. Surrey with 15 new courses planned is the second most active, and here Peter Alliss and Clive Clark have designed four courses, Barrelfield Golf Network two, while the Robert Trent Jones design at Ottershaw has not yet announced a date. Third on the most active list is Sussex with 14, four of which are by David Williams, and Essex with 14, of which three are by Reg Plumbridge, two at Brentwood and one at Chelmsford, and four by Howard Swan. These include The Village Club at Willingdale, designed as a beginners course.

Bottom of the active list is Tyne and Wear with two, a surprising Middlesex with two, Bedfordshire and a no-surprise Merseyside, each with one. Of these new courses, 68 are in Kent, Surrey, Sussex, Essex and Berkshire, a staggering 31 percent. And in Ireland, of the 33 new courses planned and already open since 1993, only three are in Northern Ireland. Ten of the new courses in the Republic of Ireland are the work of Arthur Spring, eight by Craddock and Ruddy and five have the stamp of both Christy O'Connors on them.

A list of New Developments follows after the News Round up. We are grateful to Vince Davies of the Acornbridge Golf Consultancy (Tel: 0480-411228) for the update.

NEW COURSE NEWS

** Yorkshire has a new course at Willow Valley, Clifton, the first in the Halifax, Huddersfield and Spen valley area to be dedicated solely to pay and play, designed by local businessman John Newton and his wife.

** The Carnegie Links at Skiboo in Scotland is the first links course to be built in Britain for a few decades. A Donald Steel design at the home of Peter de Savary, the construction is by Brian Pierson, one of the country's leading course builders.

** Guernsey now has a new 18-hole course at La Grande Mare Golf and Country Club on the island's west coast. The par 66 course opened at Easter, a resident professional has been appointed, and a new clubhouse is under construction.

** Golfers heading for Blackpool last summer had a new course to play. Heron's Reach, an 18 hole par 72 was designed by Peter Alliss and Clive Clark, and is owned by the Blackpool Village and Leisure Hotel, part of the Boddingtons Group. Ten man-made lakes on the 216 acre course make it a challenge, and there is also an 18-bay floodlit driving range.

** Mulligans Golf Centre in Bromley, Kent, designed by Martin Gillett, is nearing completion and features a magnificent driving range, a par three course and an aptly named "adventure" course.

** The new Chalfont Park Golf Club in Bucks opened nine of its proposed eighteen holes in June. The main clubhouse is well under way and the second nine will open in 1996.

** Lanhydrock G.C, near Bodmin, Cornwall, has a new clubhouse which opened at Easter. The course has had a checkered career since opening in 1991, falling into the hands of the receiver a few months later. It is now owned by the Bond family, who also own the clubs at St Mellion and Looe and they have embarked on an ambitious improvement programme.

** The Leeds Golf centre opened its doors in late 1993 in 150 acres of rolling countryside in the pretty village of Wike, a short drive from Leeds city centre. As well as the 6780 yard Wike Ridge course, the complex has a par 3 Oaks course, an 18-bay all-weather floodlit driving range and hosts the only David Leadbetter Golf Academy in the country.

** Work on the first new course in the Blairgowrie area of Scotland since Alyth was founded in 1894 has started. Designed by John Salveson, the new Strathmore Golf Centre is the brainchild of golf mad farmer Pat Barron. Situated in 150 acres of rolling countryside, the course will be 6500 yards par 72, and will open in early 1997.

** Burgham Park Golf and Country Club opened in May with 27 holes on 235 acres. Seven miles north of Morpeth off the A1. Membership fees are £100 a year plus £5 a round, or life membership of £2000, and Ryder Cup player Mark James, a director, plans to open a School of Excellence at the club.

** Michael Bonallack, secretary of the R &A, officially opened England's largest new golf facility at Leek Wootton earlier in the year. The Warwickshire has 36 championship holes spread over 450 acres, a teaching academy, a par three course and a purpose-built clubhouse. It is American Karl Litten's first venture in Britain and the man who created the "miracle in the desert" when he built the Emirates course in Dubai has created another masterpiece, according to Golf Fund UK, who built the complex.

** Chartridge Golf Club opened near Chesham in May, providing another 18 holes in London's commuter belt. Ladies and gentlemen are offered the same membership terms, and a policy of sexual equality ensures that all members have an equal status within the club. The course was designed by John Jacobs and is located in the Pednor Valley.

** The grounds of the Clandeboye estate, the Blackwood family seat of the late Marquis of Dufferin and Ava, are the setting for the new North Down Golf Course. Partly funded by the N.I. Tourist Development Scheme, it is located close to Belfast City Airport, will have a 43-bed three star hotel and two 18 hole courses, one of championship standard, the other a par 3 when it opens in late 1994.

** The former M.P for Scarborough, Sir Michael Shaw, is the chairman of the new Waterton Park Golf Club, scheduled to open for play in September 1995. The course was designed with the help of Gordon J. Brand, and memberships will be restricted to investors holding shares in Waterton park plc.

** Northop Country Park in Clywd opened in June, and Wales' newest championship course has agreed to sponsor the Welsh Ladies National team. The Welsh senior, under 21 and girls squads will use Northop as their training base. David LLewellyn, who teamed up with Ian Woosnam for their World Cup victory in 1987, is the club's head professional. Current Welsh Amateur champion Andrea Donne has been appointed as trainee professional.

** Frome Golf Centre in Somerset entered a new era this year when it became an 18 hole course, from an initial nine. The new course will be 4,000 yards, par 62, aimed at the golf society and the pay as you play customer. Owners Peter and Dennis Austin designed the course themselves.

** Forest Park, near York, has been extended to 27 holes with the official opening of the Old Foss course. With Moor Allerton and Malton & Norton, it becomes only the third 27-hole development in all of Yorkshire.

** Sweetwoods Park, Cowden, near Edenbridge on the Kent/Sussex border, opened its gates to golfers in spring. It is an 18 hole, 6495 yard par 72, based on a design by Neil Coles. Membership ranges from £95 plus £10 per round on weekdays to £495 for full membership.

** Pont Royal Golf Club, situated between Avignon and Aix-en-Provence in France, was designed and officially opened by Seve Ballesteros. It is a

British backed residential development by London & Metropolitan, and features Provencal homes forming three villages. A further nine holes are planned next year. The club signed an exclusive sponsorship agreement with French professional Marie Laure de Lorenzi who is aiming to qualify for the Solheim Cup.

** Kilworth Springs Golf Club celebrated its first birthday in August 1994, a course that was created out of a gravel pit site and featuring four lakes. See Awards Section later in the Almanack, entitled "Two Men and a Dream."

** The Isle of Man's prestigious new country club opened its doors in June 1994. Set in over 200 acres at Santon, the 18 hole development cost £25 million and brings the total courses on the island to eight.

** The Ryton Club at Clara Vale, Tyne and Wear, celebrated the opening in the summer of their new clubhouse. The official opening was by S.P.H. Cookson, President of the English Golf Union on September 24, and the club had marked the occasion earlier with a Gala week of golf in July with competitions every day and a Members Gala Day on July 30.

** Horncastle Golf Club added a new 9-hole course to their present 18 in April. It's a par 3 pay as you play. At only £2.50 for a round, it's a snip.

** Alnwick in Northumberland is being extended to 18 holes. The original nine were designed in 1907 by George Rochester, and the new layout has been the work of Alastair Ree. The extended course should be ready by next Spring.

** PGA European Tour Courses (IMG) Ltd has become the joint owner of Kungsangen Golf Course in Stockholm. The course, halfway between the city centre and Arlanda airport, has 36 holes and was designed by Andres Forsbrand. It also has a driving range and clubhouse, and has a membership of 1500. Kungsangen joins Collingtree Park and Stockley Park, already owned by the joint venture, which was set up to develop a circuit of high quality courses suitable for tournament play throughout Europe.

A guide to courses under construction or redevelopment in the U.K. and Ireland

Club	Location	Holes	Opening	Designer

ENGLAND

Avon

Club	Location	Holes	Opening	Designer
Farrington	Nr. Bristol	27	August 1993	J Gaunt/P Thompson
The Kendleshire	Bristol	18	1995	Adrian Stiff
St. Swithins	Bristol	18	Spring 1995	MRM Leisure
West Bristol	Bristol	27	TBA	P Alliss/C Clark
West Country Golf	Nr Bristol	9	Summer 1994	Andrew Sutcliffe

Bedfordshire

Chalgrave Manor	Luton	18	Spring 1994	Various

Berkshire

Blue Mountain	Bracknell	18	April 1993	Luff Group
Castle Royle	Knowl Hill	18	Spring 1994	Neil Coles
Donnington	Newbury	18	Summer 1993	Dave Thomas
Newbury Racecourse	Newbury	12	Autumn 1994	M Smith/Green Eagle Golf
Sandmartins	Wokingham	18	May 1993	Edward T Fox

Buckinghamshire

Chalfont Park	Chalfont St Giles	9	Spring 1994	Jonathan Gaunt
Chartridge Park	Chesham	9	May 1994	J Jacobs Golf Assoc
Harleyford	Marlow	18	1996	Donald Steel
Hartwell Estate	Aylesbury	18	Spring 1995	Hawtree
Kingfisher Club	Deanshanger	9	March 1994	Grebe Associates
Magnolia Park	Nr Oxford	18	1995	Jonathan Gaunt

Cambridgeshire

Cambridge Meridian	Nr Cambridge	18	March 1994	P Alliss/C Clark
Comberton	Nr Cambridge	18	1994	P Alliss/C Clark
Elton Furze	Nr Peterborough	18	April 1993	R Fitton
Haydon Grange	Nr Royston	27	Spring 1994	Derek Young
Longstanton	Nr Cambridge	9	Autumn 1994	T Clayton
Malton	Nr Cambridge	18	Spring 1994	Bruce Critchley
Thorney Golf Centre	Nr Peterborough	18	June 1994	Angus Dow
West Wratting	Nr Cambridge	36	April 1995	John Jacobs Assoc

Cheshire

Ashlea Grange	Lymm	18	TBA	Steve Marnoch
Carden Park	Nr Wrexham	18	August 1993	Alan Higgins
Eaton Park	Cheshire	18	Summer 1993	Donald Steel

Macclesfield	Macclesfield	18	1993	Hawtree
Marton	Nr Congleton	9	1995	Neville Pearson-ADAS
Mollington Grange	Chester	18	Autumn 1995	C&L Consultants
Styal	Styal	18	1995	Steve Marnoch
Weston Hall	Crewe	18	1995	Dave Thomas (Sth)
Weston Hall	Crewe	18	1995	PGA European Tour (Nth)

Clevland
Hunley Hall	Brotton	18	June 1993	John Morgan
Wynyard Hall	Cleveland	36	1995	Hawtree

Cornwall
Merlin	Mawgan Porth	18	1993	Ross Oliver
Roserror	St Minver	18	Spring 1995	Handmade Designs
Trethorn	Launceston	9	May 1993	Adrian Stiff

Derbyshire
Carsington Water	Ashbourne	9	July 1994	John Ludlow
Grassmoor	Chesterfield	18	Spring 1993	Golf Consultancy
Morley Hayes	Heanor	18	Spring 1993	Ray Baldwin
Barlborough Links	Derby	18	Summer 1995	

Devon
Dainton Park	Newton Abbott	18	May 1993	Adrian Stiff
Occombe	Torquay	27	1995	Donald Steel
Sparkwell	Plymouth	9	August 1993	John Gabb Associates

Dorset
Ashley Wood	Blandford Forum	9	Spring 1994	Patrick Tallack
Hyde House	Wareham	27	1993	J Hamilton Stutt
Christchurch	Christchurch	18	Summer 1994	Patrick Tallack
Knighton	Wimbourn	9	Autumn 1994	Howard Swan
Mid Dorset	Nr Blandford	9	Spring 1993	David Astle

Durham
Hall Garth Hotel	Darlington	9	May 1994	Bryan Moore
Ramside Hall Hotel	Durham	27	Autumn 1995	Jonathan Gaunt
Redworth Hall	Newton Aycliffe	18	Spring 1995	Golf Design & Mgnt

East Yorkshire
The Links	Bridlington	27	May 1993	Howard Swan

Essex
Belsteads	Chelmsford	9	Spring 1994	Howard Swan
Bournes Green	Southend	18	1995	Patrick Tallack
Burnham on Crouch	Burnham	9	1993	Howard Swan
Cranham Court	Upminster	18	1994	Howard Swan
Crondon Park	Stock	18	1994	Martin Gillett
Epping Forest	Chigwell	18	Spring 1994	Neil Coles
Highlands Park	Chelmsford	27	Summer 1994	Reg Plumbridge
Langdon Hills	Basildon	9	Summer 1993	MRM Leisure
North Weald	Nr Harlow	18	TBA	P Alliss/C Clark

St Cleres	Stanford Le Hope	27	Sept 1993	Adrian Stiff
Stonyhill	Brentwood	27	Summer 1994	Reg Plumridge
The Burstead	Billericay	18	July 1993	Patrick Tallack
The Village Club	Willingale	27	May 1994	Howard Swan
Weald Hall	Brentwood	18	Summer 1994	Reg Plumridge

Gloucestershire

Cheltenham	Cheltenham	18	1995	Simon Gidman/GDP
Minchinhampton	Minchinhampton	18	1995	Hawtree
Naunton Downs	Cheltenham	18	July1993	Jacob Pot
Rodway	Gloucester	9	Spring 1994	John Gabb Assoc

Hampshire

Barton on Sea	Barton on Sea	27	Sept 1993	J Hamilton Stutt
Cams Hall	Fareham	27	Nov 1993	P Alliss/C Clark
Dummer	Dummer	18	July 1993	P Alliss/C Clark
South Wincester	Wincester	18	Nov 1993	P Alliss/C Clark
The Hampshire	Andover	18	Sept 1993	Fiducia/Mitchell

Hereford & Worcester

Grove Golf Centre	Leominster	9	TBA	Jonothan Gaunt
Shelsley Kings	Worcestershire	9	1995	David Hemstock Assoc
West Droitwich	Droitwich	18	1995	MRM Leisure

Hertfordshire

Aldwickbury Park	Nr Harpenden	18	Summer 1994	K Brown/M Gillett
Bridgedown	Arkley	18	1994	Howard Swan
Home Farm	Little Hadham	18	1996	Howard Swan
Kingswoodbury	Baldock	27	Autumn 1995	Jonathan Gaunt
Lamer Farm	Wheathamstead	18	TBA	J Dudock Van Heel
Little Hadham	Little Hadham	18	1994	Martin Gillett
Mill Green	Hatfield	18	Oct 1993	P Alliss/C Clark
Much Hadham	Little Hadham	18	1994	Martin Gillett
Shendish House	Hemel Hempstead	9	1995	Donald Steel
Stocks	Nr Tring	18	August 1993	Mike Billcliffe

Humberside

| Cherry Burton | Beverley | 9 | Summer 1993 | David Snell |

Isle of Man

| Mount Murray | Isle of Man | 18 | Spring 1994 | STRI (Bin) |

Jersey

| Wheatlands | St Peter | 9 | Summer 1994 | Ron Whitehead |

Kent

Birchwood Park	Dartford	27	1993	Howard Swan
Broke Hill	Sevenoaks	18	1993	David Williams
Chart Hills	Biddenden	18	Oct 1993	Nick Faldo
Hewitts Golf Centre	Orpington	27	Autumn 1993	MRM Leisure
Hilden Golf Centre	Tunbridge	9	Summer 1994	Paul Wiggins
Kingshill	Maidstone	18	Summer 1995	Barrelfield Golf Network

London Golf Club	West Kingsdown	36	Sept 1993	R Kirby/J Nicklaus
Longlands Golf Park	Chislehurst	9	1994	Martin Gillett
Lydd	Lydd	18	Spring 1994	Mike Smith
Malling Heath	Malling	27	1995	Barrelfield Golf Network
Mulligans Golf Park	Chislehurst	9	1994	Martin Gillett
Pluckley	Nr Ashford	18	1995	Barrelfield Golf Network
Poult Wood	Tonbridge	9	Spring 1995	Hawtree
Redlibbets	Sevenoaks	18	Summer 1995	Jonathan Gaunt
Rotherfield	Kent	18	TBA	PeterMcEvoy
Sandwich Bay	Kent	45	1995/6	Howard Swan
Sittingbourne	Sittingbourne	9	1993	Donald Steel
Swanley	Swanley	36	1995	Fortune/Barrelfield
Sweetwoods	Cowden	18	TBA	Neil Coles
Tiffenden Manor	Kent	18	TBA	W Richardson/Sporting Concepts
Wrotham Heath	Kent	9	1995	Donald Steel

Lancashire

Blundells Hill	St Helens	18	Summer 1994	Steve Marnoch
Gathurst	Nr Wigan	6	Summer 1995	Neville Pearson-ADAS
Herons Reach	Nr Blackpool	18	April 1994	P Alliss/C Clark
Hurlston	Lancashire	18	1994	Donald Steel
Mossoch Hall	Ormskirk	18	1995	Steve Marnoch
Turton	Bolton	9	Autumn 1994	STRI (Bingley)
Walmersley	Gtr Manchester	9	Mid 1995	Steve Marnoch
Charnock Richard	Lancashire	18	Summer 1994	Oakhurst

Leicestershire

Beedles Lake	East Goscote	18	July 1993	Jelson/D Tucker
Langton Golf	Mkt Harborough	9	August 1993	Hawtree
Mkt Harborough	Mkt Harborough	9	1993	Howard Swan
Park Hill	Seagrave	18	May 1994	
Stoke Albany	Mkt Harborough	18	1995	Hawtree
Kilworth Springs	Kilworth	18	August 1993	

Lincolnshire

Briggate Lodge	Scunthorpe	27	1996	John Morgan
Gainsborough Lea	Gainsborough	18	1996	Howard Swan
Rutland County	Stamford	18	Spring 1993	Cameron Sinclair
Welton	Welton	9	Autumn 1994	David Snell
Manor Park	Lincoln	18	Summer 1995	Oakhurst Leisure

Merseyside

Thurstaston	Wirral	18	1996	John Morgan

Middlesex

Hazlewood	Sunbury-on-Thames	9	August 1993	Jonathan Gaunt
Stockley Park	Nr Heathrow	18	Spring 1993	R Trent Jones Snr

Norfolk

Caldecott	Gt Yarmouth	18	Spring 1994	Dick Scott
Dunston Hall	Norwich	9	1994	John Glasgow
Reymerston	Norwich	18	June 1993	ADAS
Weston Park	Norwich	9	June 1993	John Glasgow

Northamptonshire

Brampton Heath	Church Brampton	18	Spring 1995	D Snell/others
Overstone Park	Northampton	18	July 1993	Donald Steel
West Park	Towcester	9	Spring 1993	Cameron Sinclair

Northumberland

Belford	Berwick Upon Tweed	9	April 1993	Nigel Williams
Felton	Northumberland	18	Spring 1995	Golf Design & Mgmt
Matfen Hall	Northumberland	18	1994	Golf Design & Mgmt

North Yorkshire

Romanby	North Allerton	18	July 1993	ADAS
Rudding Park	Harrogate	18	Spring 1995	Hawtree
The Oaks		18	Spring 1996	Eagle Golf

Nottinghamshire

Bondhay	Worksop	18	1995	Donald Steel
College Pines	Worksop	18	March 1994	David Snell
Rufford Park	Ollerton	18	Spring 1994	David Hemstock Assoc

Oxfordshire

Carswell	Nr Farringdon	18	July 1993	John Ely
Frilford Heath	Abindon	18	1994	Simon Gidman/GDP
Fritwell	Fritwell	19	1995	Patrick Tallack
Rye Hill	Nr Banbury	18	1993	David Harrison
Springs Hotel	Wallingford	18	1995	Dave Thomas
The Oxfordshire	Thame	18	July 1993	Rees Jones
Witney	Witney	18	Sept 1994	Simon Gidman

Shropshire

Candles	Telford	18	1996	Howard Swan
Cleobury Manor	Kidderminster	9	July 1993	Various
Horseheath Common	Shropshire	9	1995	Howard Swan
The Shropshire	Telford	27	1993	Hawtree

Somerset

Cannington College	Bridgwater	9	1994	Hawtree
Oake Manor	Taunton	18	May 1993	Adrian Stiff
Tintinhull Forts	Yeovil	18	1995	Adrian Stiff
Wincanton Racecourse	Wincanton	9	Spring 1994	M Smith/Green Eagle Golf

Staffordshire

Bemersley Green	Stoke	9	1995	David Hemstock Assoc
Seedy Mill	Lichfield	9	April 1993	Colin Snape
Kingstone	Stafford	9	TBA	

Suffolk

Brett Vale	Raydon	18	1993	Howard Swan
Newton Green	Sudbury	9	Autumn 1994	CDC Golf & Leisure
Plumpton	Bury St Edmunds	27	1995	Henry Benz

Surrey

Bletchingley	Surrey	18	Summer 1993	Barrelfield Golf
Chiddingfold	Nr Godalming	18	Spring 1994	Jonathan Gaunt
Chobham	Chobham	18	July 1994	P Alliss/C Clark
Clandon Regis	Nr Guildford	18	Spring 1994	David Williams
Eyhurst	Nr Reigate	18	Spring 1995	P Alliss/C Clark
Farleigh Court	Biggin Hill	27	April 1995	J Jacobs Assoc
Happy Valley	Caterham	18	1996	PGA Euro Tour/N Coles
Horne Park	New Chapel	9	Autumn 1994	Patrick Tallack
Milford	Milford	18	Oct 1993	P Alliss/C Clark
Pyrford	Woking	18	Nov 1993	P Alliss/C Clark
Queenwood Farm	Ottershaw	18	TBA	R Trent Jones Jnr
Redhill	Redhill	9	Late 1993	First Tee Leisure
Reigate Hill	Reigate	18	Summer 1994	Barrelfield Golf
Sutton Green	Nr Woking	18	Summer 1994	L Davies/D Walker
Windlesham	Windlesham	18	July 1994	Tommy Horton

Sussex

Boars Head	Crowborough	9	1995	Martin Gillett
Burgess Hill	Burgess Hill	9	Summer 1994	Patrick Tallack
Castle Manor	Arundel	27	Spring1994	Philip Sanders
Chichester Golf Centre	Chichester	18	Spring 1994	Philip Sanders
Frankham Manor	Tunbridge Wells	18	1995	David Williams
Mannings Heath	Nr Horsham	18	1995	David Williams
Mid Sussex	Sussex	18	Autumn 1994	David Williams
Midhurst Whites	Midhurst	18	TBA	Patrick Tallack
Milland Heights	Liphook	18	May 1994	Philip Sanders
Newick Park	Uckfield	18	1995	J Jacobs Assoc
Rustington	Sussex	9	1995	David Williams
Singing Hills	Sussex	9	1993	MRM
Slinfold Park	Horsham	27	1993	John Fortune
Vixengrove Farm	Chailey	18	TBA	Donald Steel

Tyne & Wear

Elemore	Sunderland	18	Summer 1993	Jonathan Gaunt
Ryhope	Sunderland	9	Spring 1994	Jonathan Gaunt

Warwicshire

Bramcote Water	Bramcote	9	Summer 1994	David Snell
Canwell Park	Warwickshire	36	TBA	Donald Steel
Crocketts Manor	Henley-in-Arden	18	June 1994	Neil Selwyn-Smith
Ingon Manor	Stratford	18	Spring 1993	David Hemstock Assoc
The Warwickshire	Leek Wootton	18	Summer 1993	Karl Litten
Walton Hall	Leamington Spa	18	1995	J Jacobs Assoc

West Midlands

Aston Wood	Birmingham	18	August 1994	P Alliss/C Clark

West Yorkshire

Cookridge Hall	Leeds	18	Spring 1994	Karl Litten
Flaxby Park	Harrogate	27	Autumn 1994	David Hemstock Assoc
Leeds Golf Centre	Leeds	27	1994	Donald Steel

Lofthouse Hill	Wakefield	18	August 1994	Bob Brodigan
Mid Yorkshire	Pontefract	18	Spring 1993	Steve Marnoch
The Manor	Leeds	18	Summer 1994	David Hemstock Assoc
Willow Valley	Brighouse	18	Autumn 1994	Jonathan Gaunt

Wiltshire

Cumberwell Park	Bradford on Avon	18	June 1994	Adrian Stiff
Hamptworth Park	Wiltshire	18	Spring 1994	Philip Sanders
Teffont Chase	Teffont	18	Spring 1994	Patrick Tallack

SCOTLAND

Bonar Bridge	Sutherland	9	1995/6	Donald Steel
Dullatur	Cumbernauld	27	1995	Dave Thomas
Hospitality Inn	Irvine	9	Sept 1993	Sandy Sinclair
Loch Lomond	Loch Lomond	18	1994	T Weiskopf/J Morrish
Monarch	Gleneagles	18	June 1993	Jack Nicklaus
St Andrews	Fife	9	1993	Donald Steel
Skibo Castle	Dornoch	18	1994	Donald Steel
Whitekirk	East Lothian	18	1994	Cameron Sinclair

WALES

Caerphilly	Mid Glamorgan	18	1993	Billy Martin
Celtic Manor	Newport	18	August 1994	R Trent Jones Snr
Cottrell Park	Vale of Glamorgan	27	1995	MRM Leisure
Criccieth	Criccieth	18	1995	David Williams
Gower	Nr Swansea	18	1995	Donald Steel
Hensol Park	Minskin	9	Oct 1993	Peter Johnson
Nefyn and District	Morfa Nefyn	9	Summer 1993	STRI (Bingley)
Northop	Rhos-y-Chellis	18	June 1994	J Jacobs Golf Assoc
Pen-y-Cae	Nr Wrexham	9	Spring 1993	John Day
Pont Newydd	Llanelli	18	1993	Hawtree
St Andrews Major	Vale of Glamorgan	9	Summer 1993	MRM Leisure

IRELAND

Abbeyfeale	Abbeyfeale	9	1993	Arthur Spring
Ardfert	Ardfert	9	Summer 1993	Arthur Spring
Ballyliffen	Dunfanaghy	18	Summer 1995	Craddock & Ruddy
Ballydesmond	Ballydesmond	18	1995	Arthur Spring
Ballykisteen	Tipperary	18	1994	Des Smyth Assoc
Ballymascanion	Dundalk	9	Spring 1996	Craddock & Ruddy
Beaufort	Killarney	18	Summer 1994	Arthur Spring
Bunratty	Nr Shannon	18	1995	Handmade Designs
Clandeboye Estate	Bangor	36	1994	Simon Gidman/GDP
Connemara Islands	Lettermore	9	Summer 1994	Craddock & Ruddy
Craddockstown	Naas	18	April 1994	Arthur Spring
Druid's Glen	Kilcoole	18	Summer 1995	Craddock & Ruddy
East Clare	Bodyke	18	June 1994	Arthur Spring
Faithlegg	Waterford	18	May 1993	Patrick Merrigan

Fota Island	Cork	18	Oct 1993	C O'Connor Jnr/P McEvoy
Fota	Cork	18	1995	P McEvoy/J Miller
Galgorm	Ballymena	27	1995	Handmade Designs
Glasson	Co West Meath	18	Sept 1993	Christy O'Connor
Grey Abbey	Newtonards	18	TBA	Peter McEvoy
Kilrush	Kilrush	6	Summer 1994	Arthur Spring
Lee Valley	Cork	18	1993	Christy O'Connor Jnr
Limerick	Co Limerick	18	Summer 1996	Craddock & Ruddy
Makree Castle		18	TBA	Peter McEvoy
Newcastlewest	Ardagh	18	April 1994	Arthur Spring
Newtownmountkennedy	Co Wicklow	18	Summer 1996	Craddock & Ruddy
Parknasilla	Sneem	9	Summer 1994	Arthur Spring
Portmarnock Link	Dublin	18	Summer 1994	Bernhard Langer
Rathsallagh House	Co Carlow	18	Spring 1994	C O'Connor/P McEvoy
Saggart	Dublin	18	1994	Christy O'Connor Jnr
Sligo	Dromore West	9	Summer 1996	Craddock & Ruddy
Temple Patrick	Co Down	18	1995	Handmade Designs
Wicklow	Co Wicklow	9	Summer 1995	Craddock & Ruddy
Woodstock	Ennis	18	Sept 1993	Arthur Spring

Women Golfers
and the Voice of Reason
by Patrick Armstrong

Watching Channel Four's Cutting Edge programme some months ago was like taking a step back in time, several hundred years, it seemed. Not so, it appears. It's all true, and rather than a cruel look at an anti-quated golf club run by a bunch of old fogies, it is claimed to be an accurate picture of most present-day British clubs. Women not allowed to vote? Nonsense, old boy. Women barred from sitting on committees? Stuff and nonsense.

Unfortunately, it's only too true. There are exceptions, of course, but the general run of golf clubs in the British Isles a) restrict the numbers of women allowed to join, b) bar them from sitting on committees, thus effectively denying them a part in the club's management and c) limit the times they can play at weekends. So there you are, ladies, and what are you going to do about it?

It has to be said that there are thousands of ladies who are happy with the situation. One lady golfer, married to a surgeon, told me that she has no wish to play at weekends. "It's the only time my husband or his friends can play. They often work six days, and I don't want to get in their way on the only day available to them." Other ladies confirmed that view. "Really, my children have all left home, and apart from my charity work, and the odd bit of babysitting for grandchildren, the time is my own," said a member of a Midlands club. "I play several times a week and John is busy at the office, except weekends. Why should I demand equal playing rights with the men when I can play weekdays when I like?"

That view, without being unkind, is held by most women a) whose hus-bands are successful in their careers, b) who don't need to work and c) who are fifty-ish plus. It is my view also that, very generally, men feel a need to play golf, and the game of golf is the prime goal. With the majori-ty of women, the need is for company, for conversation, and the game is secondary. Until the fabric of the working society patterns change, as they have in the US, not much will change in the UK.

And it is in the US where the pressure for change is being demanded. With more businesswomen striving for success, there exists a need for women to use the golf course as a place for closing deals, as much as men. Businesswomen are rightly invading the old haunts where men excluded them, but not, it seems, in the golf clubs of Britain. Working women as a group are not a factor in golf clubs. Whether this is because they have increasingly demanding careers, and often families, to take care of is one argument put forward for their absence. Another is that the golf clubs have made no attempt to recruit them as members. But then very few clubs like Northwood have any need for a recruiting drive.

They have a waiting list. Why bother?

The USA may provide a clue as to what the longer term future holds for British clubs. The Executive Women's Golf League, started in 1992, has over 60,000 members. Forty percent of these subscribe to the League's newsletter. There are over 60 branches in different states. Also 40% of all new golfers are women in America. A large number of the US members are Executives in Sales, Advertising and Marketing with large companies. They are on the lookout for new business opportunities, and where better to find them than at the golf club? It is an informal way of doing business that has been part of business culture for a century and more and more women will discover its merits in Britain, as they are doing in the US.

So where do we go post-Northwood? The sad thing about the programme is that the committee saw the film before transmission, thought it was excellent -so we are told- and then were exposed as absolute fools. One wonders how they could have been guilty of such self-delusion. And even after the exposure, it's difficult to see a lot of change in Britain for a good many years. Many clubs are run by Ancient Mariner lookalikes who have no intention of giving up the control they've had down the years. The same clubs have members who are too crippled by arthritis to play, but won't give up their membership, as it's now part of the fabric of their social lives. They want to preserve that intimacy, that exclusivity that has always been their club. But the same doddering old fools will sit on committees, where they've sat for decades, and block any moves by the younger elements to change things. Any invasion by businesswomen - Heavens above, she tried to get my business before I'd finished my soup! - would be blocked, nay, strangled at birth.

There are increasing numbers of clubs where women are welcome, and treated as equals. These are generally newish clubs some of whom have abandoned "gender golf" completely and opened their competitions to men, women, old and young. Chartridge, the new club in Chesham, has a policy of treating men and women as equals. Many British golfers feel that the abolition of gender golf is nonsensical, that it would be like making Athletics, Rugby or Basketball unisex. And they're absolutely right. What women really want is to be allowed to join, pay the same as men, have the same playing options as men, and be allowed to sit on committees and play a part, however small, in the running of the club. In essence, that's a fairly simple request. They're quite happy with their ladies competitions, as are the youth with theirs, and the seniors with their own. Women are more influential nowadays at home, even the Church (now there's a can of worms!) and, increasingly, in business, especially sales, and in politics, so why not at the golf club? The question is, how can that simple request be satisfied, and how long will it take? Since Adam and Eve days, we all know that when women demand something as a right, men dig their heels in and say NO. Anne Boleyn only asked Henry for an increase in her palace allowance, and look what happened to her.

The sports psychology view is an interesting one. Sarah Puri, Professor of Psychology attached to several golf organisations in the USA, sees the threat of an increase of women in golf clubs as a rapier at the heart of the male ego.

"When a man stands with his pals on the first tee, takes a huge divot and trickles the ball a few yards, he feels a fool. When his partner slices his drive out of bounds, he doesn't feel so bad. Men support each other through little crises like fluffed bunker shots, three putting and topped drives. They have to, because they all take turns at feeling foolish. It is a fact, however, that women are much more critical, and men simply don't want that. When a man comes home from a golf game, having struggled to break 110, he can tell his wife he didn't play too badly. If she had witnessed his air shots on the third tee, his three putting on every green, and the tee shot that hit the ladies tee and shot off like a rocket at right angles into the River Avon on the 12th, his golf life would become a nightmare, and his personal esteem would fall. So men do not want to share these failures with their wives, although they're almost totally unselfconscious about these failures in the company of other men."

Social psychologists will confirm that the Northwood-style club is a haven of tranquillity and tradition, where the real British world of football louts, child molesters, Gloucester body burying and video nasties has no place. It is the last great security blanket, a world where Freddie Trueman still bowls them at your right ear, Lord Ted isn't a failed selector but an arrogant, regal batsman, Georgie Best, Bobby Charlton and Pele still stride the world stage, JPR Williams and Phil Bennett are still first on the Welsh teamsheet, Typhoon Tyson is still the world's fastest and Roger Bannister's famous run was just last week. It is a peaceful place, where you meet the same golfers you've played with for the last 30 years. It's also a place where, like the rugby club, you can get away from women. When a man is retired, he feels a need for a place where he doesn't get under his wife's feet, and the club fulfils that need beautifully. They don't want change, they don't need it. And change, in the not unattractive shape of women, will be fought on the beaches, the fairways, the bunkers and, of course, the committees, where, we know, the women have no vote. What Northwood succeeded in doing was to expose a long lost world where change, though much needed, isn't really wanted at all.

GOLF FOUNDATION
Junior Golf - Alive and Kicking?

Chris Plumridge looks at the work of the Golf Foundation, and sounds a warning.

As a result of its unprecedented success in recent years, European golf is experiencing an explosion in popularity, with more and more people succumbing to its lure. Nowhere is this more evident than among young people, those who have witnessed the deeds of the modern-day heroes and are motivated to try to emulate them. Junior golf in Britain and Ireland has its roots in the 2500 golf clubs distributed through the British Isles. Most of these clubs have thriving junior sections where young golfers are encouraged to develop their skills.

At the heart of this lies the Golf Foundation, the national body for the promotion and development of junior golf. Founded in 1952 and originally the brainchild of the late Sir Henry Cotton, the aims of the Foundation were to introduce golf to schools to try to combat the dwindling club membership which was a factor at the time. Six schools responded to this initiative and now, forty years later, more than 2000 schools and junior groups benefit from instruction via the Foundation's Coaching Scheme.

This scheme forms the basis of the Foundation's work through subsidised instruction by qualified members of the Professional Golfers' Association to students of schools and universities, and to junior members of golf clubs who are in full-time education. This enables schools which do not have golf as part of their sports programme to take advantage of the chance to give their pupils an introduction to the game and a solid grounding in its techniques.

From the 40000 youngsters who pass through the scheme each year, there emerges a number of talented youngsters who go on to make their mark at senior level. Such players include Ryder Cup captain Bernard Gallacher, Solheim Cup captain Mickey Walker, Brian Barnes, Peter Oosterhuis, Paul Way, Michael McLean, Ronan Rafferty and up and coming players Darren Clarke, Ian Garbutt and Lee Westwood. It is not the Foundation's role, however, to discover an elite group of future champions. Its prime function is to ensure that as many young people as possible become involved in the game and thus form the next generation of club membership.

While the Coaching Scheme is the main part of the Foundation's work, young people's interest in the game must be sustained. Running in tandem with the Coaching Scheme is the Merit Award Scheme which rewards juniors as they progress and their aptitude develops.

The Foundation also organises two important tournaments, the Golf Foundation/Weetabix Age Group Championships which are relevant to a player's physical development, and the Golf Foundation Team Championship for Schools which attracts entries from over 2000 schools from around the world, culminating in an International Final for the R & A Trophy. The Foundation also supports sponsored tournaments for juniors such as the Daily Telegraph Junior Golfer of the Year tournament.

The implementation of all these activities costs a great deal of money and the Foundation relies heavily on club golfers, as well as commerce and industry for its income. The main contributor is the Royal & Ancient which donates a percentage from the Open Championship, but in general terms grass roots golf is under-funded.

Another underlying problem for young people is lack of access onto private golf courses, particularly in cases where the parents are not members. There is access to public and municipal courses, but these are outnumbered by the private ones. Such courses depend largely on green fee income from visiting golfers and they are loath to reduce their charges for young people. So, unless the parents are members and are prepared to pay for junior membership, the financial restrictions are inhibiting.

Despite these problems, junior golf is in a healthy state, but there is no room for complacency in the face of a dwindling youth market and fiercer competition from other activities. The future of the game lies with the young golfers of today. It is up to everyone to make sure that future is secure.

Further information may be obtained from the Golf Foundation, Telephone 0920-484044.

H.R.H Duke of York with Rebecca Hudson and James Hull at a charity dinner hosted by London Clubs International in aid of The Golf Foundation in April.

Seniors . . .

"The days of older people holding hands and strolling off into the sunset for a happy retirement is a thing of the past. The older generation are now much fitter, youthful thinking and looking for an active life, not one in a rocking chair." So says Barry Edwards, Executive Director of the Senior Golf Association.

With increasing numbers of all ages taking up golf, the game is an ideal pastime for those retiring. It's got an excellent social side, it's not too energetic, but great exercise, and affords a chance to travel abroad in escorted groups with like-minded people. So the Senior Golf Association was set up in January 1994 after a test marketing campaign gave an encouraging response, and already has retained the services of Tommy Horton, Bernard Hunt and Beverley Lewis.

Edwards, who started the Women's European Tour with Vivien Saunders in 1979, is enthusiastic about its prospects. "Our aim is to bring together like-minded people together for competitions, open days, and travel. It will not happen overnight, but the beginning is encouraging, and we have organised a range of benefits which include health insurance, pensions, holidays, discounts."

He has watched the growth of the Seniors Tour here and in the US. The events are well supported and this support will grow. "Older people - the grey market, as they're referred to - have more disposable income, their children are no longer a financial burden, and it's now time to spend a little money on themselves." He estimates that there are 600,000 golfers over 50, and therefore potential members of his fledgling association. He is a keen golfer and a member of Coombe Hill. At 60, he is also a member. "I'm sure it will be a success, and even if only a small percentage of the potential members actually join, it will still be worth it, and be a valuable addition to golf in the UK."

. . . and Juniors

You're never too young, it seems. FOUR year old Jason Hobday astonished golfers at his father's golf club, by hitting a hole in one at an 83 yard par three. Only 44 inches tall, the youngest ever to get a hole in one used a specially shortened five wood. Jordan, of Popley Four, Hampshire, has played since he was just over two years old, and is said by his father Andrew to be completely golf-mad.

INTERNATIONAL
GOLF ALMANACK
1995

AWARDS
FOR GOLF EXCELLENCE........

The International Golf Almanack 1995 set out to make awards for excellence in all areas of golf. We were looking for outstanding achievements throughout the world of golf, and we examined the claims of some unsung heroes as well as the acknowledged kings and queens of the sport.

In this our first year of publication we decided to make awards in the following categories:

1. Lifetime Achievement Award. Our first Award is to South African legend, Gary Player
2. Golf Coach of the year. We have chosen Owen McKenna, a teaching professional at Earls Colne, near Colcester Essex
3. Best new golf course in the UK, open for less than a year. Our first award is to Kilworth Springs Golf Club, near Market Harborough, Leicestershire
4. Best new golf course in the United States: Lake Nona.

Features on these Award winners appear elsewhere in the book.

A FANTASY GOLFING TOUR
by RICHARD BAKER

We set out to find a list of courses that a keen golfer, on winning the pools in a modest (say £50,000) way, could indulge his hunger for the game on a grand USA tour of public golf courses where he'd be treated with courtesy and be able to get on without the need for references from the local County Sheriff and Chamber of Commerce. The Grand Tour would take in at least one truly spectacular course and eleven courses where he'd get the most for his money without compromising his wish to have lifetime memories. The list below represents our idea of a "Fantasy Golf Tour". Unlike Great Britain, where we're lucky enough to be able to play throughout the year, the extremes of climate in the USA mean that courses are often closed from October till April. The other factors to consider are the extreme heat, often over 100 degrees in July and August, and the huge distances between our chosen venues. So our fantasy tour starts in mid-September in Orlando and ends five weeks later in Colorado. If any reader tries it, please let us know, and tell us if you share our judgements on the venues.

1) SIMPLY THE BEST
THE MOST SPECTACULAR GOLF COURSE IN USA

The IGA award goes to the Lake Nona development in Orlando, Florida, owned and operated by the Sunley Homes Company of London, England. The course itself is a Tom Fazio designed spectacular, and the abundance of natural beauty and serene surroundings seems a contradiction to its highly accessible location. Lake Nona is only 20 minutes from downtown Orlando and just 9 minutes from Orlando International Airport.

The complex is all the more amazing when one considers that it was only in 1984 that John Sunley, chairman of one of England's oldest home builders, obtained almost 7000 acres in southeastern Orlando for the most ambitious project in the history of the company. The ultimate goal was a self-contained community with residential areas, resort hotels, other golf courses as well as Lake Nona, shopping parks, offices, schools and hospitals. The private estate to the north of Lake Nona, Buck Lake and Red Lake has now been completed.

Membership at Lake Nona is by invitation only, limited to 300 Equity members. Family membership entitles the member and immediate family to full use of the club facilities. Recognised by Golf Magazine as one of the top golf courses in the world, it is 7011 yards set in an amalgam of rolling fairways, lakes, ponds and liberally sprinkled with bunkers. Designed by the man who put his signature to Butler National and Juniper Hills, Fazio used 600 acres to build a golf course to dream of. There is no modern trickery, just pure golf with water, bunkers and undulating greens. Some say the 578 yard 15th is a masterpiece, others rave about the short par 4's, and even the stroke index one 2nd, a monster at 543 yards. The 440 yard 18th is a spectacular finishing hole.

The wildlife haven't been told about the club's ultra civilised atmosphere. There's a family of bald eagles, often seen swooping through the oaks and pines, as well as hawks, ospreys, herons and a great variety of ducks. Deer, raccoons, rabbits, wild pigs and the rare red fox make occasional visits.

The club has several honorary members, including John Jacobs and Dennis Thatcher. David Leadbetter is Director of Golf and the pro shop is run by Gregor Jamieson from Turnberry. It is a classic example of privacy, privilege and prestige and an elegance and charm about the wooded enclave by the lakes sets it apart from other golf-oriented communities. The course has played host to amateur events, including the Florida State Amateur, and the professional World Cup, won last year by Fred Couples and Davis Love III.

Country Club Magazine called Lake Nona "simply beyond first class." We found it staggeringly beautiful, a stunning community of homes and golfers. We've never seen a finer golf facility and the course itself is best summed up by recent visitor Bob Hope, "It's a beautiful golf course. I'm coming back next year to try out the fairways!"

2) ALMOST THE BEST
THE PUBLIC GOLF COURSE OF THE YEAR (USA)

The IGA award for the American Public Golf Course goes to Montauk Downs State Park Golf Course, on Long Island, New York. It's 120 miles from New York City on the easternmost tip of Long Island, but well worth the drive. Break your trip at The Hamptons, where P G Wodehouse lived in retirement and wrote some of his best golf stories. F. Scott Fitzgerald also lived nearby. Montauk's green fees are around a paltry $20, and there are reductions for twilight play! The course itself has beautiful sea views, but the wind, the dunes, the big greens and the hills make it a stern test for any handicap standard. It's been described as a smaller Shinnecock Hills, which is close enough to play both courses on the same day. Avoid in July and August because of the heat and the queues, other times it's well worth the visit.

3) There were two very close runners up. One was the **Breckenridge Golf Club, Colorado.** With green fees of $50 weekdays, and reduced fees for twilight play, it represents mountain golf at its very best. Jack Nicklaus designed this spectacular course, his only public one, and it's an excellent test, perhaps too demanding from the back tees, and tough for the 18-handicapper and above. At 7279 yards, par 72, visitors have described this course as "awesome, incredible, never to be forgotten". If you're smart, get there in October and stay for the skiing, which is equally spectacular.

4) The other was the **Eaglesticks Golf Club, Zanesville, Ohio**, around 50 miles from Columbus. Green fees are around $30 with reductions for weekday twilight play. It's an elegant course with a need for accuracy and over 100 bunkers. With several short par fours, it's not a long course, (6412 yards, par 70), but it's challenging and the staff are outstandingly helpful.

5) Heather Glen Golf Links, North Myrtle Beach, South Carolina. Less than eight years old, there are three loops of nine holes, all par 36 all around 3400 yards. It's a well groomed complex, as you'd expect, with difficult, unique holes and spectacular setting. Well designed to suit all handicaps with green fees $50-$99. The original 18 holes were named as the Best New Public Course of 1987.

6) Timberton Golf Club, Hattiesburg, Mississippi. This 7000 yard par 72 is a beauty, currently ranked No.3 in the state, with green fees of around $30, less on weekdays. Our man rates it as a future US Open venue, and especially liked the staff, who, he says, actually like golfers, and nothing is too much trouble for them. Less than 100 miles from New Orleans, so if you're into jazz and golf, don't miss it!

7) Sugarloaf Golf Club, Carrabasset, Maine. This 7000 yard par 72 costs around $30, less if you play on weekdays late in the afternoon, and is less than 100 miles from Portland, Maine. It is a staggeringly beautiful mountain course, where you have got to be straight and long, a cart is a must and you may see the odd bear prowling around, as well as moose and deer in a natural wildlife setting. Its outstanding beauty, especially in the New England autumn make Sugarloaf the best course in Maine, if not in all the Northeast states.

8) Bethpage State Park Golf Course, Farmingdale, Long Island, New York. There are five courses here to choose, but the Black Course is a supreme test of golf, suitable perhaps only for 16 handicappers and below. At under $20, less if you play late afternoon, it's probably the best value in America. Some holes require carries of 200 yards, the rough is horrendous, and, at 7000 plus and par 71, it is physically demanding. (No carts). If you want a less demanding course, try the Red one, at 6750 yards and par 70.

9) Bryan Park and Golf Club, Brown Summit, North Carolina. The Champions Course is over 7100 yards and par 72 with a superb layout. The large lake and the winds are factors, and you have to be a straight hitter. At $30, with reductions for twilight play, it's only ten miles from Greensboro.

10) Sugarbush Golf Course, Warren, Vermont. A classic mountain course, designed by Robert Trent Jones, with drama around every corner and wonderful views. Make sure you go there before October and after May, else you'll find yourself surrounded by hordes in psychedelic outfits with long strips of metal on their feet. Only 45 miles from Burlington, it's 6500 yards, par 72, and you can play for $30, less on weekdays and for the resort guests.

11) Olde Mill Golf Course, Laurel Fork, Virginia. A hilly, spectacular jewel in the Appalachians, 90 miles from Roanoke. It's difficult to find, so you may be the only one on the course, but it's so beautiful and enjoyable, each hole is so different, that you might just want to give up your detached house in Cheltenham and move there. The 6800 yards, par 72 course has lots of water as well, just to keep you thinking! It'll cost you around $25.

12) No fantasy tour would be complete without a round at the Walt Disney World Resort in Orlando, Florida. There are five 18-hole courses to choose, plus a nine hole Oak Trail Course, the only course where you can carry your clubs. It'll cost you from $50 -$99, less if you play at twilight, and the best course is the Osprey Ridge, a Fazio designed 7100 yards par 72. It's just a beautiful course with lots of rolling fairways and interesting holes. Some holes require long carries, and it may be too difficult for seniors. The drawback here is the risk of a six hour round.

So there you are. A modest pools win cheque has just been presented by Jimmy Tarbuck and he asks you, "Will this change your life?" You shake your head, no. But when the tickets come through, and you start with Lake Nona, follow on with Walt Disney, then Mississippi and on to the Carolinas, then Virginia, Ohio, New York, Maine and Vermont, finishing at Breckenridge, you'll have played Baker's Dozen, and your life on the golf course will never be the same again!

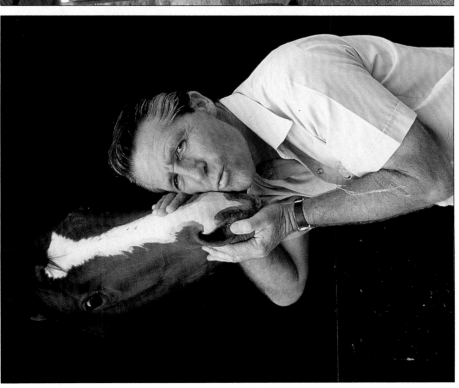

Gary - Down on the farm

Gary Player accepts his Lifetime Achievement Award at Royal Lytham from
Blandford Editorial Director Rod Dymott.

The stunning 18th at Lake Nona in Orlando, Florida.

Owen McKenna shows Alex Jamieson the ropes at Earls Colne

Two holes from the stunning new course at Kilworth Springs

John Daly strides out at the British Open

It's mine! Greg Norman at the British Open 1993

Nick Faldo. Not impressed with Peter Alliss or Ernie Els?

Laura Davies. Top of the Ping Leaderboard

Ian Botham in swinging mood at Collingtree Park

Spot the celebrity ?
The Variety Club present a Sunshine Coach at Selsdon Park

Tom Watson captained the 1993 US team to victory in the Ryder Cup
at The Belfry.

First win in over two years at St. Mellion for Ballesteros

No Simple Simon. Iain Pyman turned pro in 1994

The world's leading Guru at Lake Nona with club professional Gregor Jamieson

Player of the future ? Gary Harris, Brabazon Trophy winner

Gary Player,

the First Hero for many.

A look at the life and achievements of Gary Player. Ben Clingain talks to John Cook, Director of Golf at Collingtree Park Golf Club, Northampton, who knows Player well.

He is a small man, a little 'un who beat all the big ones. His success has been all about determination. He didn't start with any privileges, he got there with sheer hard work. That was Ian Woosnam's opinion of his first hero in golf, Gary Player. It was also the opinion of millions who watched the little man in black, dubbed The Black Knight, the Milk Tray Man without the dangling from helicopters, plunging off cliffs and diving through windows who carved his dramatic way through the sixties and seventies taking on giants like Palmer and Nicklaus and beating them. A man who impressed those millions, and still does, with his composure and dignity. And he's still the idol of modern golf superstars like Bernhard Langer. When the German realised he had a gift for the game, the man he wanted to emulate was Gary Player.

He first came to the notice of the world in the late fifties in the British Open. At the age of 23, he won the first of his three Opens in 1959 at Muirfield, beating Flory van Donck and Fred Bullock by two strokes, coming from behind and finishing the last eighteen with a brutally courageous 68. With 36 holes to play on the last day (who said older golfers had less stamina than today's superstars?) the South African was eight strokes off the pace. His display of dogged determination that would characterise the whole of his career won him a host of new admirers as he slowly closed the gap on the leaders. His final 17-hole total stood at 62, and he needed only a par at the last to be virtually certain of winning. The 448 yard par 4 eighteenth at Muirfield is arguably the most demanding finishing hole of all the Open Championship holes, not a hole most golfers would relish having to par if they needed a 4 to win. That was the situation facing Player. High drama ensued as he put his drive into a bunker, summoned all his resources to reach the green in two more, then agonisingly three putted for a six and a total of 68. "I thought I'd given it away," he said, many years later. "I'd done everything right all day, then poured all the hard work down the drain." He sat, almost inconsolable, head in hands, weeping unashamedly, while his wife Vivienne tried to comfort him, for a long 120 minutes. Two hours aged him ten years, he was to confess later, then his nearest rivals faltered and left him a relieved champion, a winner by two slender strokes. He was on his way.

Peter Alliss has said that when Gary Player first began to compete in British tournaments in the early 1950's, his talent looked limited. He lacked "feel" for the game, and with his chipping and putting there wasn't the delicate flow to his game that one would see in other good golfers. But, he concluded, in "Supreme Champions of Golf", published in 1986 by Collins, that if dedication, tenacity and making the most of natural ability are the yardstick, nobody worked harder at improving his golf than Gary Player. Alliss went further, citing Player's ugly flat swing and huge hook of his early days. But Player learned from Dai Rees amongst others, made adjustments and improved, although there was still a problem with his balance, which Alliss rightly says is usually death to consistent golf. Many of Alliss's contemporaries thought that the young Gary should go back to South Africa, get a proper job and play golf for fun.

With all that as background, one would wonder how Gary Player ever won a single tournament, never mind the litany of championships that made him a legend alongside Palmer and Nicklaus. That winning group was dubbed "The Big Three", for their accomplishments.

But he won his first tournament in Britain in 1956, the Dunlop at Sunningdale. The same year he finished fourth in the British Open. Buoyed by this success he tried the US Tour in 1957, eventually winning the Kentucky Open in 1958, then finishing second to Tommy Bolt in the US Open. That year he finished seventh in the British Open. He was moving up the ladder to become one of the leading figures in world golf. But when he won the Open in 1959, the critics said he had won because of the faltering of others and remained unconvinced for a while.

Player remained impassive. He continued to practice, and he continued to win. His determination to succeed and to win in convincing fashion, shaped the rest of his career. For Player, the obstacles that he overcame in the formative years of his life were what made his great success so remarkable.

Gary Jim Player was born the third child of Harry Audley Player, a gold mine captain on 1 November,1935. The family's means were modest and his mother died from cancer when he was eight. Fifty years later, Player still remembers the pain of loss. "Even now I can still remember her vividly. I remember her voice, the things she told me. All that I am and all that I have become is in some way a tribute to her. It has been a means for me, as it were, to settle some unfathomable debt. What I know is that for all my success, fame, fortune, my own delightful children and grandchildren, the burning regret is that she never saw what I had made of myself." But his father Harry played golf off 2, and, despite his lung complaint, the sad legacy of a lifetime spent down the mines, insisted on watching Gary play later in life whenever possible. There was a great bond between them. His brother Ian, eight years his senior, taught him how to box, lift weights and climb. The resulting strength, stamina and physical conditioning were things that concerned few golfers of the time, but they served Player well as a professional.

Even now he will not go to bed without doing his exercises, no matter how late he gets back to his hotel room. The long trips to tournaments in the old propeller planes - over 45 hours from Johannesburg to the USA! - made him a pioneer, learning to play under all sorts of conditions and weather, without having the best of equipment. What today's players have in shoes, clubs and clothing was unheard of in the early days of his career. Estimates are that he has flown over eight million miles in his career. And, despite his worldwide popularity, his early solitary life stays with him. "I travel a lot on my own, " he confesses. "I live alone on tour in motel rooms, I eat alone, I practice alone. And even though there may be thousands of people watching a tournament, I am by myself out there. It's just me against the rest."

By the age of fourteen, he was practising his golf shots most of the available daylight hours. And he was later to say:" The harder I practice, the luckier I get." He realised that his build would not make him a power hitter, so he concentrated on his short game. He spent hours practising bunker shots, as John Cook was to discover when he visited him early in his own career. "Gary was a perfectionist and we would spend hour after hour in bunkers," says Cook. "He'd make me stay in the bunker till we had both holed five shots. Then we could break for a while and start again. Even now, years later, it's the best part of my game, and it's all down to Gary Player."

His body in peak condition, Player turned his thoughts to the mind. He believes in the power of positive thinking."Convince yourself that you are in peak form and you have the right attitude to do battle with the course. Convince yourself that every shot is going to be a good one and success will be the outcome." Even clothing is important, and along with Sam Snead's straw hat, Bobby Locke's plus fours, Gary Player's trademark was an all-black outfit. Black absorbs sunlight and, he felt, helped to keep him warm and give him strength. It created the Black Knight image and logo, which came to represent fierce determination, while always remaining a gentleman.

1959 was full of successes. Along with the British Open, he won the Dunlop Masters, the South African PGA and four other tournaments in South Africa. In 1960 he repeated his success at the Dunlop Masters and the South African PGA, but added the South African Open and repeated his wins of the previous year at Natal, Western Province and Transvaal. At the US Masters in 1961, he became the first man from overseas to win the Augusta tournament, beating his good friend Arnold Palmer in a dramatic last hole finish. Player's bunker practice paid off in style. At the final hole, his second shot drifted into a bunker to the right of the green, but he got up and down in two. Palmer had started his famous charge and, four behind the South African on the final day, led by one on the eighteenth tee. But his second fell into the same bunker as Players and he took four more shots to get down, and Player had won by a single stroke.

The following year he won the US PGA and in 1965 at Bellerive, Missouri, he beat Kel Nagle with a 71 in a playoff to win the US Open. He thus became a member of a select band of Grand Slam winners - all four Majors - which included only Sarazen, Hogan and Nicklaus. The excluisive trio had now become a quartet. All doubts were removed as to Gary Player's ability. In South Africa, his success was staggering. He won the South African Open thirteen times, the South African PGA three times and the Masters ten times. He won on every continent, with seven Australian Open titles and five World Matchplay championships. On the

US Tour he had 21 victories, an astonishing total for a man who never played in the USA full time.

His career is a litany of wins all over the world, with over 150 events. He was inducted into the World Golf Hall of fame in 1974 and in 1990 he was awarded Sportsman of the Century in South Africa. He captained the South African team back into international golf in 1991 and they were narrowly beaten by Sweden in the final of the Dunhill Cup at St Andrews. As early as 1966, he won the Bobby Jones Award from USGA for Distinguished Sportsmanship in Golf and has been widely recognised as the International Ambassador of Golf. He's still winning, standing fifth on the Most Senior Tour Victory scoreboard with 21 Senior international.events

Away from golf, he lives on his ranch near Johannesburg with his wife Vivienne, whom he first met at the age of fourteen. Player soon made up his mind. "As soon as I saw her I decided that we should marry, even though I was only fourteen at the time," he says. "She has been my greatest inspiration ever since." They were married in 1956 after he won the $14000 first prize in an Ampol tournament in Australia, and he sent her a cable: "Buy the wedding dress." He named his home "Blair Atholl," after his Scottish ancestry. He and Vivienne have two sons and four daughters, Theresa, Michelle, Jennifer, Amanda, Marc and Wayne. They also own over 100 thoroughbred horses and pursue a passionate interest in breeding race horses. They now have a ranch at Colesberg, about 200 miles from Capetown, where their string of horses are trained, and all are frequent visitors to the Newmarket sales.

His love of the horse began in childhood and has never left him. What started as an enchantment with all the Western movies developed into an abiding passion. He first rode at the age of nine at a friend's farm outside Johannesburg. He had a talent for riding, an instinctive feeling for the horse that went beyond Tom Mix and the Cisco Kid. At the age of seventeen he bought a horse with his boss, Jock

Gary and Vivienne

Werwey, his future father in law. Later in life, the boy who sold programmes at Turffontein race track for pocket money would return to that same track as owner and breeder. His boyhood celluloid dreams were realised when he discovered the Quarter Horse and he took dozens back home to breed. But he soon learned that the way to make money in horses was by breeding thoroughbred racehorses, and a few years later he moved to a more ideal location at Colesberg, in the Karoo region of cape Province, on a ranch of 4000 acres, in an area that ranks with Lexington, Kentucky, or Newmarket, as one of the world's great breeding centres for thoroughbred horses. The lure of horses remains strong, as does the Player dream of breeding another Secretariat or Northern dancer. His experience with horses mirrors his life in golf. He was good, he had an instinctive feel, but always had to work at it.

Player recognises that the newer generation of golfers has more scientific knowledge available in their search for perfection. "I did it all by trial and error," he says in his book "To Be the Best,"

Gary and some of his grandchildren.

published with Michael McDonnell by Pan in 1991. "But it still comes down to sheer hard work. Sometimes there would be a temptation to put my exercises off till tomorrow, but the old cliche is true: it never comes."

John Cook saw that determination at close quarters. Cook had won the English Amateur championship at the age of 19, and was the only golfer to win that title and the British Youths championship in the same year. That was in 1969, the year he turned professional. He met Gary Player two weeks later at Sunningdale at the World Matchplay, and the great man asked him what he was doing that winter. Cook was going to play in the Nigerian Open, an event he won, and Player invited him to stay with him in South Africa. An intended short visit turned into a four-month stopover, and Cook returned every winter for the next seven years. From 6am every day, they practiced bunker shots for two hours. There was no let-up for Cook as they played for 5 cents nearest the hole and a rand for every bunker shot holed out. "It cost me a fortune over those seven years," Cook recalls with a wry smile. "But it made me a more than useful bunker player. It also made me appreciate the the amazing dedication of the man. He would go out of his way to help young players in any way he could, hoping some of his single-minded determination would rub off on them. He was warm and generous with his time and his hospitality, and that made him special, even to his greatest rivals on the professional circuit."

The constant practice paid off, and Cook's first four years as a professional were promising enough to lead Tony Jacklin to rate him as one of the best prospects in the country. A short time later, he played in a tournament in Morocco to celebrate the King's birthday. Cook was caught in the middle of a violent coup that overthrew the monarch and the event changed his life. He felt lucky to be alive, but the experience shook him and he never won anything major afterwards. He realised then that he lacked the killer instinct, that he would never be the best as a pro, and set out to be the next best thing, the best club professional. Gary Player understood his reasons. His advice? "Don't look back. Just work now at being the best. Like everything, you'll make it if you're determined enough and practice enough."

While Player's golfing days are finite, his contributions to the game will be everlasting. Two years ago Player purchased Gary Player Golf Equipment, which produces clubs composed of the unique alloy aluminum bronze. The complete line of men's and women's clubs are now distributed throughout the world. Player also oversees the Gary Player Design Company which boasts over 100 golf courses around the world. The Gary Player Foundation with its Blair Atholl School provides an education for 600 underprivileged children in South Africa.

The publishers of the International Golf Almanack are delighted to make an award to Gary Player for his lifetime achievements in golf. We are honoured that he has accepted and added our award to the countless ones he has collected over the years as an ambassador and a lifetime winner. But he himself never thought that one day his empire, including travel, real estate, golf course design and management, would attract as much attention on the financial pages as his golf exploits would on the sports pages. He never set out to be rich, that was never the purpose of all that relentless dedication. He wanted to be simply the best. He's achieved that, and a whole lot more.

Gary toning up . . .

TWO MEN and a DREAM
New Course is Award Winner

When Paul Stevenson and Roger Vicary bought land in 1989 for access to 250 acres on which they intended to build a golf course, they had a lucky break. They discovered that they didn't have the 200,000 tons of gravel they thought, they had over 3 million tons! So they took out enough gravel to create the course. Then they found that there was a huge demand for materials to build the nearby A1-M1 Link road from Market Harborough to the motorway, so the gravel they took out was sold as road materials. Not only did they get the course they wanted to build, but they also can claim to have helped build the important motorway link road that opened last July.

Stevenson was a keen golfer in the early 1970's. "There wasn't the wide range of choices for the golfer then," he recalls. "The explosion in new courses has only happened in the last few years, so there was really no option if you wanted to play the game. You had to get your name on a club list and wait." He waited and waited, then, disillusioned, gave up the game. His business life as a developer and builder was also a factor in the decision. His partner, Roger Vicary, was an agricultural contractor and had never played the game. The twosome have been together as business partners since 1985 with companies in England and France. Their French project involved building houses on a course in France, and the idea of building their own course surfaced again.

They called in Ray Baldwin, now 79, from Droitwich, Worcester, an accountant by profession and explained what they wanted to do. He had been a scratch golfer most of his life, and had recently been involved with the English Golf Union and helped get their Golf Design manual off the ground. He was one of the principal development officers with the EGU and they leaned heavily on their unbiased opinions and steered the partners in the right directions. Baldwin is now the president at the club.

"There was no point trying to build a Florida course in the middle of England," says Stevenson. "A lot of highly paid designers try it, and it just doesn't work. The land we had suited the product. All our research was done by looking at other courses all over the country. We finally knew what we wanted and went off and did it. We wanted a traditional British course. Links courses are so great, they're wonderful and can change character every time you play them, sometimes in the middle of a round. And, if your drainage is right, you can play all year round. We've got a course built on 135 acres of free-draining soil with its own water supply"

Since they opened in August 1993, there has been a nationwide catalogue of week after week of rain, with one course in Torquay closed for five weeks, other courses closing for several days every week, or playing with winter greens. Many of these courses are almost a century old. Despite the rain deluges, Kilworth has not closed once, nor had any winter greens. Their free-draining soil and their choice of grass for the greens has a lot to do with their ability to stay open and offer golf all year round.

And what the owners conceived is exactly what the golfer gets. "The average golfer in the UK is an 18-handicapper," claims Vicary. "We've tried to build a course with a bit of imagination that Mr. Average can play. And yet it's not that easy. Kevin Dickens, our touring pro, who recently finished fifth in the Midlands PGA at Moor Hall behind winner Paul Broadhurst, has been to other new courses and shot 66's and 67's. His best score here is 70. We're fairly high up, and the wind can change the character of several holes in a matter of minutes. I've seen some 18-handicappers shoot 39 on the front nine, then come home in 51. And that makes it an interesting course. Target golf it's not."

So what does an average golfer think of the course? John Wiffill plays off 21, and has been a member since opening day. "The margin for error on most holes is greater than most other courses, especially on the front nine," he says. "It's the kind of course that eases you into your round, and gets a little harder as you progress."

Tony Worthington joined recently, playing off 17. "Most golfers rush frantically to a golf course, and before they know it, they've have a nine, and their round is ruined," he says. "Kilworth starts you off with three fairly straightforward holes, then a tough stroke index one, then a few more easy holes. The wind can change the character dramatically. It makes it a very interesting course to play. There aren't many bunkers on the front nine, but the water on the back nine, and the increasing number of bunkers means that you have to concentrate hard on the last eleven holes. And there are no really boring holes anywhere on this course."

Ian Wilson (13 handicap) agrees. "It's a very forgiving course, but it's easy to be lulled into a false sense of security, especially on the fourth, and even the Devil's Toenail, the par-3 sixth. The wind can make it a pitching wedge or a five iron!"

The psychology of the Kilworth course is subtle, and it's well thought out. From the yellow tees, the tenth is a long par five 523 yards with out of bounds, water and bunkers guarding the green. Then a par-3 of 148 yards where the wind becomes a critical factor. The twelfth, however, is a "real son-of-a-bitch", in the words of 17-handicapper Andrew Wright, another recent member. "There's a lake in front of the tee, out of bounds on the right, the River Avon further away on the right, and, if you're a long hitter, a hidden dyke 230 yards away on the left. Parring it is a minor miracle."

Then there's the 388 yard 16th, with a canyon in front, two ditches 300 yards away and, if the wind's behind, you need to be careful not to overshoot the green with your second shot. "Our greens are twice the size of normal ones," claims Paul Stevenson. That's true, but it's no help on the 379 yard 17th, where the giant McKenzie green twists and turns more than News of the World photographers chasing Princess Diana on a night out. And then there's the finishing hole, a par-3 177 yard nightmare over a lake, with a sneaky, deep bunker to punish the short hitter and a two-level green.

"Who ever heard of a par-3 finishing hole?" commented one dubious player before starting his round.

I stood with him on the eighteenth as he swished his 5-iron. "177 yards, wind against. Easy-peasey," he snorted. "You might just need your wood," I commented. "No way. It's an iron shot," he said. His shot soared up into the wind and dropped into the bunker. He got out well onto the top level, ran his putt past the hole and finished this "easy" finishing hole with a five. It's not a stroke index 4 for nothing.

Kilworth Springs celebrated its first birthday last August with a programme that included the world-famous Noel Hunt Exhibition. The putting green is now open as is the only "sunken" driving range in Europe, with 20 floodlit bays below ground level, and 20 above. So are the two practice bunkers and chipping area. It's still a pay as you play course with membership at £100 and rounds priced at £9 weekdays, £12 weekends. The owners have also introduced a flat membership fee with annual subs of around £500.

A final word from Paul Stevenson. "We've set our stall out to be an amateur championship course. We hope to attract these kind of events because the course is good enough. In time it will happen. We don't need fancy marketing to make it a success. The course will do all the shouting we need, once people play it and realise just how good it is," he says. At the International Golf Almanack, we couldn't agree more.

OWEN McKENNA
The Boy from Belfast done Good...

Ben Clingain talks to Golf Foundation Award winner Owen McKenna to find out what makes him such a successful teacher.

Owen McKenna has had a golf career that is hardly the traditional one. Not for him the rarified atmosphere of the youth section at the local golf club or playing off scratch at the age of fourteen. Anything but. And yet, he has become one of the leading teachers in the country at the age of 33, an expert on the golf swing, and a tutor of the handicapped, respected for his methods all over the U.K and a winner of a Golf Foundation award a few years ago.

One of seven children born in Belfast, N. Ireland, he was brought to live in Hatfield at the age of six months. He grew up mad keen on all sport, especially football. He first picked up a golf club at the age of 21 and found he liked the game, and had an obvious talent for it. By the time he was 23, he had a handicap of five, had left his job as a motor mechanic and got a job with Peter Jones at Old Fold Manor Golf Club in Barnet as an assistant. He turned professional soon after, but never played on the circuit.

"I could play, but I found I had a talent for teaching," he says. "I gave lessons and people improved as a result. Teaching people to swing properly, whatever their size and build, was much more interesting than going out and playing. And once I could initiate simple modifications in their swing, they were much more confident going out on the course."

McKenna stayed at Barnet for two years, then went to work for Jimmy Burns at Warley Sports Centre at Brentwood. The experience added to his golf and general sports management education and he found that his ability to initiate change in his pupils' performance was improving. He studied all aspects of sports therapy, hypnosis, visual and audio cues and used the techniques to good effect. "That side of teaching fascinated me. Jimmy Burns must take a lot of the credit. He showed me why you get success with some pupils, and not with others, and that sometimes, as professionals, we have to change ourselves first and adapt more, working with the material we've got."

It was there that McKenna started to teach golf to special schools and found he really liked the experience. Teaching those with mild, or even severe, learning difficulties was a different situation, but one he discovered a talent for. After a short spell with Vantage Leisure on the business side, organising company days and teaching clinics, he was offered the head professionals job at the newly opened Earls Colne Centre, near

Colchester. He moved there with his wife Joanne in 1990 and has never looked back. The centre itself is an amazing complex, owned by the Hobbs family. Eric and Margaret Hobbs bought what was the old Earls Colne airfield in 1965 and farmed it. The site had been a large wartime air base with one of the longest runways in Essex. Bob Hope, Glenn Miller and Frances Langford had entertained US troops there in 1943 and Flying Fortresses, Marauders, Liberator bombers and Mustang fighters were based on the site. The golf course, designed by Reg Plumbridge in 1990, is now part of a complex which includes a nine-hole par 30 course, a four hole teaching academy plus a 20 bay floodlit driving range and indoor bunker practice area as well as the 18-hole championship course. There is also a clubhouse and leisure centre, an indoor swimming pool, conference suite and restaurants and bars.

Here Owen McKenna found free range for his talents. He offered open access to golf for those who didn't have it, schools, ladies groups, and all the community. He wanted to create an environment where everyone could come, learn and play, where husbands could play 18 holes without feeling guilty. Their wives could come, play tennis, swim, use the beautician and leave the children safely in the creche. He organised golf tournaments for school children with learning disabilities, added a buffet and disco, and generally tried to make golf a lot of fun for everyone. The children's tournament is now an annual one, and last year McKenna took 70 of his students to the PGA at Wentworth. He preaches his methods to his assistants and they now teach seven schools a week on average, all of them with some form of learning disability.

The school children are important to him. (He now has two of his own, Harry and Charlotte.) But his philosophy is simple: golf should be available, affordable, effective and fun. And his attitude comes through in his instruction. I watched him give instruction to Alan Jamieson a 27-handicapper, and a member at nearby Gosfield Lake. Jamieson had been playing the game for three years, but was having problems, like most high handicappers, in being consistent. He'd follow a good shot with a bad one. I watched the lesson in McKenna's purpose built video room with a facility for indoor or outdoor instruction. Four videos follow every movement of the student's motion, making it easy for the instructor to spot and correct flaws. His style is simple, patient and direct. He'll only make you do what your own body can cope with. He relates the golf swing to baseball and tennis. He'll then show you a breakdown on the screen, and you can see all the elements in slow motion and in graphic form.

He talks about leverage, balance, rhythm, pre-swing and the critical control points in an easy to understand way. You get the feeling he's not teaching you HIS way, he's correcting YOUR way, doing what your body can cope with. I can't say what effect the lessons will have on Alan Jamieson's game long-term, but what he was hearing was having a galvanising effect on him. A lot of what he was doing in his golf swing would be dramatically improved, he was sure of that himself. And he was coming back for more.

Sean Connery at St. Andrews in 1990 with Malcolm Campbell

CONNERY BONDS WITH GOLF
"Tough competitor," say rivals

The movie screenplay is ready. It's been written, rewritten and checked for accuracy by the R &A, the USPGA, Tony Jacklin and the WPGET. It tells the story of a professional golfer who gives up the game at the age of 49, having won nothing on the USPGA Tour or the Volvo Tour, apart from the Morocco Open in 1976. After 25 years as a pro, his claim to fame is hitting a spectator in Bermuda shorts in a painful place at the Bob Hope Classic and finishing 39th to Dave Stockton at the Greater Hartford Open.

Sick of travelling and living out of suitcases, tired of the demands of his three ex-wives, and annoyed with the press who habitually describe him as a "journeyman", he is grateful for the offer of a job as Director of Golf at a new course near St Andrews. He packs up the tour and tries to settle down. But the daily grind of correcting the herky-jerky swings of the club members and his clumsy efforts to attract corporate interest in the new complex soon begin to wear him down. He hated life on the tour, now he misses the adrenalin, the uncertainty of it all. He misses the banter, the easy friendships, the rivalry, the ribaldry and the bed-hopping groupies. He also misses the bottles of Becks and Budweiser.

He hits the bottle, hard. But then he meets a disillusioned golf guru who talks him into going on the Seniors Tour. He hires a girl caddy at Royal Lytham, a beautiful ex-professional golfer trying to make ends meet, and his life changes. He starts winning and stops drinking.

There is a lot of discussion who the Hollywood moguls want to play the roles of the Guru and the Caddy. Mac O'Grady and Glenn Close are among the front runners. There is no dispute who is the choice to play the lead role. If they can't get Sean Connery to play the old pro, there won't be a movie at all. This is no surprise to anyone who knows Connery. His credits as an actor are a mile high, and his ability as a golfer is well known. Ask Malcolm Campbell who's played against Connery twice. Both times were in the final stages of the R &A Jubilee Vase, the club's matchplay championship at the Old Course at St Andrews.

"We played in the 1990 semi-final. I managed to beat him by one hole, but it was a struggle. Then I lost in the final," recalls Campbell, a six-handicapper. " But the following year he got his own back. I met Sean in the final, the last two out of 158 entries, and he beat me by one hole. It was tense. He loves to win. He's quite a competitor, won't give an inch."

James Walker, a keen photographer who lives in St Andrews, took the photo of Campbell and 007 in 1990. Campbell was one up at the time, which may explain why his opponent didn't look too pleased. Connery hit his second out of bounds, but the ball struck a van on the roadway and bounced back onto the green, and he made par. Campbell's drive landed on Granny Clark's Wynd, which runs across the last fairway and from which there is no relief, but he made par to stay one up. According to Campbell, it was all a bit exciting, and Connery wouldn't talk to the press afterwards. The Sunday Mail ran a pretty wicked picture of a dejected 007 making his way back to the hotel above a caption: " Is THIS the World's Sexiest Man?"

And the wicked Auric Goldfinger discovered just how competitive Connery could be in the scene filmed at Stoke Poges Golf Club. Not even a gold bar as a bribe could put the smoothie James Bond off his stroke. 007 proved more than a match for Goldfinger and beat him eventually by out-cheating him, convincing his rival that he had played the wrong ball by cleverly switching them. The golf theme has found a way into a few Connery movies, including his latest, "Rising Sun." He plays a police lieutenant trying to solve a brutal murder in the headquarters of a Japanese corporation in America. Connery breaks down the culture barriers by playing golf with the president. "I shall look forward to our game tomorrow. Perhaps you can find a new way to let me win," are among the final words spoken in the movie, after the murder is solved. Like many golf enthusiasts, Connery is reputed to have clauses written into his movie contracts giving him free time and access to nearby golf courses. And many friends and acquaintances attest to his fondness for the game and his liking for a wager on the course.

Bob Warters, now editor of EMAP's Fore! Magazine, met Connery in 1993 while the star was partnering Paul Broadhurst at a pro-am in Gibraltar. "He has few challengers when it comes to competitive play," Warters says, then editor of Today's Golfer. At the time, Connery was playing off nine, and determined to get down to seven. He had just returned from a gruelling six months filming in the USA, and had been "playing like a drain." He was hoping his new Lynx clubs, bought in America, would help him get his handicap down. "I think you could call Sean a frustrated professional golfer," says Warters. "He's good, he's got no nerves and he's got the will to win. Given more time, and an earlier start, he might have made it as a pro."

Which brings us back to that screenplay. Malcolm Campbell sent the idea to him some time ago. It may be still in the pending tray. Campbell is the author of "European Golf Courses", just published by Pryon in hardback at £19.99. It is an analysis of the top seventy courses in Europe. "I'd like to get Sean on some of those courses. I might just have a chance of beating him. And I could convince him that the script and the role are just what he needs to maintain that sex symbol image!"

As we say in the "Golf at the Movies" section, there have been few films with the game of golf as a serious theme. Golf, as television ratings executives have discovered, is a sexy sport. Film moguls have only seen the game as a Dean Martin/Jerry Lewis/Caddyshack-type comedy. So come on Sean, give it a shot, you'll get to play golf and make a movie at the same time.

From Tee to Jelly

Or why some of the world's leading show business and sports stars turn wobbly on the first tee

Bob Hope said it a long time ago: "I hate the first tee." But then he was playing with US Presidents like Dwight Eisenhower, Gerald Ford and George Bush. If he ever played with Richard Nixon, he never admitted it, although no doubt he would have scrutinised his scorecard. Some observers say that it was Hope and Bing Crosby who made the world realise that golf could be a great fun sport for everyone. Johnny Carson helped by swinging an imaginary golf club on the Tonight Show, every night for over twenty years. When the watch-

Peter Purves of 'Blue Peter' fame

ing world saw President George Bush swinging on the White House lawn in the middle of yet another global crisis, the image was complete. Even Harold Wilson got into the act, supporting Great Britain and Ireland in a Ryder Cup match, although nobody ever saw him swing a club. So there has been a link between politics, show business and golf for a long time. But what about that first nervous tee-shot?

Russ Abbott and Nigel Mansell have a love of golf in common. They also share a common nightmare- a flubbed tee shot when their legs turn to jelly and the 3-wood has as much feel as a crowbar.

"As actors, cricketers, singers or whatever, we are all performers," says Abbott."And we've rehearsed and are experienced at what we do for a living. But when we stand on the first tee at a charity golf tournament, we are usually quivering wrecks. Unfortunately, the public expects us to be as professional at golf as we are at our other careers. I can play a role at the London Palladium in front of thousands and be relaxed. Put me on the first tee in front of fifty spectators and I can be like jelly."

Mansell confirms this. "I can drive at Silverstone with ten thousand spectators willing me to win. That's no problem. How Greg Norman can stand on the first tee at the British Open and not turn to jelly is beyond me. I don't know how the golf pros do it."

Rachael Heyhoe Flint, handicap 10, captain of England's women's cricket team for twenty years, has had similar problems. "I was playing with some novice lady golfers in a Bernard Cribbins charity day when I topped my first shot a few yards off the tee. There was a painful silence, then a spectator muttered that she thought I'd be a lot better."

Rory Underwood, England's leading try scorer, once topped his drive at the Terry Wogan Classic at Waterford in front of a big gallery and took four more shots before he was able to get his embarrassment out of sight over a hill. Mike England, ex- manager of the Wales football team, and a legend at Tottenham Hotspur, was playing in a charity match at St Pierre when Ian Woosnam's group arrived, complete with well over a thousand spectators. England then topped his first shot into a pond in front of the tee.

First tee nerves can have disastrous consequences for spectators, too. Mike Redfern, a character actor, best known perhaps for his role as the father in the Oxo commercials, was playing off 14 in a charity competition at Croham Hurst. His full blooded drive on the first hit a woman spectator and she had to be taken to hospital. Luckily she was alright. Spiro Agnew, vice-president in the days of Richard Nixon was legendary for his ability to hit spectators wherever they stood. He is quoted all over the world for his immortal "I know I'm getting better at golf. I'm hitting fewer spectators!" Henry Cooper, despite his 10 handicap, also has a talent for hitting his audience. "I've done it several times, but the most embarrassing was when filming for TV. I hit one of the female production assistants on the right breast. What can you do except say Sorry?"

But it's not just first tee nerves that can embarrass the victim. Jeremy Guscott, the glamour boy of Bath and English rugby, was playing off 12 at La Manga in the Henry Cooper Classic. After a cracking drive, he took a 6-iron and struck it sweetly into the hotel swimming pool 30 yards past the 18th green.

Most of the big name sporting and show-biz stars play on the Celebrity-Am tournament which has become very big business in raising funds for a variety of recognised charities. There are over 70 events in Britain alone and golfers who want to rub shoulders with the famous pay £100-£200 for the privilege. The day usually ends with dinner and an impromptu cabaret. The Variety Club of Great Britain Golfing Society, whose 1994 vice captain is Jasper Carrott, has raised several million pounds to provide Sunshine Coaches for underprivileged children from entry fees and the inevitable charity auction. One of the main events is the Henry Cooper Classic at La Manga, in Southern Spain, a popular fixture since 1984. The legendary former British, European and Commonwealth heavyweight champion now attracts well over 100 competitors. Cooper took up the game when he retired from the ring and now plays off 12, left-handed.

"It's a game you never master, and provides a constant challenge," he says. "And just when you think you've got it licked, it'll catch you on the chin."Jerry Stevens has been the Variety Club's Tournament director since 1986 and estimates that the Club has raised over £4 million in the past eight years."We're presenting our 500th Sunshine coach sometime this autumn," says Jerry. "It's a very special vehicle, costing around £47000, with life-saving equipment on board, including a transport incubator support system which will be presented to King's College Hospital."

Started in 1965, with Jeremy Hawk as captain, the Variety Club Golfing Society was formed to raise funds for the purchase of "Sunshine Coaches" for handicapped children. It grew dramatically with support from showbiz and sports personalities and now has almost 500 members, with some 100 of them celebrities. It raises more than £500,000 every year just from golf events all over the UK. The present Chairman is Henry Cooper and the President is Lady Sheila Butlin, widow of the much loved Sir William, himself a past President. Recent captains have included Russ Abbott, the late Bernie Winters, Bobby Charlton, Roy Walker, Duggie Brown of Brookside fame, (who raised £606,000 in his year of office), and the present captain is the incomparable ex-Spurs and Arsenal hero Pat Jennings.

The list of past captains reads like a Showbiz Hall of Fame, with Frankie Vaughan (1986), Frank Carson (1981), Jimmy Tarbuck (1971 & 1980), Dickie Henderson (1974), Ronnie Corbett (1973), Sir Harry Secombe (1972), and Sir Stanley Baker (1969) all holding office.

If you want more information on this dedicated band of golfing fund-raisers, talk to Jerry Stevens at the Wembley Park office, at Fulton Road, Empire Way, Wembley, telephone 081-900-2226.

So what's the great attraction of golf for them?

Like most mere mortals, once bitten, four putting, as Eric Morecambe was reported to have said at the height of his fame. The volume of Morecambe wisecracks about golf widows would fill a few paperbacks, but the fascination of the game for him was always in his mind:

"The wife says she'll leave me if I don't give up golf."

"That's terrible," replies Ernie Wise.

"Yes, I know. I'm really going to miss her."

Golf widows have been around as long as there have been golf nuts. George Houghton was arguably the greatest writer and illustrator of the golf nut syndrome, and his work is featured elsewhere in this Almanack. US Presidents, especially Eisenhower, Gerald Ford and George Bush have been bitten by the bug. So what is golf's great attraction?

"The frustration of the game is perhaps its greatest fascination," says Snooker's John Virgo, who has been playing for 11 years, handicap 18.

"The bonhomie of the game. You meet such nice people. I wish I had started earlier." Singer Frankie Vaughan, who's only been playing since 1986, handicap 24.

"Your game can desert you, then come back, just as suddenly. Golf will take longer than my lifetime to conquer." Cricketer Rachael Heyhoe-Flint, who has also represented England at hockey and is rated as one of the best after-dinner speakers in sport. She has been playing only six years, handicap now 10.

"It's one of the few games where you are playing against yourself, and if you cheat, you are only cheating yourself." Actor Johnny Briggs, who plays the ever-nasty Mike Baldwin in "Coronation Street". He plays off 16.

Kevin Whateley. Plays off 24.

"I enjoy golf's easy pace and sociability. My wife Wendy has now taken it up, so it's a game we can enjoy together." Rugby's Rory Underwood, who plays off 20

"I would love to get my handicap down to 2 and go round a course with a realistic chance of making par. It would also be very satisfying to go out and attack a course, instead of just trying to hit the ball down the middle." Snooker's Stephen Hendry, who claims his putting action is like Zorro waving his sword, but is reckoned to be a bandit off a handicap of 12.

"My best shot is my practice swing. The real beauty of this game is that you'll never crack it, nobody ever will." Jasper Carrott

"Golf is a great equaliser. You can play with sheiks, princes, politicians and miners. The only important thing is not their social standing, or their Swiss Bank accounts, but how many shots they take to get that little white thing in the hole." Bob Hope.

Celebrity Golf Handicaps

ACTORS

Johnny Briggs	16
Sean Connery	9
Ronnie Corbett	15
Paul Henry	10
Christopher Lee	8
Kenny Lynch	14
Mike Redfern	16
Mike Reid	11
Eric Sykes	16
Kevin Whateley	24

SINGERS/ENTERTAINERS

Tony Christie	14
Bruce Forsyth	10
Con McCluskey	11
Shakin' Stevens	19
Rick Wakeman	14
Marty Wilde	14

COMEDIANS

Jasper Carrott	13
Roger de Courcy	8
Bobby Davro	14
Gareth Hale	22
Eddie Large	10
Tom O'Connor	8
Mike Osman	24
Norman Pace	21
Jimmy Tarbuck	5
Roy Walker	9

CRICKET

Rob Bailey	18
Chris Balderstone	11
Ian Botham	7
David Capel	18
Brian Close	9
Ted Dexter	6
John Emburey	13
Mike Gatting	10
Desmond Haynes	12
Rachael Heyhoe-Flint	10
Allan Lamb	18
Wayne Larkins	11
David Lloyd	10
Mal Loye	14
Gladstone Small	15
Greg Thomas	7
Fred Titmus	8

RUGBY

Nick Beal	3
Barrie Corless	16
Jeremy Guscott	12
Gavin Hastings	12
Simon Hodgkinson	18
Ian Hunter	21
Tim Rodber	7

FOOTBALL

Dave Beasant	18
Liam Brady	14
Bobby Charlton	12
Martin Chivers	11
Steve Coppell	14
Kenny Dalglish	8
Mike England	6
Ryan Giggs	22
Mark Hughes	20
Pat Jennings	6
Kevin Keegan	6
Frank McLintock	10
Martin Peters	14
Lee Sharpe	12
Alan Shearer	17
Frank Worthington	22

OTHER SPORTS		T.V/ RADIO PRESENTERS	
Bob Anderson (darts)	10	Richie Benaud	9
Henry Cooper (boxing)	10	Trevor Brooking	15
Stephen Hendry (snooker)	12	Alan Hansen	4
Brian Jacks (judo)	11	Tony Lewis	12
Dennis Taylor(snooker)	14	Desmond Lynham	16
Eddie "the Eagle" Edwards	18	Michael Parkinson	13
		Mary Parkinson	18
		Ed Stewart	18
		Ralph Dellor	24
		Kenneth Wolstenholme	18

Mike Gatting

Kenny Lynch

Celebrity Stories

Bernard Cribbins is a keen (17 handicap) member of the Water Rats Golfing Society. One day he was playing at Kingswood in the London Business School Alumni Celebrity Golf Classic, and was striking his tee shots very well. His playing partner, Gordon Bull of Chalfont St Giles complimented him after a few holes. "Ah," said Cribbins,"This is my rabbit club", and went on to explain that when shooting rabbits at his home club Foxhills, he had stumbled across a dilapidated driver deep in the woods, presumably flung there by some despairing golfer. He took it home, restored it and found that it suited him very well.

Play continued until the 13th, when Cribbins hit a real daisy cutter along the edge of the wood. His partner thought he saw something leap into the air and when Cribbins reached his ball there was a luckless rabbit stone dead beside it. This aroused great hilarity when retold at the ensuing dinner. Hard luck on the poor rabbit, but an amazing coincidence!

(Contributed by Gordon W Bull, Chalfont St Giles, Bucks)

Jasper Carrott is the vice captain of the Variety Club of Great Britain Golfing Society. He was playing at Stoke Poges with Brian Barnes when he smacked a spectator with his tee shot and broke his wrist."It was his own fault," claims Carrott, who plays off 13. "If he had stayed in front of the ball, I'd never have hit him. I gave him a couple of tickets for my show, and he showed up and made me autograph the plaster"

Fore! Magazine

Ivan Lendl, the tennis player, is a rabid golfer. His wife Samantha says that his fascination with the game extends to manic preoccupation. Lendl grew up playing soccer and hockey, is a formidable bicycler as well, and has regularly entertained newspaper writers in Toronto with details of his golf rounds. Part of his agreement with various tennis tournaments includes providing a golf window at the nearest championship-quality course. Lendl plays off 8 and is a member at the local club Stanwich, near his home in Cornwall, Connecticut.

Johnny Mathis, the singer, is also well known for his golf mania, and plays off 15. His concert contract, in addition to accommodation, sound arrangements, financial guarantees, and food and beverage specifics, has a stipulation that he has a free round of golf at the nearest local club. When he sings at the Oakdale Music Theatre in Wallingford, Connecticut, he plays at the nearby Farms Country Club.

Lendl and Mathis details provided by Greg Garber, Hartford Courant, CT, USA

Irishman Theo Foley was a noted player and coach with Arsenal Football Club. His passion for golf almost finished his career. Whilst playing at Northamptonshire County Golf Club, his second shot at the par five eighteenth landed on the roof of a shed used for storing mowers. Unworried about the awkward lie, he climbed on the roof and played a fluke shot to within a foot of the pin. Sadly, he overbalanced and fell through the roof, injuring his shoulder and knee, and was out of football action for six weeks. But all the way to hospital in the ambulance, he was seething, because he'd missed his one and only chance in the game for a birdie!

> *Contributed by Joe Kelly, Northampton Town and County Irish Golfing Society.*

Oliver Hardy and W C Fields were said to be deadly rivals on the golf course, although both were duffers and Stan Laurel was of the opinion that they hit more spectators than greens. But they played for $100 a corner, huge amounts in those days, despite the fact that neither has the ideal build for golf, and each struggled to break 100. On one game, Hardy bet his house that he could beat Fields, and lost. He duly signed the house over, and it was only later that Fields discovered that Hardy's house was rented!

> *Contributed by Michael Linville, Cleveland Plain Dealer, Ohio, USA*

Gary Myers, the Australian actor who rocketed to fame as the dashing hero of the Milk Tray ads, is also a golf fanatic. The ex-soldier jumped off fast trains, dived off cliffs and did many of his own stunts, all because the lady loved...He retired home to Australia a rich man in the mid eighties but unhappily was recently diagnosed as seriously ill with a brain tumour. But he continues to pursue his first sporting love, golf, although he collapsed last May on a Sydney golf course.

Jerry Stevens, the Entertainer and Events Director of the Variety Club of Great Britain Golfing Society, was playing golf one day with Eric Sykes at a course in Surrey. As they approached one of the tees, Eric said "you know Jerry in all the years I've played this game, on certain courses there are some holes that no matter how many times I've played them, I've never played them well".
As he stepped on the tee he said "It so happens that this one we're about to play is one of my worst 19 holes in golf". Jerry said "Really Eric, and where are the other 18".... "Wentworth!" Said Eric.

Nigel Mansell, armed with his £8 million Indycar contract, and £1 million per Formula One appearance, is strongly rumoured to be in the mood to buy his own golf club. He flew into Devon in July to see the Woodbury club, near Exmouth, before jetting off to compete in his first Grand Prix for over a year in Paris.

CELEBRITY SPEAKERS

On a Budget...

So what do you organise for your annual golf club or society dinner? The usual round of prizes can be enhanced if you can get a well-known after-dinner speaker to tell a few yarns and take the mickey out of the captain's swing. But where can you get a speaker that won't cost the earth? Forget Faldo, Woosnam, Gallacher, Jacklin. They're way out of your price range. Some "stars" will set you back £100 a minute, or £3000 for a quick half-hour. As for other well-known golf nuts from the world of show business, like Tarbuck, Wogan and Forsyth, unless one of them's your secretary's uncle, forget that as well.

There's a solution, however. Chris Plumridge, an accomplished speaker himself, who covers golf in the Sunday Telegraph, and who has written for Golf Weekly for a number of years, formed Golfspeakers in 1990. Billing it as "The Talk of the Game", he has a list of golfing personalities who will light up your annual do for £350 upwards. For that you can get a half hour of witty and amusing golfing anecdotes from the likes of Michael McDonnell of the Daily Mail, Renton Laidlaw of the London Evening Standard and Sky Television, Sandy Jones, executive director of the PGA, based at The Belfry, John Wild, former president of the English Golf Union or John Stirling, the professional at Meon Valley, Hampshire.

Plumridge has tried to keep the organisation a regional one, to keep costs down and has developed a network throughout the country. So if you live in Manchester, you'll probably choose John Wild, who lives in Wigan, and avoid having to pay travelling costs and hotel bills. These are the costs that could make your annual speaker prohibitive. And Plumridge doesn't use showbiz or pro golfers because of the high cost factor.

John Wild, in fact, has made quite a name for himself on the after-dinner speakers circuit. IMG asked him to do a series of four functions in Australia recently. "It was a marvellous opportunity to see a country I'd never been to before," he said. "My wife Judy and I were treated wonderfully." His first engagement was at the Australian Open Championship, with Doug Sanders and Rolf Harris as fellow speakers. He began his after dinner career in 1966, and averages 60-70 occasions a year. He is best known for his campaign to get the Open Championship played at Wigan, his home club, even though it is only 9 holes. Ever the optimist, he is a witty after-dinner speaker.

Plumridge, based in Bucks, has written eight books on golf, as well as editing and packaging them for other writers. He also acts as Press and P.R man for the Golf Foundation. So when you start planning your annual golf awards night, give Chris a call on 0494-873137.

HOBBIES OF THE FAMOUS

Paul Newman likes fast cars, Nigel Mansell is a golf nut. But what about pro golfers? Extracted from the Official Tour Guides, here is a list of off-course activities that turn on the men and women of professional golf:

Bible study - Bobby Clampett
Bungee Jumping - Muffin Spencer-Davis
Club making - Arnold Palmer
Cycling - Seve Ballesteros
Dancing - Bernhard Langer
Duck shooting - Jim Gallagher Jnr
Eating - Russell Claydon
Fast cars - Laura Davies
Ford Mustangs - Fred Couples
Gardening and landscaping - Tom Kite
Guitar playing - Tom Watson
Parachuting - Eduardo Romero
Safaris - Jane Hill
Scuba diving - Greg Norman
Soccer - Bernhard Langer
Skiing - Craig Stadler
Swimming - Sandy Lyle
Wine collecting - Ronan Rafferty

Sandy Lyle - swimmer?

SONGS FOR SWINGING GOLFERS

How many times have you arrived home after a medal in the pouring rain, soaked to the skin, teeth chattering, ears full of water, to find your wife busy in the kitchen, humming "Singing in the Rain" quietly with a look that says-"You Fool"? When she says sweetly, "But I thought you said it never rains on the golf course, dear," you can find no words to answer her back. As music is supposed to soothe the savage beast, instead of clipping her ear with your Ping 3-wood, or stuffing three Topflite Magnas into her mouth,we urge you to give some thought to the hundreds of songs that are out there over the years, and present here our Top Twenty songs for swinging - and not so swinging- golfers. We've ignored the obvious ones like the horrible "Birdie Song" and Jane Morgan's song from the sixties, "The Day that the Rains Came Down". If all you readers out there can think of others, please let us know and we'll include them in next year's edition.

1. Straight Down the Middle, Bing Crosby
2. Love Letters in the Sand Trap, Pat Boone
3. 19th Hole Nervous Breakdown, Rolling Stones
4. Swing Low, Sweet Titleist, Vienna Boys Choir
5. Any Old 7-Iron, Peter Sellars
6. The Green Green Grass of Turnberry, Tom Jones
7. One Tree or Another, Keef James
8. Turn, Turn, Turn, The Byrds
9. 40 Shades of Green, Johnny Cash
10. Rhythm and Greens, The Shadows
11. Sunday, Bloody Sunday, U2 (Wives No.1)
12. Dimples, John Lee Hooker
13. The Twist, Chubby Checker
14. Fool in the Rain, Led Zeppelin
15. Straight Ahead, Brian Auger's Oblivion Express
16. I Wanna Break 100, Freddie Mercury and Queen
17. I'm Coming Home (in 39), Dave Edmunds' Rockpile
18. Simple Game, The Four Tops
19. Splish Splash, Bobby Darin and Charlie Drake
20. Sorrow and Pain, Unit 4 plus 2

AND AFTER THE GAME, THE CLUBHOUSE BLUES:

1. Don't Cry, Guns and Roses
2. Was it worth it? Pet Shop Boys
3. Poor Me, Adam Faith
4. Keep on Trying, Bobby Vee

5. Nightmare Returns, Alice Cooper
6. All in your Head, Hilton Valentine
7. Good Morning Heartache, Diana Ross
8. Green Swearwords, Booker Tee and the G-Men
9. Rough Boy, Z Z Top
10. Raining in my Heart, Buddy Holly

AND WHEN YOU GET HOME.....with apologies to the Beatles

It's been a hard day's golf
And I've been putting like a schmuck
It's been a hard day's golf
My tee shots were all right out of luck

But when I get home to you
You say," Dear, how did you do?
And was your game all right?"

It's been a hard day's golf
I was beaten 5 & 4
It's been a hard day's golf,
I'm not playing anymore.

I tried the Wilson Firestick
I could hit it a fair lick
Only one time out of four.

When I play, everything seems to go wrong.
When I putt, I always hit it too long
Or short.......

It's been a hard day's golf
Back to basics I must go,
When the assistant sees me swing
He knows I won't make a touring pro.

But when I get home to you
I know what I've got to do
I'll give it one more go,
TOMORROW.

AND WHEN YOU'RE IN LOVE..with more apologies to the Beatles.

She was just seventeen, you know what I mean,
And the way she putted was way beyond my dreams.
Now I'll never play with another
When I saw her on the green.

Well she took her five wood, I took my three
And she smacked it 200 yards off the tee,
When she got down for a birdie,
She had my love eternally.

Golf

By Gary
Norman

at the Movies

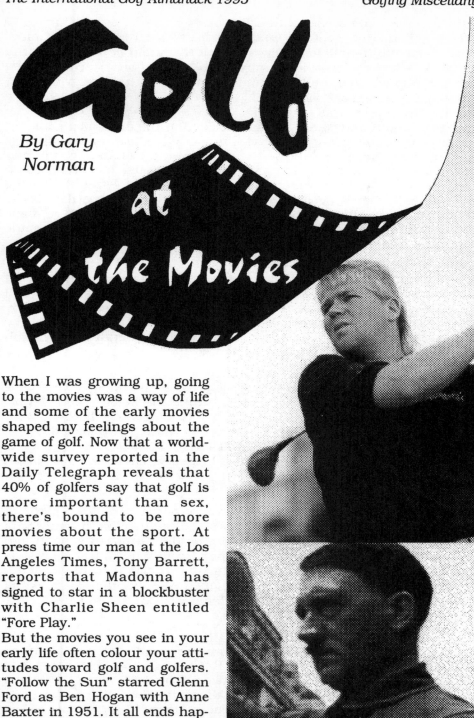

When I was growing up, going to the movies was a way of life and some of the early movies shaped my feelings about the game of golf. Now that a world-wide survey reported in the Daily Telegraph reveals that 40% of golfers say that golf is more important than sex, there's bound to be more movies about the sport. At press time our man at the Los Angeles Times, Tony Barrett, reports that Madonna has signed to star in a blockbuster with Charlie Sheen entitled "Fore Play."

But the movies you see in your early life often colour your attitudes toward golf and golfers. "Follow the Sun" starred Glenn Ford as Ben Hogan with Anne Baxter in 1951. It all ends happily, of course. Prior to that there had been odd scenes with golf courses as background, starring W C Fields, Katherine Hepburn amongst others. Then came "The Caddy" when Dean Martin and Jerry Lewis were at the height of their popularity in 1953. A few songs, a few funny faces and Pebble Beach. But the appetite was whetted, and "Goldfinger" set golf on its way, with Bond cheating Goldfinger and vice versa.

(See CHEAT story in this Almanack).

"M.A.S.H" and "Caddyshack" established golf in the mind as a game for off-duty medics or vicious and spoiled property speculators. Now the age of video stars Canadian actor Leslie Nielsen as a golf cheat. I'm sure that true golfers feel cheated by the way their beloved game has been treated over the years by the movie moguls. For sports fans, especially boxing and baseball, there's been plenty of movies in the last two decades to keep them more than happy. It's about time more movies were made about golf, so we've invented some, as Hollywood might have made them, and here are some of my favourites, old and new:

LADY CHATTERLEY'S SAND WEDGE (1962)

When Lord Chatterley suffers an accident with a bunker rake at Carnoustie, his wife, a 5-handicapper, has to deal with his moods and his inability to consummate the marriage. Her gardener shows an unexpected talent for golf and she gives him lessons so successfully that he makes it to the Ryder Cup. Stars Abe Mitchell, Gerald Bailey, Bob Andrews, Madonna and Tom Hanks. Rating ****

PSYCHO HILLS (1963)

Alfred Hitchcock's masterpiece with Tony Perkins as motel owner Greg Norman-Bates who develops the land behind his house into a 9-hole course. A mixed group of society golfers including Janet Leigh-Janzen, Sandra Dee, Mike Bletsoe-Brown and Bobby Darin arrive for a day out, bodies disappear and are later found in the lake by the ninth hole. Suspect weapon is a Ping Zing putter. Incredible climax as they watch the US Masters. Rating ***

WAR AND PEACE (1993)

Director Stanley Kubrick's dramatic account of the Ryder Cup battle at Kiawah Island when an Iranian terrorist cell kidnaps both teams and seals off the island. Jasper Carrot stars as the European captain and Larry Hagman is the Marine Colonel who blows up the 18th hole just as Bernhard Langer is about to putt in his crucial match with Paul Southworth . Robert Powell has a cameo role as the "Man in the Envelope." Nancy Sinatra as Debbie Couples steals the show with her table dance. Rating *****

MURDER ON THE ORIENT EXPRESS (1974)

Agatha Christie's classic story of murder and intrigue as Mark McCormack takes his troupe of IMG stars to Venice for the Michaelangelo Masters. Albert Finney plays Tony Jacklin, Jack Nicklaus as Arnold Palmer, Lauren Bacall as Mickey Walker with Sarah Puri, Jack Lemmon, Frank Sinatra and Spencer Tracey in a taut tale of lost balls, clubs, innocence and virginity. Rating **

THE BERLIN BUNKER (1945)

Stephen Speilberg's Oscar winning thriller about an Austrian painter who becomes the German Open champion, thanks to the skill of his blonde caddy, Eva Braun. Dramatic footage of North Africa, Sicily, Poland and the Russian Front. But his meteoric rise to fame is curtailed by his inability to play out of sand traps, and when he fails to get out of the Berlin bunker, he falls on his one-iron. Co-stars John Wayne as Henry Cotton, John Hurt as Bobby Jones, Eric Cantona as the French Resistance Open champion and Trevor Howard as a young Alex Hay. Rating ****

COBRA (1989)

Sylvester Stallone wrote, directed and starred in an all-action yarn of the rivalry between equipment manufacturers on the USPGA Tour. Brigitte Nielson, Becky Linville and Tony Curtis play leading roles as the trio who invent the golf ball with a silicon implant that can fly up to 500 yards when hit with a pitching wedge. The R &A ban it on the basis that is has nipples instead of dimples. Derek Loud, Peter Jones and Ian Morris are convincing as the evil scientists who try to steal the formula. Rating ****

BILLY LIAR (1963)

When a 12-handicapper accidentally changes his handicap to 22, he begins winning matches against the best his club can throw at him. When Julie Christie, as the lady captain, discovers the error she is torn between exposing Giles (Tom Courtenay) and exposing herself. Astonishing sex scene at the golf club's kitchen sink and Christie's agonising dilemma won her an Oscar. Co-stars Jill Wiffill, Jane Maxwell and Sian Richardson as Solheim Cup players. Rating ***

GOLDPUTTER (1968)

Auric Goldputter is a crook and a cheat at golf. He plans to steal all the putters in the world and force golf to become a game of 13 clubs. Sean Connery challenges him to a game at Stoke Poges Golf Club where Leslie Nielsen is the professional. Together they unmask the dastardly plot with the help of Shirley Temple, Shirley Eaton, Shirley Valentine, and Bill Heeps and the pompous Gert Frobe comes to a sticky end in an unraked bunker on the 12th. A classic. Rating *****

THE ACCIDENTAL GOLFER (1991)

Comedy starring Benny Hill as a one-armed taxi driver at St. Andrews who is asked to caddy for the great Jack Nicklaus, when the great man's caddy dislocates an elbow swilling McEwans. He steers the Golden Bear to victory around a tricky course and is asked to be Jack's permanent caddy. Together they travel the world, Nicklaus can't lose. Then the Caddy breaks his leg. Can Nicklaus win without him? Taut melodrama, co-starring Rita Hayworth, Rita Wilson and Rita Coolidge. Rating **

FATHER OF THE BRIDE (1991)

Steve Martin plays the lead role as a golf nut in East Sussex whose daughter arranges her wedding on the day of the golf club's annual championship. Martin organises the reception at the golf club, mayhem ensues as the guests mingle with a party of inebriated golfers from France who think the reception's in their honour. Dustin Hoffman, Sallyann Wilson, Kim Novak, Roger Mapley, Lewine Mair, Geena Davis and Francois Mitterand are the stars in this piece of harmless hokum. Rating ***

CARRY ON SLICING (1980)

The familiar gang invade a seaside golf course in Skegness for their company day out. Usual off-colour jokes and naughty scenes in the woods, with Hattie Jacques as the lady captain, Sid James, Charles Hawtrey, Bernard Bresslaw as Peter Alliss, Kenneth Williams as the club captain, Michael McDonnell as the journalist, Kelvin McKenzie as a TV reporter and Barbara Windsor as the caterer. Gene Kelly makes a cameo appearance and performs "Swinging in the Rain" on the first tee at Little Aston. Rating *

ROBIN HOOD- THE LEGEND OF MEN IN PLUS FOURS (1966)

When Robin is playing in a medal at Sherwood Forest, two of the Sheriff of Nottingham's lackeys accuse him - in a letter to the committee - of cheating, once of moving his ball on the fairway, and twice of dropping a ball down a hole in his green tights. He is exonerated by the committee, but the duo refuse to apologise, so he takes the case to the Sheriff himself. John Buckingham stars as Robin, Richard Greene as Will Scarlet, Laura Davies as Maid Marian, and a menacing Renton Laidlaw as the sheriff. Gripping courtroom drama. Rating ***

THROW YOUR GOLF CLUBS OFF A TRAIN (1990)

Danny De Vito is a fed up tour pro who has just failed to renew his Tour Card at Qualifying school. On his way back to Minnesota and a job at the local dingy municipal course, he decides to end it all and throw himself and his clubs off the train on the suspension bridge over the Mississippi. But a blonde waitress, on an exchange scholarship from Inter-City, played by Kim Bassinger, herself a low handicap golfer, sees his predicament, seduces him into playing one last celebrity tournament in Brooklyn, which he wins in spectacular fashion against the British champion Jim Bob Green, and his confidence is restored. Great family entertainment. Take plenty of tissues. You'll cry a lot. Rating ****

THE SAND PEBBLES (1967)

John Wayne is an ex-Marine who turns to golf and makes it to the US Open. Stuck in a bunker on the 10th at Winged Foot, he impatiently kicks some pebbles out of the way in a greenside bunker. Underneath the pebbles lives a family of leprechauns who've been trying to get out for a decade. They grant Big John three wishes and he wins the US Open, the Masters and the PGA all in the same season. But in the British Open he's locked in a tie with Irish Legend Christy O'Connor, and the leprechauns have to choose between their promise and their native son. Gripping drama with Rachael O'Vass, Jim O'Noble, Maureen O'Hara, Piers O'Bickley, Darby O'Gill, Joe O'Kelly, Declan O'Betts and Peter O'Bedwell as the leprechauns. Rating ****

THE SANDS OF IWO JIMA (1958)
Two US marines in the South Pacific find a half-dead 16-year old Japanese soldier in a sand trap on a deserted island. They adopt him and take him back home to California where he learns to play golf and becomes the greatest bunker player of all time. John Mitsushiba, Billy Nolan, David Green, Paddy Loughnane, Tony Kelly and Tommy Nakajima star with Jumbo Osaki in the lead role. Subtitles. Rating *

SHARK'S TREASURE (1975)
The moving story of Greg Norman's climb to fame from humble beginnings as an inept Sydney waiter and beach bum. Paul Hogan plays the lead with Ben Elton as his caddy, Jeremy Reed as his arch rival, Oliver Reed as Craig Stadler and Diana Dors as the tart with a heart who shows him the way out of the slums. Not a dry eye in the house. Rating *

BASIC INSTINCT (1991)
Michael Douglas plays a Ryder Cup star who visits the disco at The Belfry, picks up a lady golf pro during a Motown medley, wines, dines and beds her. To him it's only a one-night stand in a trail of casual affairs across Europe. To Glenn Close, however, it's a lot more serious and she follows him from tournament to tournament, putting spiders in his golf bag, smearing his grips with superglue, poisoning his caddy and burning his Ram Tour favourite woods. Ben Crenshaw saves him, but not before a succession of devastating eagles and albatrosses, as well as some horrible bogeys, attack him on the cliffs at Pebble Beach. A real cliffhanger. Rating *****

HOOK (1991)
Peter Pan and Tinkerbell befriend the dreaded Captain Hook, curing his fade, draw, slices and hooks. Animated Disney cartoon that will delight junior golfers everywhere. Rating ***

WHITE MEN CAN'T PUTT (1992)
Woody Harrelson and Wesley Snipes play the lead roles in the story of the integration of Augusta National Golf Club. Only Blacks and women are allowed to join and "The Masters" becomes "The Mistress". Heady stuff as Whoopie Goldberg sinks a 40 foot putt to become the first winner of the Pink Jacket. Co-stars Betty Grable and Betty Place. Rating *****

THE STUD (1976)
Classic Jackie Collins novel on the big screen with Oliver Tobias as the US amateur champion who wins the Masters, beating all the big names. Joan Collins stars as his agent who has designs on more than his swing after she sees him in the showers, and the story moves from Shinnecock Hills to Hollywood Hills as he roams from bed to bed, course to course, drinking and carousing his way to fame and fortune. John Daly co-stars as a Budweiser salesman who straightens him out. Rating ***

HAVE YOU GOT A FAVOURITE GOLF MOVIE? IF SO, PLEASE WRITE TO THE INTERNATIONAL GOLF ALMANACK 1996.

"CAN THIS BE THE SAME CONFIDENT
CAREFREE HUSBAND WHO ONLY AT
BREAKFAST TOLD ME HE HAD COMPLETELY
MASTERED THE PALMER METHOD?"

The genius that was

George Houghton

Bob Hope once said of his friend George Houghton, "In the game of golf, he discovered laughs. I can't, all I get is tears"
George Houghton, sadly, died last October at the age of 88, working to the last.

Anyone who knows golf and can read will know about George. Every Christmas from 1952 to the mid-1970's, at least one of his books on Golf Addiction had found its way onto bookshelves across the world. Titles such as "The Golf Addicts Omnibus", "Golf Addict among the Scots", "I am a Golf Widow" and "Addict in Bunkerland" will be familiar to any reader over fifty.

But the "Addict" series wasn't his only contribution to the world of books. His first few (1936-49) were about the military, amongst which was "They Flew through Sand", about the RAF in the Western desert. This was dramatised for the BBC and twice televised. Even in wartime, however, his interest was golf, and he set up a three hole course in the Western desert which Major Randolph Churchill strenuously tried to get banned, but was overruled. By the end of the war he had risen to the rank of Group Captain, and was awarded the OBE by King George VI. Whether this had anything to do with his golf exploits is unrecorded.

He launched his own brand of humour on the golf world in 1952 with "Confessions of a Golf Addict", and then took his addict on a tour of USA (1958), Ireland (1965), the Far East (1967), and Wales (1969). Various compilations and omnibuses have been published in the last 20 years.

"This is my crusade to make a world of happy hackers who will spread their gospel far and wide. "To hell with nuclear physics and megatons..." they will shout. I agree. Let the moon keep shining serenely, without having to duck our rockets. Get priorities right - golf first, skylarking later." That was George Houghton's introduction to Golf Addict Strikes Again, published in 1963 by Country Life Limited, and it sums up his whole philosophy to golf. He cornered golf addiction as a permanent theme for his writing and cartoons, making shrewd analyses of golfing emotions along the way. He ferreted out foibles and characteristics, drew the characters involved and offered many predicaments as a cartoon comment on the golf mores of over forty years.

And he found rich material all over the world. He would often recount the story of the Catholic priest on a remote island in the Philipines who used the church collections to maintain nine holes for his congregation of golf addicts! And they loved his cartoons in every corner of the globe. Bing Crosby, perhaps the best known golf addict in the world, arranged that over a hundred Cartoon Calendars by Houghton should be sent to his friends in Hollywood, Madrid, Paris and London every year. Bob Hope promptly accused Crosby of trying to buy their friendship, so highly did he rate the work of George Houghton. Jack Benny's meanness was also a Hope target. "He only sent out one Houghton calendar this Christmas, and that was cash on delivery!" he claimed.

As his wife Kay explained in a foreword to Sean Arnold's book, "The Best of George Houghton," published in 1991, "A golf addict takes his wife to Paris to see the shops, but he is more interested in the Arc de Triomphe and the possibility of clearing the high archway with a 9-iron. That did actually make one of his cartoons."

Cartoons

Houghton was a prolific writer, particularly in the sixties when he wrote eleven books within a decade and he drew his own cartoons. His Cartoon Calendar for Golf Addicts has appeared annually since 1952 and is still published by Collins. Sales of his golf-humour books total well over two million, by far the largest of any writer-cartoonist in the sports field. He also spent some 15 years as associate editor of the magazine "Golf World" where his "Hackers Corner" had an immense following. And an unusual side to his ability was his creation of brand logos for advertising agencies. Few people know that it was George who created the Polar Bear for Fox's Glacier Mints, still on the wrappers 30 years later.

Hole in One

Many of his books are now out of print and collectors items. During the last few years, he concentrated on painting golf landscapes- he was a professional artist- in oils and watercolours. In the mid-Sixties he founded the Golf Addicts Society of Great Britain, and, though far from a first class player, he travelled the world in search of material for his books along with his non-playing wife and personal assistant, Kay. His material was drawn from the sort of incidents and confessions that only a true addict could relate, such as hitting 600 balls in a one day attempt to get a hole in one at the 200 yard second at Letchworth.

He failed, but the attempt provided another anecdote for yet another book. His wife Kay recounts that, despite his failure at Letchworth, George did achieve TWO holes in one, the first while playing with the Governor of the Isle of Man and another at Worthing Golf Club, which was at the time his home club.

George Houghton has been called the golf addict of the civilised world. For Bernard Hunt, the Golf Addict books made him realise that golf isn't always the serious business the professionals imagine. Henry Longhurst summed him up as the "little man of golf who likes to think himself as, and he is, the backbone of the game. Golf cuts us all down to size and George's books strike a chord of sympathy among golfers all over the world." Tony Jacklin is another Houghton fan.

"Golf is fun. Laughs at the end of the day act as a healing balm on the wounds made by sclaffy shots and missed putts." And the Daily Mail's Michael McDonnell commented that only George Houghton came close to defining golf's eternal challenge.

For any writer, his books are his legacy, his gift to the world. George Houghton has managed to leave a rich treasure trove of laughs for golfers in every single corner of the globe. His timeless portrayal of every situation on the golf course has given him legions of fans. And surely future generations of golfers will discover his unique brand of humour for as long as golf grips nations, as it has all of us over the years. Houghton's portrayal of golfers in love matches anything PG Wodehouse has ever written: "They strolled along beneath the moon. It was teed up on a great cloud and looked exactly like a brand new Dunlop 65 waiting to be walloped. Freda sat on the stile.

"I'm glad they're widening the tenth," she whispered. Matt didn't reply, but he squeezed her smooth white hand - the left, which was usually gloved. Without speaking they gazed on the rolling terrain. After a while, Matt murmured: "Your brassie shots are divine." It was the highest praise he knew. "

We all toy with golf for a while, like a child tugs with the jowls of a St. Bernard. Then one day, we are converted to the three knuckle grip. Before we even realise it, golf gobbles us up and handicap erosion sets in, one stroke at a time, down from a despised 28. When that happens, forget the weekly lessons and start reading George Houghton.

He'll make you laugh at yourself, at the dreaded golf addiction and keep you human.

"SO THAT I SHAN'T BE LATE ON THE TEE"

"HE"S JUST WONDERING WHETHER TO HAVE A GO
WITH HIS BLASTER - OR PRETEND IT'S A LOST BALL"

THE RISE AND RISE
OF THE GOLF SOCIETY

Summer is now over and the lush fairways of the British Isles have been crawling with golfers. The Ryder Cup is not far away and the aspiring Faldos, Woosnams and Watsons are all hacking away at their handicaps with a vengeance.

The recession has hit golf as it has most things. Some golf courses have gone into receivership, Slaley Hall near Newcastle, Staverton Park in Northants, Broome Park in Kent, Aldershaw near Hastings and the £20 million Quietwaters complex in Essex. Others, like Collingtree Park in Northampton, have risen Phoenix-like from disaster to success.

But the older, more established courses remain almost impossible to get into. Waiting lists are long, sometimes five years, and organisations like the Golf Club of G.B. and the recently revamped Tony Jacklin Golf Club have jumped into the gap and offer members the opportunity to play some of the great courses as well a providing them with a handicap.

But there is an easier way. Thumb your nose at the golf club and its waiting list. It's so simple, and tens of thousands of maniac golfers have done it already. It's legal, sociable and doesn't cost the earth. Just form your own golf society. Or join one that's already in existence.

It is now a matter of historical coincidence that the recession has witnessed a dramatic surge in the formation and membership of golf societies. Whether this is simply an accident is for the social analyst to agonise over, but the facts are these:

1. There are currently 330 golf societies registered with the English Golf Union. Conservative estimates are that there are at least 12 times that amount of active golf societies not registered, a total of approximately 3960 societies in England alone.

2. The Scottish Golf Union lists 150 societies, and the Welsh Golf Union 15 societies.

3. Each registered society has an average of 35 members, though this is misleading because of the larger numbers in the older societies. A typical golf society has around 25 members.

4. Of the 330 registered societies in England, 237 were formed in 1987 or later. Of these, 177 were formed after 1990.

5. The total of 495 registered societies in the UK (excluding all of Ireland), plus the estimated 5840 unregistered societies means a staggering total of 6335 societies and an estimated 221725 golfers playing as part of societies.

6. What is difficult to calculate also is the number of golf club members who play as part of "casual societies" within the club and who play as often as six times a year at some of the premier clubs in the UK. This we estimate to be in the region of 10000.

7. The Playing Card Club has 9000 members, the Golf Society of Great Britain has over 10000 members, and the Tony Jacklin Club similar numbers.

8. The total number of society golfers could be in the region of 260000, a figure we consider to be a conservative one.

Society golf began in 1911 with the Bank of England G.S. and there were only five in existence by 1939, all formed as a social side to working in a large company. One more society followed in the forties, none at all in the fifties, only nine in the sixties. Then the gradual rush began with 35 in the seventies, growing to a total of 65 by 1986.

Then the stampede began, with 237 formed in the six years between 1987 and the end of 1992. From 1987-1989 inclusive, societies were being created at the rate of 20 a year; then, from 1990-1992 inclusive, it was 59 per annum, a staggering three-fold increase.

The oldest society, as mentioned, is the Bank of England Golf Society, still thriving with 242 members, holding 20 events a year. Second oldest is the BBC, formed in 1928.

Currently with 257 members, it is not known whether Mr Wogan or Mr Tarbuck are members. What is known is that the shortest golfer in its history, and still the record holder, is Mr Ronnie Corbett. Joint third oldest are the Old Chigwellians of Essex (90 members) and Western Motor Industry of Avon (50 members), both formed in 1929.

The largest society is the BBC with 257 members. It was larger last year, but Ronnie Barker, who counted as four members, has now retired. Of the 150 Scottish golf societies, 20 are in Glasgow and an astonishing 72 in Edinburgh.

Among the most active societies are the Sheffield 30 Club with 28 events a year; Stockbridge Village Cricket Club on Merseyside with 30 events (whenever do they get the time to play cricket?); but the most active is the Ford Laser GS with 31 events a year for a membership of 32. Pass the Philosan tablets, please.

On the other side of the activity coin, several societies have only 2 or 3 meetings a year. The Beech Tree Inn from Cheshire with 25 members has only one event, obviously preferring sinking pints to sinking putts. But at least they do have one event, unlike the Palmers Green GS from Middlesex who have 28 members and NO meetings. But the prize for laziness must go to the aptly named Idle Golf Society from Yorkshire who have 24 members and, again, not a single meeting. No, nary a one. The mind truly boggles, answers on a postcard, please.

Some societies take their names from their local pub. 39 do, and 20 take their names from animals or birds. But some names are unfathomable, like the Green Sneakers from Glasgow, and the 1-62 GS from Symington. All walks of life are represented, and you'll find a few here to puzzle over.

There's Bellringers from Staffs, Colliery workers from Notts and the Home Guard GS from Eastham in Cheshire. I leave you to guess how long it takes them to play 18 holes. Their secretary is a Mr R.E.Jones. Not a corporal by any chance, is he? There's Grasshoppers from Dorset - I thought they'd play cricket, ha,ha! There's stockbrokers from the James Capel GS - do they "share" their clubs, I wonder?

Prison officers from Lindholme in Yorks- is this an "open" prison? The Old Leamingtonians from Warwicks- do they use the old school "tee"? The Old Whingers from Sussex speaks for itself, as do the Whigs GS from (where else?) Surrey.

There are the strange gentlemen of the Hate Cup G.S in Oxon, the Nadgers, the Newts and the Oddfellows; the Pig on the Wall GS from Warrington and the Shell Cracking GS from Merseyside. Or try the U to Me GS from Welwyn, Herts; or the Flying Scud GS of Surrey, formed in 1991. Is Stormin' Norman a member? Then there's the Happy Hookers GS from London who must be fun to play with. If I tell you there's 23 members, there's no pun intended.

There are societies for every trade, profession and walk of life. The Abbey Panels from Coventry- they're unbeatable; The BP Nutrition GS- that's food for thought; The Likely Lads GS- president James Bolam? There are societies for ambulancemen, bus drivers, police, although we understand that the West Midlands Police GS has been suspended on full handicap, pending a countback. There's the Burnham Cabs GS of Berkshire. Do they yell "Fore" or "Fare"?

There are Boilermakers from Gwent, Clergy from Glasgow, Dentists from Edinburgh, Railway workers from Perth, the Abinger Roughs from Surrey with the only lady secretary in the country. And, of course, the Ga Ga Mumfa of Kent. What next? There is even a society in Maidstone with a knowledge of Latin, the Semper Circantes, whose secretary Neil Webber assures me that it means " Forever Searching", presumably for lost balls. As Butch Cassidy said to the Sundance Kid when they were being doggedly tailed by the posse that wouldn't let go-" "Who are these guys?"

There are also societies for nationalities, with the Scots and Irish especially active. There is a national union of Irish golf societies, with local societies in Luton, Oxford, Northampton, Notts, virtually everywhere, in fact.

I had a call last week from a society in Bournemouth, asking for a match with my own Pitsford group. It seemed a good idea till they told me their name. They're probably very nice guys, but I wouldn't know whether to go all out to beat them or throw the match. In the end I declined and asked them to contact the Duke of York GS or the Prince of Wales GS.

Now that the Royals are paying tax, it seemed only fair that they should also share other burdens, especially now that Andrew plays off a respectable 10. So if you, like me, get a call from the Bournemouth &

Southampton Inland Revenue Golf Society, don't say I told you so, but refer them to the Duke of York or the Prince of Wales

After all, you never know, do you?

FORMING YOUR OWN SOCIETY

There are two ways to start. Firstly, the casual way. Does anyone in your office play golf? Find a few partners and you've got the beginnings. Organise a few competitions, or challenge another company, or another office. Or even enter a team in your local newspaper's annual competition, if there is one. Many local pubs also have their own team or full-blown society. Join them or challenge them, and your landlord is a good place to start.

Secondly, there is the organised way. Contact the Scottish, Welsh or English Golf Unions, (EGU telephone number is 0533-553042). They're very helpful but you'll need to have 20 active members, and they'll send you a copy of the rules. These are not very complicated, and it'll cost you about £3 a head to become a registered society in England. They'll explain how to issue handicap certificates, which is a critical area. You'll also have to elect a captain, a secretary,a treasurer and a committee, but again this is the essence of simplicity. You can charge your members £20-£30 per year. That should cover the cost of printing, letters, stamps and telephone calls. Open a bank account locally in the society's name, with at least three signatories (any two of three will do). Decide on a name. That's a lot of fun in itself, see the examples above.

By this time you will have your letterheads and handicap cards via a local printer ready to give out to your members and you're ready to go.

The first question is- Where do we meet? What's wrong with the local pub? Most societies seem to have a common meeting place - usually work or the local.

The next question is- where do we play? In any of the golfing magazines, especially Today's Golfer or the new Fore! magazine, there are pages and pages of golf clubs advertising their rates for societies. These range from £30 to £40 for a days golf including coffee, light lunch, dinner and 27 holes. There are other, more spectacular and expensive courses like Woburn, Wentworth or The Belfry where you'll pay around £80-£120. They're superb courses but better saved till your society has found its feet, and a format is established around more humble courses. The recession means that there are very few golf clubs who turn away society bookings. Twenty golfers will easily spend upwards of £1000 on a day's enjoyment, and this is vital revenue for the golf clubs today. Or simply contact your local golf club secretary. You'll find him anything but stuffy, and he will bend over backwards to help make it an enjoyable day. Try to choose a course that's no more than an hour's drive away from home, so you can all be on the tee around 9.30 and home by 9 or 10 o'clock.

Now you've organised the venue, what is the best format for the day? I mentioned 27 holes earlier because we have found that the best formula for a day's golf is nine holes in the morning playing a Texas scramble, and then 18 holes stableford or matchplay in the afternoon. That way nobody falls asleep during the presentation. "What presentation?" you say. Well, it's a good idea to build into the day some prizes for, e.g., the-longest drive, nearest the pin, the highest stableford score, and a few booby prizes like the lowest stableford points or the shortest drive!

Society golf is a lot of fun, but there are three main things to keep at the front of your mind. One is to appoint a captain who can play reasonable golf and who can keep members straight about the rules and etiquette. Also appoint a secretary who will make sure that everyone turns up on the day. But the most important thing to instill into your members is to respect the rules of the course you have chosen to play, especially dress rules and general course etiquette. Simple good manners, like replacing your divots and letting quicker golfers play through will go a long way to ensure that local club members do not resent giving up their course to a society. After all, you'll want to go back next year, won't you?

"WHAT A LIFE ! - FIRST MY WIFE
LEAVES ME - NOW THIS SLICE!"

"HE'S TRYING OUT AN OVERLAP GRIP"

ROYAL GOLF
The most exclusive Golf Courses in the world

How do you get to play some of the world's most famous golf courses? It's usually quite simple. With Pebble Beach, Augusta, Wentworth, Doral, Woburn, St Andrews and the like, it's not that difficult if you're willing to pay the course fee. The resourceful Golf Society secretary can, with a bit of experience, get his member on to any course in Europe at a reasonable fee.

Royal Golf Courses, however, are a different ballgame, as Alex Hay is wont to say. There are two only in the U.K, at Windsor Castle and Balmoral, both for the exclusive use of anyone serving the Royal Family, whether a Civil List employee or on the Royal staff, with friends by invitation. From the 1920's there was also a twelve hole course at Sandringham but this was ploughed up in 1940.

It is known that senior members of the Royal Household played the Windsor Castle course from 1901, when it was laid out on the instructions of King Edward VII by Muir Ferguson, who also made alterations to the course in 1905. It is a nine-hole course with eighteen tees. Ferguson was a distinguished amateur player who had laid out a course at Woking, called New Zealand. He sketched out the Windsor Castle links with the last hole ending up just below the East Terrace, and men with stakes marked where the bunkers were to go. Instructions were then given to the farm bailiff to have the bunkers made.

Two months later Ferguson received an irate telegram from the King to the effect that the course was ruined and that the bunkers were to be raised to the ground. The man who had made the bunkers had no knowledge of golf and the result was that the course looked like a graveyard with tombstones dotted about. Muir Ferguson was summoned along with the professional from nearby Datchet, the bunkers were rebuilt and the King was finally happy.

Leading golfers were invited to play with the King. First of all Alexander Kircaldy came down from Scotland, but the occasion proved too much for him, he got rather drunk and was sent back home. Then Ben Sayers came and was a great success. He was always keen to praise the King's shots, and once, when the Royal topped his drive he exclaimed, "Very good direction, Your Majesty." Once when the King said he would play at three o'clock, Sayers teed up two brand new balls ready, but received a message that the game was delayed till four, so he went away.

Meanwhile Queen Alexandra came out to play and, finding the new balls, proceeded to play a sort of hockey with them till they were battered into a three- cornered shape. She then replaced the balls on the tee and went in.

At four o'clock the King came out and asked Sayers if he had any golf balls. Sayers said that two new ones were on the tee, ready. When the King saw the battered balls, he thought Sayers was trying to be funny and was not amused. Luckily Sayers had plenty more, but it wasn't till teatime that the King found out that the Queen had played at three and understood why the new balls were so battered.

The Balmoral Castle course is also nine holes with eighteen tees, and is much used by those on duty when the Queen is there in August and September. It was laid out by Jimmy Gibb in 1922, using natural landscape. It is a pleasant hill course with attractive slopes and hollows with fine trees, measuring 2235 yards and a par of 33. There are four short holes, ranging from 96 to 233 yards and one par five.

The Windsor Castle course is 4560 yards off the eighteen tees, par 64, with eight par threes, and no par fives. The longest hole is the 406 yard sixth, the shortest the 107 yard fifth.

In the 1920's and 1930's the sons of King George V played golf, and it is known during his brief reign that King Edward VIII played on the Balmoral course. The only member of today's Royal Family who plays golf, however, is the Duke of York.

JUST ONCE IN YOUR LIFE
A GOLFER'S FANTASY

There are courses to play and some to dream about. You see them on television. John Daly drives the green on a four hundred yard par four, Greg Norman plays a nine iron out of deep rough on to the apron and Bernhard Langer, stuck up a tree, takes the tiger line out of trouble. Tom Kite plays a loose shot at Pebble Beach and ends up in the rocks, his ball retriever useless in the foamy surf. Mark Calcavecchia loses his nerve and slices his drive into the water at Kiawah. But what are they like to play, these manicured courses with the magnolias and the island greens?

The short answer is, they're murder. On the nerve ends and also on the pocket. Try a round at Pebble Beach in California for upwards of $100. The site of three US Opens, 1972,1982 and 1992, it's awesome in every sense of the word. Friends who've sampled the course come home marvelling at the scenery, but with advice: "Don't shop there," or "How much is scenery worth?" or "The greens are poor from too much play."

Much the same is true of The Blue course at Doral Resort and Country Club in Miami. A round there, on the site of the Doral-Ryder Open, will set you back $100 at least. And the comments from those who've been range from: "Pure class" to "Great hype, poor greens" and "Green fees are outrageous, not worth the high price."

The Ko Olina Golf Club in Oahu, Hawaii is the site of the LPGA Hawaiian Ladies Open. The 6870 yards par 72 course will cost you $100 and up. More reasonable (less than $100) is the Kapalua Golf club on Maui, Hawaii, venue for the USPGA's Kapalua International. Even better is the Greenbrier, White Sulphur Springs, West Virginia, site of one Ryder Cup, where you can play for around $60 on a course designed by Jack Nicklaus. Comments here were "spectacular" and "thrilling."

The Tournament Players Club of Scottsdale, Arizona is the home of the Phoenix Open. Again cost was over $100, it's murder in the summer months and the greens are slow. It's a similar story with the Players Club at Sawgrass, in Ponte Verde Beach, near Jacksonville, Florida. At least $100 is needed for your green fees and comments range from "Intimidating, too hard," to "Overpriced and overrated." It's a similar story at the PGA National course at Palm Beach Gardens, near West Palm Beach, Florida. Although you can play four different courses, each with a green fee of around $50, the Champion course will set you back over $100, and again the comments range from a gushing "Just wonderful" to a caustic "Too expensive." The Broadmoor at Colorado Springs is slightly better value for money. The USGA Women's Open was played here in 1995, and there is a choice of three different courses, all par 72 and close to 7000 yards in length. The scenery is beautiful, the only drawback is that you have to stay at the resort hotel in order to be allowed to pay your $99 green fees.

But by far the best value of all the courses on the USPGA Tour was the Torrey Pines Golf Course, near San Diego, California. The home of the Buick Invitational of California, it will cost you around $50 to play the North or South course, both with great coastline views and the crashing of the Pacific Ocean as backdrop. And if you remember the drama of the missed putt by Bernhard Langer in the 1991 Ryder Cup, you can pay a nostalgic visit to Kiawah Island, near Charleston, South Carolina. There are three courses at the resort, costing around $50, and the Ocean course, with green fees of $100 and upwards, designed by Pete Dye, in an area of staggering beauty. Described as the "Pebble Beach of the East Coast", it's reckoned to be the toughest course in the world, with wind a significant factor, just to add to the general difficulty of the place.

So the general feeling of many who have played the legendary courses in the USA is that yes, they look good, some of staggering beauty, some of horrific difficulty. The common denominator is that if they've been on the tour or television, they're going to cost you at least $100. Some can wreck your score, a few can wreck your pocket. But if it's thrills you're after, there's nothing like Pebble Beach in June, or Kiawah Island with the wind blowing strong in your face. Just take plenty of dollar bills and a sackful of balls......

The Weirdest Golf Clubs
in the World?

The Teeth of the Dog Golf Club, Horse Thief Country Club and other strange names...

There aren't many golf clubs in the British Isles where you raise an eyebrow at the name. The vast majority reflect the area in which the club is located. When you travel, however, you realise that there are some weird and wonderful names given to golf clubs, some of which are beyond logic and belief. Many are named for animals native to the area, like Moose Creek, some for geographical landmarks, like The Pines. Many are American Indian unpronounceables. A few obviously feel that golf is a lazy man's game, like the Sleepy Hole Golf Course in Portsmouth, Virginia, where dogs still serve as forecaddies, finding and retrieving lost balls! The International Golf Almanack proudly presents its list of the Weirdest Golf Clubs in the World. If any reader comes across any stranger names, please let us know, and send us a card of the course.

Medium Weird.

Pheasant Run, Ontario, Canada.
Buffalo Valley, Johnson City, Tennessee.
Lion's Paw, North Carolina.
Owl's Head, Quebec, Canada.
Wolf Creek, Alberta, Canada.
Falcon's Lair, South Carolina.
Fox Run, Plymouth, Michigan.
Ruffled Feathers, Chicago.
Steeple Chase, near Chicago.
Trysting Tree, Oregon.
Chardonnay Club, California.
Fox Chase, Lancaster, Pennsylvania.
Fox Squirrel, Southport, North Carolina
Hounds Ears, Blowing Rock, North Carolina.
Possum Run, South Carolina.
Raccoon Run, South Carolina.
Sun Dance, Minneapolis, Minnesota.
Wind Dance, near New Orleans.
Kicking Bird, Oklahoma.
Hanging Rock, Roanoke, Virginia.
Blackwolf Run, Kohler, near Milwaukee, Wisconsin.
Hell's Point, Virginia.

Honey Bee, Virginia Beach, Virginia.
Sudden Valley, Washington.
Ghost Creek, Cornelius, Oregon.

Very Weird

Spook Rock, Suffern, New York.
Wind Watch, Hauppauge, New York. (You have been warned.)
Kayak Point, near Seattle, Washington. (There must be water here somewhere.)
Whirlpool Golf Course, Niagara Falls, Canada. (There IS water here.)
Walking Stick, Pueblo, Colorado. (Take a buggy.)
Three Little Bakers, Delaware. (The food is good here.)
The Witch, Conway, near Myrtle Beach, South Carolina.
My Old Kentucky Home, near Louisville, Kentucky. (Take your banjo.)
Big Sky, near Bozeman, Montana.
Trappers Turn, near Madison, Wisconsin. (Davy Crockett hat optional.)
The Mirage, Nevada. (If you've got a handicap from this club, nobody believes you.)
Bald Head Island, North Carolina. (Leave your toupee in the clubhouse.)
Superstition, Arizona.
Bent Tree, Sunbury, Ohio. (Watch out for the wind.)
Breakers, Palm Beach. (Where car thieves retire to?)
Hard Labor Creek, near Atlanta, Georgia.
Swan Lake, Manorville, New York. (Tu-Tus are optional.)
Stanhope, Prince Edward Island, Canada. (What we all do on the first tee.)
Dead Horse Lake, Knoxville, Tennessee.
Gator Hole, North Myrtle Beach, S. Carolina. (Just don't look for your ball in the lake.)
French Lick Springs, Louisville, Kentucky.
Licking Springs Trout & Golf Club, Newark, Ohio. (No, I don't believe it either.)
Hecla Golf Club, Manitoba, Canada. (Sounds like the House of Commons at question time.)
Grapevine, near Dallas, Texas. (Catch up on all the gossip.)
Jeckyll Island, Jacksonville, Florida. (A very open course, with nowhere to Hyde?)
Page Belcher, Tulsa, Oklahoma. (Don't eat there. The noise of the other diners will put you off.)
Cochiti Golf Club, New Mexico. (Members of Sherwood Forest don't play here.)
Ole Miss, Oxford, Mississippi. (Watch the two foot putts here.)
Miracle Hill, Omaha, Nebraska. (The place for high handicappers.)
Teeth of the Dog, Casa de Campo, Dominican Republic. (I think something's got lost in the translation? Shouldn't it be the Hair?)
Robber's Row, Port Royal, Hilton Head, South Carolina. (Where you padlock your clubs.)
Sentryworld, Stevens Point, Wisconsin. (Your clubs are safe here.)

Intercourse Golf Club, Bird in Hand, Lancaster, Pennsylvania. (No comment. Just dress for the occasion, and send lots of postcards home.)
Horse Thief Country Club, near Bakersfield, California. (Don't leave your car there.)
Leather Stocking, Cooperstown, New York. (Politicians and ex- ministers welcome.)

"I HAVE A FEELING THAT YOUR FRIENDS WOULD RATHER BE SOMEWHERE ELSE . . ."

"HE ALWAYS PRACTICES DURING SIESTA!"

HOOKED ON GOLF

Last year I became hopelessly hooked on golf because of the betting. I'm not ashamed to admit it.

The morning after watching yet another re-run of the famous James Bond film "Goldfinger"—remember how they cheated their way around a golf course? – I stood, as a new, happy owner of a 27-handicap certificate on the first tee with a trio of pals, 26, 22 and 17 handicaps respectively.

"Pound a corner, chaps?" enquired Phil, the 17 handicapper, innocently. We all made "Yes" nods, including me. I didn't really want the others to know that I hadn't a clue what a corner was. I had, in fact, previously assumed that a corner was somewhere a Pakistani built a shop. But that was before being introduced to the jargon of Golf.

"And nearest the pin on par 3's for a pound?" inquired the 17-handicapper.

"Good idea!" we all chorussed. At least here I was on safe ground -I knew what the bet was this time.

The first hole was a nightmare. 4 shots to the green and 3 putts left me with a 7 on a hilly par 4. "That's 7 -less the 2 shots you get-so it's 5 for a point," said Phil, the 17 handicapper.

"What do you mean?" I enquired with some trepidation.

Phil explained patiently that we were playing Stableford, off three quarters of full handicap, so I'd get at least one shot every hole and two shots on the most difficult 3 holes. This system gave me 21 strokes on 18 holes. I was a bit mystified but I knew they'd keep me right as there was money on the game. As the first was stroke index 3, I got two shots, hence a nett 5. A nett par would get me 2 points,a nett bogey scored one point.

I began to feel quite pleased with myself. If I could keep this up, I'd have 18 points at the end of the game.

The second hole was a par 3,190 yards over water." You'll need a 6-iron here," volunteered Phil,who was being very helpful. The water looked a bit daunting so I took a 4-iron. The ball soared low over the pond, skipped on the bank and rolled to 6 feet from the flagstick. The others were all off the green, one in a bunker.

Phil clapped me on the back. "Super shot. What did you use?"

The others were equally enthusiastic. I waited while they all chipped on to the green and had plenty of time to line up my putt. I did what I'd seen Woosnam and Nicklaus do on television, holding my putter in line with the hole while crouching on my haunches.

I hadn't a clue why they do this but it seemed to help Nicklaus sink all those long putts.

The 17-handicapper, Phil, was chewing vigorously on his cigar, the 26-er was sucking loudly on mint imperials, the 22-er jingled coins in his pocket. I closed my mind to the background noise. I'd be like Freddie Couples—nothing could faze me. I stroked the ball from 6 feet, it slid up to the hole, seemed to pass it, then fell in sideways.

The crunch of mint imperials stopped, the pocket change fell silent and the puffs of stale cigar smoke hung heavily over the flagstick.

"Well sunk, old boy," choked Phil, the 17-er.

"Side-door job," muttered Charles, the 26-er.

"That's a quid from us," smiled Bill the 22-er, "and double for a birdie, of course."

I didn't know about that rule, so I kept quiet. I simply nodded. "How many points is that?" I choked.

"Let's see. You got a 2, less your shot, so that's a net one for 4 points," said Phil, the 17-er. "Well done. That was a real pressure putt."

The drizzle was starting as we walked to the 3rd. "Your honour," said Bill. I gulped.

It was an awkward par 4 famous for its shark shaped bunker whose tail started 140 yards away right in the middle of the fairway. I decided to forget my driver and stick to my trusty 3-wood. The ball went straight up in the air and landed 15 yards short of the bunker.

"Safe shot," said Phil.

"Got ice on that one," said Bill.

"Good lie," chomped Charles and drove his ball 75 yards past mine, into the deepest part of the shark bunker. Phil hit his tee shot over the tail of the shark and safe. The best drive was Bill's, landing 200 yards away, over the middle of the bunker, to a chorus of "Well dones".

"I was lucky there," he said. I began to notice that golfers say that a lot after hitting stunning shots.

My second shot looked difficult and I tried not to think about the shark. The trees on the right obscured my view of the green so I decided to play safe and use a 5 wood. The ball soared up, clipped the tallest tree, soared on and landed in the shallow bunker at the front of the green, 220 yards away.

"Super shot," growled Phil. I could only gulp, never having hit a golf shot quite like it before. "That was almost big trouble," I finally managed to squeak, overcome by the majesty of the old game, not to mention my narrow escape from the trees. It was still drizzling.

Phil shanked his second into the trees on the left and threw his cigar after it.

Charles took 3 shots to get out of the shark and was now in serious danger of breaking his teeth on his mint imperials.

Bill topped his fairway wood 20 yards further on.

"You lifted your head," said Phil. "Bad luck," volunteered Charles.

"Bollocks," said Bill and put his next shot into the hedge.

My ball was lying near the front of the bunker with a nice wide flat exit point in line with the pin. I took out my putter.

"Ah, the old Bronx wedge," said Phil.

"I'd use a sand wedge" said Charles.

Bill was silent, jingling his change.

Careful not to ground the putter in the sand, I clipped the ball toward the exit point. It scurried out, up the slope and stopped six inches past the hole.

"Never seen a shot like that," growled Phil, lighting another cigar.

"Bloody good putt," crunched Mint Imperial.

Bill was silent, his eyes glazed. I carefully avoided their eyes and kept busy, raking the bunker.

I walked slowly to the ball and tapped in. "How many points is that?"

"That's 4, nett 3, for 3 points," said Phil. It was still drizzling.

"That's 8 points after 3 holes," I thought. "This can't go on."

But it did. Apart froms the 8th and 12th where I took 8s, and the par 3 14th where I had three shots to the green and 4 putts, every tree shot rebounded out, poor shots slid out of bunkers and avoided ditches and ponds by inches. I was leading a charmed life. The drizzle had gotten worse.

Much later, with my tally standing at 33 points after 17 holes, we came to the fateful 18th. Phil had run out of cigars by the 13th and his temper was worsening by the minute. Charles had a bottomless bag of mints and was chewing 3 at a time. Bill's game had deteriorated and he had hardly spoken a word for 3 holes, content to sip from his hip flask.

It was my honour—again. My tee shot missed the ditch 150 yards away by a matter of inches.

"Bloody Hell," said Phil.

"Not again," groaned Charles.

Bill's eyes narrowed and he put his drive 60 yards past mine.

"Bloody good shot," we all chorused.

"About **$^@!%@* time," muttered Bill, offering us a sip from his hip flask for the first time.

Both Phil and Charles had good drives and put their second shots on the edge of the green. Bill took a 5 wood for his second. The ball screamed high toward the green, clipped the edge of the deep bunker to the right and rolled to 15 feet from the pin.

"Super shot," croaked Phil.

"Wonderful ball," congratulated Charles.

"About **$@%@** time," said Bill, offering his flask again. It was empty.

Bill suddenly became very chatty. Charles offered his mints around. Phil accepted one of my Silk Cuts. He'd previously dismissed them as cotton wool balls, unworthy of the attention of a true smoker. The drizzle stopped. Phil clapped me on the shoulder. "Don't worry about that last shot," he said sympathetically, "It happens now and then."

That was some consolation. I'd topped the ball that had landed a few inches short of the ditch right into the deepest part of the ditch, taken a drop and hooked a 5-iron into the trees right of the green. This time there was no lucky bounce, no ricochet, just the sound of wood. I managed to find it in a good lie and chipped on to the side of the green, into the bunker that Bill's ball had just missed.

I'd now had 5 shots, played out and 3-putted for a 9—nett 7 and zero points.

Phil chipped on and sank a 9-footer for par.

Charles used his putter from 30 feet, hit the stick and rolled 4 feet past.He sank the putt for a par.

Bill—silent again—lined up his 15 foot putt. There were no mints a-chewing, no change a-jingling, no smoke a-puffing. Bill's putt slid ever so slowly up to the hole, passed it and then dropped in sideways for a birdie.

"Absolutely brilliant," said Phil.

"Superb putt," said Charles.

"Lucky, very lucky," beamed Bill. "Fancy a snifter?"

Back at the clubhouse, Phil totted up the points on the cards. "Well done, my lad, that was a very useful 33 points. I'd won by 3 points in my first real competition and—as it turned out—£9 plus £3 for the miracle birdie on the second hole.

We repaired to the bar for a welcome shandy. There was no longer any talk of my fluke shots, my ricochets off trees or the way my ball had refused to go into lakes or bunkers. It was all about the 18th, two pars and a birdie, no mention of my 9, thank heavens. Bill basked in the praise heaped on him for his pressure putt and, on the strength of the acclaim, bought two rounds in a row.

The early horrors were forgotten in the glory of that last hole. Other golfers just finished were subjected to the drama of Charles hitting the flagstick and the unbearable tension of Bill's 15 feet putt. I noticed that something strange had happened. Charles had chipped on from at least 50 yards out and Bill's putt was now a 35 footer.

As for myself, I was totally hooked. I had never encountered a game where I could start badly, play flukily, finish badly and win £12 in the process. Never had I encountered a trio of golfers who could play badly all day, lose £12 between them and end up in such high spirits, thanks to a collectively brilliant last hole.

Funny old game, golf.

Golf with a Gallic Flavour

All Gaul is divided into three pars, 3, 4 and 5. Or so a wit remarked some years ago, although there is historical evidence that Julius Caesar was much too busy building straight roads to have contemplated creating dog-legs in France.

Since the mid-eighties, there has been a commitment to develop golf throughout France. There is an now excellent choice of challenging courses and the golfing world has begun to recognise the quality of golfing holidays now available. Outside the British Isles, it has more courses than any other European country, and most are often uncrowded.

There are dozens of companies who offer a bewildering selection of "Transmanche" short break golf packages, and the Channel Tunnel will not only increase the number of companies in this market, but will also speed up the journey time to the closer parts of France. The Tunnel has been the subject of hundreds of years of speculation, planning and disputes between the French and English, but the reality now is that the Pas de Calais is virtually an adjoining county to Kent. All of this is good news for the avid golfer who wants to get away from winter greens and soggy fairways, and British enthusiasts are sure to swarm in even greater numbers to Hardelot, Le Touquet and Wimereux. And the prices are excellent if you're prepared to spend time wading through the brochures.

To make it easy to get through the maze, we picked on a golf society in the middle of England and challenged them to organise a trip to France before 26th May- prices go up alarmingly thereafter- for a group of eight, play the maximum amount of golf in two days with one night's accommodation for around £100 each.

Peter Bedwell, president of Pitsford Golf Society, arranged two trips to choose from as follows:

Trip One.

Brittany Ferries, Portsmouth to Caen. Left Northampton Tuesday 5a.m (that made the wives happy!), arrived Portsmouth 7.30. Ferry 8a.m. Arrived Caen 3p.m. (France is one hour ahead). Played 18 holes on the Golf de Caen course, 18 holes par 72, a course with high quality greens and a modern stylish clubhouse, only a few minutes drive from Caen. Cost £10. Food after golf at course plus beer £12. Arrived Hotel Mercure, Omaha Beach,10 pm, 26 miles from Caen. More visits to bar, cost £10. Next day, Wednesday, continental breakfast, packed all the gear and teed off 9am on the Golf de Bayeux, a challenging Scottish style links 18-hole. Spectacular views over the landing beaches. A quick lunch (£8 including coffee and the obligatory beer), then on to the 9-hole American style course, finishing around 5pm. As the main course was now empty, another 9 holes ending at 7.45 pm. Dinner in a restaurant in Caen (£18 including wine) and back to the ferry 11.15 pm for a crossing at 11.59.

Arrived Portsmouth 5am,- remember the hour's difference- home to Northampton by 8.30 Thursday.

Total time away 52 hours. Total time in car 7 hours plus. Total time on ferry 12 hours. Total time golfing 13 hours (54 holes). Total cost, basic £81, plus £10 for the first day's golf in Caen, plus £48 food, plus £40 incidentals (food on ferry, petrol etc). Total £189.

Verdict? Many of us felt that a ferry crossing which left Caen for Portsmouth on Wednesday about 6pm would have been ideal. It would have given us 27 holes and got us home around 2.30a.m. Brittany ferries, take note. The courses were excellent but too much time was spent in the car or on the ferry. We were also shattered. Our advice? Spend two nights away. It's easier on the system!

Trip Two.

Left Northampton at 4.45am for Folkstone to Boulogne via Seacat at 8am. Time 55 minutes at sea. Arrived at Le Touquet (Le Manoir Hotel) and teed off at 11am. 9 holes on the Sea course, a quick sandwich and then 18 holes on the same course, finishing at 7.30. Dinner at the hotel-set menu - was around £16. Beers at hotel £10.

Next day Wednesday, hearty English breakfast (included), then 9 holes on the Forest course, teeing off 10am. Soup and baguettes for lunch (£10), then teed off at 2.30 for another 18 holes. Left Le Touquet at 7.00 for Boulogne, time to visit the Supermarket-although we should have left more time- caught the Seacat at 9.15, Folkstone by 9.10- the hour's difference, remember?- and home by almost midnight.

Total time away 43 hours. Total time in car 6 hours. Total time on ferry 2 hours.

Total time golfing 13 hours (54 holes). Total cost, basic £122, including £10 extra each for Seacat, plus £48 food, plus £40 incidentals. Total £210.

Verdict? Less time on the ferry gave us more time to enjoy the golf, and we were less tired. We could have played 36 holes each day, but we found that 27 was just right. Both courses were excellent, the Forest a real test. The 9pm Seacat departure time from Boulogne was also ideal, and the midnight home arrival time meant we could go to work on Thursday without too much "jetlag". A friend from another society advised us to take the pain out of disturbing the whole family in the middle of the night, leave at 7pm the previous evening and stay within 20 minutes of Folkstone, as he did, at the Kings Head, Deal, an old smugglers Inn, for bed and breakfast. It'll add around £30 to the cost but worth it to keep marital peace!

THE ALTERNATIVES?

Longshot Golf Holidays offer 3-night short breaks via Air France to the Chantilly region, north of Paris, staying at the Mont Griffon Hotel. With flight and bed/breakfast included, prices start at £219 up to 31/3, rising to £229 up to 30/6. Golf is extra, but green fees start at £19 per round on the Mont Griffon course. Other nearby courses are the renowned Chantilly which will set you back FF 350, and Apremont which costs FF 200.

If you decide that the mad rush to the continent and playing 27 or 36 holes a day is too tiring, a more leisurely two nights at Le Manoir, with bed and breakfast, will start at £129 - but only during February! May prices are from £265 - £295 and include free golf. If you want to stay longer, then three nights midweek b/b accommodation might suit with Longshot's £135 (up to 31/3, then £159) jaunt to the Hotel Les Ormes in Northern Brittany via P & O. Again, watch the extras and shop around for the best green fees.

For those with a bit more time, you could be tempted to try Brittany Ferries overnight to St Malo from Portsmouth. The old fortified town of St Malo has three superior courses within 20 minutes of the ferry, Dinard, a links course, Le Tronchet, and the chateau course at Des Ormes, so you could be tempted to stay put. Two hours drive south, however, and you can take advantage of the South Brittany "Green Pass", with parkland courses like Queven and St Laurent, or links style courses at Kerver and Baden to choose from. The pass is available all year round and for five days costs from £60 in low season to £95 in July and August and you can choose from eight nearby courses.

(Available from BDH Golf, Tel: 081-644-1225). Accommodation is relatively inexpensive, auberges should cost no more than £30 for dinner, b&b.

TIPS FOR THE TRAVELLING GOLFER

1. MAKE SURE you have pre-booked tee times. A group we met had, the previous year, run into a traffic jam on the first tee because of a competition. And that is no way to start a golfing break where time is always of the essence.

2. Get the course scorecards in ADVANCE. This is free and will save you a lot of time. Just request them on your booking form.

3. Ask for DISCOUNT. Companies will give a free place for every 20 booked on one-night trips, 50% off the 12th player on trips of 2 nights or more.

4. If you're intending to have prizes at dinner, you can request a PRIVATE dining room, generally at no charge. This is a good idea if you have a large noisy group and don't want to disturb the other hotel diners.

5. MAKE SURE your price includes Breakdown cover.

6. Watch out for French HOLIDAYS. Hotels, golf etc will cost extra. These are 3/4, 12/5, 22/5, 145/7, 14/8, 15/8, 30/10, 31/10.

7. BEWARE of LE WEEKEND. Trips are more expensive and the Free Golf offers are less liberal.

8. Breakfast in France tends to be croissants and juice. Le Manoir Hotel at Le Touquet was once owned by Brent Walker and serves a full English breakfast.

9. Finally, LEAVE ENOUGH TIME to get to the ferry! And coming back! The M25, as we all know, can be sometimes brilliant, or more often a large parking lot.

Information was correct at press time, further details from BDH Golf (081-644 1225), Longshot Golf (0730-268621), Brittany Ferries (0705-751833).

" I FANCY WE'VE GOT A REAL PROBLEM HERE, SIR "

Poles Apart
...or Vivienne Fuchs off to the North!

Just what do you give the golfer who has everything? And no jokes about penicillin, please. I've got a choice of two tours that will do what Nissan claims to do, i.e. make your jaw drop. The first is an exercise in total luxury for the golf nut, the second so unbelievable that my jaw has remained on the floor despite photographic evidence, and actually meeting the people who have to qualify as the golf nuts of the year. So fasten your seatbelt and hear this:

Trip One. A refurbished luxury DC-8 leaves Atlanta for Palm Beach, Florida with 68 golfers on board on 29th August, 1994. the plane has been reconfigured to hold just 70 passengers in utmost luxury, and features the finest in catered cuisine, business communication and entertainment equipment. It flies around the world in 24 days, taking in Jack Nicklaus courses all around the globe, including Palm Beach, Austria, Japan, China, Spain, Hawaii, Ireland and more. Perry Golf have designed the Jack Nicklaus Design World Tour for around $35,000. Starting with a reception and dinner party hosted by Nicklaus in Palm Beach, the group will be accompanied by Jack Whitaker, an American TV commentator who will offer insights and anecdotes throughout the tour.

"This tour is designed for the avid golfer who demands the finest golf experiences on the planet," commented Jess Taylor, executive Vice President of Perry Golf. "We have designed it to visit great hotels worldwide, and play some of the most outstanding courses in the world, while travelling by the ultimate private jet." For the price, naturally, all hotels, meals of the gourmet variety, and golf are included, plus some special activities. Handicap certificates advisable, but not critical.

Trip Two. A charter plane with ten golfers aboard takes off from Ottawa, Canada, just after Easter 1994 for the North Pole. They're on an 8-day golfing trip that includes wildlife study - (The Northwood Golf Committee that retired recently are now part of the endangered species that live there) - plus travel by dogsled and helicopter. All special equipment and clothing is included for around £10,000 from Accessible Isolation. It's a once a year trip, the next one scheduled is 21st April 1995, so book now. Now I know that queueing is a problem these days, but the North Pole? Alastair McLean of the seven year old company assures me that it is a popular adventure/golfing holiday. So here's an opportunity for a clothing company to prove that their waterproofs are better than anyone else's.....But don't take bets on the first Eskimo golfer to win the Masters.

GOLFING DOCTOR?

Doctor Vernon Coleman, a household name through his articles as the "Agony Aunt" for The People, is also a golf nut and a prolific author on cricket, golf and other subjects. He trained as a doctor in Birmingham, but is now a full time author and lives in Devon.

His output is prolific and he has written over 50 books which have been translated into 17 languages and sold around the world. As well as his newspaper column, he edits the European Medical Journal.

He first played golf at the age of 12, and his initial drive resulted in a lost ball. He claims there has been little noticeable improvement in his golf since that day. Despite his noticeable lack of success on the golf course, his ability with the ball is better shown by his lifelong interest in cricket, a subject on which he has written several books, including "Thomas Winsden's Cricketing Almanack", "Diary of a Cricket Lover", and "The Village Cricket Tour".

His medical books are of significant interest to the golfer, with such titles as "Addicts and Addictions", "Backache", "Stress Control" and "Mindpower". He has also written books on sex, including " Complete Guide to Good Sex". His most recent novel is "The Man Who Inherited a Golf Course", published in 1993. It features Trevor Dunkinfield, a young journalist who suddenly inherits a golf club. There are two small snags, however. His uncle stipulated that, in order to keep his inheritance, Trevor must play a round of golf in less than 100 strokes, and that he must find a partner to help him beat two bankers in a match play competition.

As his only previous experience with golf had been on a crazy course in Weston-Super-Mare, it's not going to be easy to keep his inheritance. The entertaining book reveals all.

Tee off for Tommy

A new golfing challenge was initiated for 1994 by Skoda, called "Tee off for Tommy" Open to all lady club members throughout the UK, the challenge was designed to raise money for St Thomas' Hospital, to help the establishment of a Research centre for Fetal health. It was sponsored by Skoda UK Ltd and supported by the WPG European Tour.

Peter Titterton, Operations Director for Skoda, was sure women golfers would support the campaign. The club raising the most funds will receive the New Skoda Challenge Trophy and a major prize of a Favorit pick-up truck. There is also a trophy and a round of golf with Alison Nicholas for the highest fund-raiser in the winning club.

GOLF WOMEN
by Gary Norman

There are no other sports in which women are as much maligned as in the great game of golf. Such male dominated sports as basketball, soccer and wrestling have their own women stars and there have never been such cries of prejudice in these sports as emanate from the average golf club on a Saturday morning up and down the country.

And whoever heard of prejudice in Athletics? Or the London Marathon? Or horse riding? I asked my friend Delaney, who knows all about women (married three times) and golf (plays off two), if he knew why golf was so unique.

"It's easy, really," he said without a moment's hesitation. "Have you seen any women athletes? Or women basketball players? What do you notice about them?"
I replied that they all seemed very tall or quite well muscled.
There was a gleam in his eye as he shook his head impatiently.
"You've never noticed their long legs and short pants?" he asked me in a tone that suggested I was a pitiful unobservant wretch.
"Well, now you mention it....."
"That's the reason," he said triumphantly.
I was lost. There I'd been, thinking that there was a deep-rooted anthropological - or even psychological - reason, and Delaney had reduced the root cause to long legs and short pants. But then I thought about Fatima Whitbread, and found Delaney's theory a bit weak.

I decided to research the subject a bit further and posed the question to the captain of the local golf club. "What a load of piffle," he boomed. "Our lady members are treated as equals. They even have their own morning -Tuesday- when we men aren't allowed on the course. Unless, of course none of the ladies are playing. They have their own lounge, and the men aren't allowed in. Absolute piffle, old boy."
As we spoke a member and his wife passed by, obviously in the middle of a row.
"For Heavens sake, Dorothy, be quiet. You just go on and on. Now shut up or you'll drive me out of my mind."
"That," snapped Dorothy, " wouldn't be a drive, that would be a putt."
The captain shook his head sadly. " They're always arguing. She plays off 10, he's off 18, and she always beats him. He's had hundreds of lessons, but it's not done him any good. He can't stand being beaten by a woman."

"Does your wife play golf?" I enquired. " Certainly not, old boy. Absolutely hates the game. Lucky for me."

A few of the members wandered over and joined in the conversation. "The real trouble with the ladies is that they like to talk," ventured one. "When you see a group of three or four men at a golf club, it follows the format of a group of men anywhere in the world. If one of them is talking, the others are listening. When you see a group of four women at the club, it's the same all over the world, they all talk at the same time. The bloody noise is deafening, dear boy, and all that cackling as well."

"You're right, Forsyth," said another. "But it's the same on the course. I followed a ladies fourball last week, and they talk, talk, talk, God knows what about. And when they play their shots, well, you can't believe it. One hits her ball to the right, another to the left, another down the middle, one into a bunker. Now we men walk to our own balls. Not the women. They walk in a group to every ball. I watched them, all four went to the left, still yakking, then to the bunker, then to the right, then down the middle. No worries about holding us up. The same thing happened on the second shot. It's as though they're afraid to miss something."

"I miss the good old days at Little Aston," sighed another.

"Why Little Aston?" I was intrigued.

"A few years ago, I was sitting in front of the clubhouse by the eighteenth with Colonel Bletsoe and his old batman. A couple of lady members passed by and we gave them a few wolf whistles. They complained to the committee. Can you imagine that? Accused us of ribaldry, no less."

"What happened?" I asked

"Committee sorted the whole thing out. Banned the lady members from walking in front of the clubhouse. Now they've got to go the long way round, silly moos."

"I hear you're leaving us," said the captain to one.

"F'raid so, had enough of this women's lib business. I'm going to a club where men are men, and they keep the women where they belong, doing the breakfast dishes."

"Where are you going?" I asked, intrigued.

"Northwood, of course."

SKEGNESS MON AMOUR
The Golfing Stag Tour

PART ONE . . . Pre Tour.

The decision to go to Skegness for a stag weekend was a strange and impulsive one.Somehow when two illogical and separate strands of conversation come together, anything can happen. And so it was with Skegness and the golf stag tour.

It all began with Sam, whose stag night was fast approaching. He was in one little circle in the pub, talking about his forthcoming nuptials with Billy the Geordie, Declan the Muscle, Ben the Yank, Jim Bob the Parcel and Gary Oh. As men do, they were talking about the great stag nights they'd been on and reminiscing about the time Graham the Grecian had got off the coach on the way back from Oxford to relieve himself. He'd tripped over in his alcoholic stupor, fell into a ditch and slept there till morning. His claim to fame was that whilst falling he hadn't spilled a drop, although how he knew that was anybody's guess. He was still annoyed because none of his so-called mates on the bus had missed him.

In another circle in the pub were the girls including Tracy the bride to be. They were also talking about the wedding and the honeymoon (none planned), babies (none planned), house (not yet finished) and mothers in law (not met). It's a well known phenomenon that men and women - given the same broad subject -tend to approach it from different directions.The girls are more practical, the boys more humorous. Anyway the wedding was planned for the 16th of September and we were keen to set a date for the stag night as well as the venue. These key events in a marriage must be planned carefully and - as the best man was working in Hawaii - we thought it was worth talking about. The girls, meantime, were asking the bride to be about the places she'd like to go for a honeymoon. Tracy manages a book company and, as everyone knows, the three months before Xmas is one long mad rush. So they were trying to plan a 3- day honeymoon somewhere in the U.K. "Besides," said Tracy, as she leaned across to ask me for a light, "We can't really go away for longer. Sam has to go and close up the caravan he's got at Skegness for the winter by the middle of September."

"What do you mean?" I asked. "Well, we've got to go and clean it up, take all the bedsheets and linen away and close it up for the winter." Billy the Geordie said, "Never been to Skegness." "Me neither," said Jim Bob the Parcel, "What's it like?" Declan the Muscle had been there. "It's an absolute armpit of a place," he offered in his usual inoffensive way. Standing over 6 ft. and 15 and a bit stone, Declan was a Mercedes dealer, light on his feet at discos and a snappy dresser. Not flash as car salesmen can be but too bulky to be really elegant.The first time I met him I'd dared to ask him how many people were trapped inside his sweater. That he didn't brain me at once with one of his meathook hands is a tribute to his temperament. We'd been friends since.

"How long have you had the caravan?" I asked Sam, really curious about this side of life that was a bit foreign to me. "Oh, it's been in the family for ages. In actual fact, Skeggy isn't too bad. Nice beach and a few nice golf courses there."

I stood there , as Cortez must have done when he first saw the Pacific; as Lester Piggott must have stood when he saw the buff envelope from the tax inspector; and as Richard Branson must have done when his hot air balloon pilot jumped out and left him to it over the Atlantic. Transfixed, you might say. There is always a moment when the brain works faster than computer, when all the ingredients -taken singly-just don't fit. But when taken together are pure dynamite. I heard the conversation going on around me, oblivious. Billy the Geordie jerked me back to reality. "Another pint?" This was such a rare offer that my attention immediately focussed. "Yorkshire bitter please."

I added up all the elements. A caravan meant accommodation.It was also different.We'd all been to the usual places for stag parties. Pub crawls, night clubs and strippers were all old hat. Skegness was an armpit of a place with a beach and golf courses. I'm afraid to confess that the attraction of playing golf in an armpit near a beach with caravan accommodation thrown in was too much to resist. The big question was how could I sell the idea to the girls?

With an idea like this one, it would have been churlish not to try. So in I went feet first. "What're you doing for your hen night?" I asked Tracy." I thought we might do something different," tossing her blonde mane, "and go to a health farm overnight." "Brilliant" I said enthusiastically. "Tres different" opined Declan in his huskiest French accent. "Great idea" said Gary Oh. "Smashing" said Billy the Geordie "Soooper" said Fi-Fi Le Bon Bon.

Her real name was Fiona, but her husband Mark the Teabag had a penchant for French. Such was his mastery of the language that, years before, a college friend Peter, who was madly in love with a Parisian girl, went over to meet her parents and pop the question. Unfortunately she chose that weekend to blow him out and he returned home to the flat he shared with Mark, truly miserable beyond words. Mark has a keen instinct for saying the right things in these situations. He got Peter bombed during a lengthy pub crawl and was heard to say - many times - "Don't worry, there are plenty more poissants dans la mer." Declan reported this heartless misuse of the French language to me and I'm sure it's true.

But I digress. Also I should have mentioned that all the men in the pub were members of the Pitsfield Golf Society and were -in varying degrees-golf nuts. Their golf abilities, however,weren't always in direct proportion to their enthusiasm. Declan the Muscle always played golf dressed entirely in black. His resemblance to Gary Player was - even to the kindest eye - non-existent. Jim Bob the Parcel was of similar rotund, though less lofty, build as Declan and played to a similar golf standard. There were worse players than these two, but more of that later.

The parameters were now set. The girls were discussing very seriously the prospect of a night on the health farm. The big moment had arrived - almost. "How many does your caravan sleep?" I asked Sam casually. "Six easily, eight at a push." Quick mental arithmetic. "Could it sleep ten?" "Couple on the floor, but no problem. Why?" A sudden gale of laughter from the corner told me that Declan had caught on. So had Mark the Teabag and the others. Billy the Geordie was the first to speak. "Are you seriously proposing" (strangled voice) " that we all go off to Skegness for a pub crawl?" "Yes and a game of golf." "When?" "Sam's stag night. We have a few beers and finish it off with a round of golf the next day." My wife was the first of the girls to catch on. "Are you serious?" "Never more." Sam stepped into the breech. "Don't see why not. You girls can go pamper yourselves at the health farm and we may as well go off and play a bit of golf. I can close up the caravan while we're there and the boys will give me a hand. It'll also save us a trip, Tracy."

His words fell like sweet music notes on a hushed concert hall. It was settled there and then with little argument from the girls. But Skeggy itself was the master stroke. Poor unfashionable Skegness, where we couldn't get into much mischief. I mean, what possible harm could we come to there? Little did we know.

PART TWO .. SKEGNESS

Golf is like a religion. Few would deny that. It has its rituals, its rules, its Plus Fours and Twos and its Rupert Bear trousers. On the course players wear coloured garments which, if worn while shopping down the High Street, would cause one to be stared at, maligned and even arrested. Once this religion has got a grip on you, it seldom goes away. Those who do manage to lapse usually convert to Judaism because the rules are easier to understand. We of the Pitsfied Golf Society got hooked by accident two or three years ago and are now addicts forever. To us the phrase " threescore and ten " means the usual par for an average golf course. Saint Jude, he of hopeless cases, is our patron. Skegness was becoming an obsession because, although we'd had a few day-long tournaments at nearby courses, we'd never managed an overnight stop. The thought of the stag night, sleeping over and then 18 holes of golf was becoming intoxicating as the day approached. There were now 8 of us going with another joining us on the Sunday morning.

But I was becoming uneasy about our overall standard of play. Most of us were DIVOTees more than devotees. Sam, the groom, was a hairdresser and had booked us into the fashionable Seacroft Golf Club as a Hairdressers Society and in his optimism had assured the club that we all had handicaps. In other words, he lied. But in our own unique way we did have handicaps. In our tournaments- usually played over 9 holes- we had stumbled on a very effective way of handicapping each other. There were 12 of us to begin with and we simply graded players as either O.K. or useless. I suppose even the R.& A had to start some-where. Depending on how you played in the previous tournament, your handicap was adjusted. This caused much argument and hilarity as the "handicapping committee" kept changing in both size and personnel. As players of my ability had a handicap of 22-ish, Declan the Muscle's first handicap (he'd never before picked up a club, or so he said) was 48. Jim Bob the Parcel was 44, later changed to 30 when we found out he'd had a couple of sneaky lessons. Sam the Groom's was 36. He was stupid enough to admit he'd played before. We also encouraged the girls to join for fear of retribution, so FiFi le Bon-Bon's was a generous 56. In a nor-mal golf club or even a society, these would have been ludicrous handi-caps. But for us they worked.

When Declan the Muscle won his first tournament, his handicap was adjusted down from 48 to 28. Next time out he shot a 116 and, after much court room argument, the handicap committee (on which he sat) raised him again to 46. For myself the committee (from which I was barred) couldn't decide. I was deemed to lie somewhere in the middle range of mediocrity, between 20 and 24. A coin was flipped and I lost every time.

Our recruitment policy was a simple one. All were welcome to join. It was then merely a question of setting an initial handicap. Any newcomer was automatically assumed to be off 28, unless our legion of spies reported otherwise. Then the questions would begin."Have you got a set of clubs?" If yes deduct two handicap points. "Have you got a trolley?" If yes deduct two points. "Spikes?" If yes deduct 3 points. "Have your woods got head covers?" If yes deduct 3 points. "Have you played in the last 6 months?" If yes deduct 2 "Have you ever had lessons?" If yes deduct 3 "Do you know the rules of golf?" If yes deduct 10 "What make are your clubs?" If Ping, Ram or MacGregor we'd deduct 10 points "Do your parents play?" If yes deduct 2 points. So you see, by clever ques-tioning, we could take a complete stranger and whittle his handicap down by 16 or 18 points without seeing him play. Anyone seen wearing Pringle or Lyle & Scott was immediately in serious trouble with the handicap committee.

All this was the cause of much hilarity but a far cry from the handicap-ping standards laid down by the fathers of golf. Existing members approached the problem creatively. They took secret lessons. Nobody really noticed as somehow the lessons didn't seem to work. By the time we re-formed the golf society and joined the E.G.U we had learned to handicap properly. But all that was long after the Skegness weekend. Perhaps you can now understand a little of my uneasiness in contem-plating the prospect of our golf members daring to play on a manicured up-market course in the guise of a hairdressers outing. I will draw a veil over the stag night itself. Suffice to say that we endured in rapid succes-sion the usual concoctions - greasy chips, mushy peas, spiked drinks, and purple nasties. This last item is an evil drink consisting of half lager, half cider topped with Pernod and blackcurrant and must be drunk in one long swallow. On stag nights and other occasions it was awarded for any wrongdoing such as drinking with the wrong hand, not buying your round or such similar trivial offense. We also endured the obligatory disco visit where one member danced all night with one of the room's support poles. We even paid a late visit to the Helter Skelter at Skeggy's pleasure beach, not a wise move in our advanced state of inebriation. We had also decided on a dress code for the evening's outing around the bars - blazer and greys. In a town where the standard dress-up code is tee shirt, jeans, dockers and tattooed arms (and that's just the girls), we stuck out like a sore thumb. We did have some pretty big guys in our party, however, and what saved us from innumerable scrapes, I think, was the suspicion amongst the locals that we were one half of a touring rugby club and the other half might show up at any minute. So back to our cramped quarters we went in a fragile but unmolested state by 3 a.m. where the author slept in what seemed like a shoe box and the others alternately belched, laughed, drank, argued over the bed sheets and passed wind. All the good things, in other words, that men do when there are no women around. I merely passed out.

By 7am we were all miraculously awake and somehow managed to shave and brush teeth without too many arguments in the confined space. We also washed up the teacups and loaded Sam the Groom's car with sleeping bags and bed sheets and blankets as well as putting on our Pringles in readiness for the serious business of the day. The only minor irritant came when Declan the Muscle produced his hair dryer at the last minute and insisted that he simply had to wash his hair. By 8 o'clock we had swallowed our supplies of Anacin, Anadin, Aspirin and Hedex, loaded the last car and posed outside the caravan for a team photo. Noone admitted to a hangover, the caravan was locked and we were off. We motored serenely past the Lingalonga cafe for the final time looking at the rows of caravans stretching as far as the eye could see. From the raised seat of a Range Rover it looked like a complete city made of tin. The sunlight glinted off the metal as we looked over the acres of the Tin City. We put our Ray-Bans on and left Skeggy in our wake. Sam the Groom had recommended a little village cafe not far away for breakfast where the full works cost only £2.50. You may be wondering about the contents of our stomachs by this time. An X-ray would have revealed copious amounts of beer, lager, mushy peas, chips, fish, sausages in batter, vodka, gin, port and even candy floss. We were now going to increase the pressure with eggs, bacon, sausages, fried bread, tomatoes, toast, marmalade, tea and coffee. We sat in the September sunshine contemplating the steaming plates. No one flinched.

The air was balmy, even the wasps were friendly. Or at least one seemed as he swam in the warmth of Declan's fried tomato. He whacked it senseless with his copy of the News of the World, scraped it to the side of his plate and finished his tomato without a word. One final drama was to unfold before we reached the golf course. Our ninth member Ian the Tall had not yet appeared. We assumed he'd meet us at the course. On the way there John the Whiff decided to stop and ring his wife who was pregnant. We gathered around the roadside phone and listened, as you do. "Where are you?" we heard Jill ask. "Skegness." "Where did you sleep last night?" We saw John pale, then redden. "In the caravan." "No you didn't." "What do you mean? We were in Sam's caravan." "Well, Ian the Tall went there this morning and nobody was there." "We were all gone by eight." "Ian said there weren't any car tracks at the site." "Who the hell does he think he is, Tonto?"

We all then decided to phone our wives. Jill would have told them and they'd be worried. Worse than that they'd be on the warpath, all wondering where 8 of their husbands had spent the previous night. A few calls later our worst fears were confirmed. The girls were all indeed on the warpath. We had a quick council meeting. Unlike the meetings of the handicap committee, there was no bickering and little argument. We resolved to disembowel Ian the Tall if we ever saw him again. At that moment his car appeared. He'd been to the caravan, then the golf club, then Skegness beach, then back to the golf course and still no sign of us. Although we were still mad at him, the handicap committee was hastily convened. They cut his handicap from 36 to 16 but let him keep his bowels. We also made him ring Jill and explain that he'd found us, that we had indeed slept at the caravan and that Indian tracking was not his forte. All was well again.

By now we were desperate to get on the course and forget our wife troubles. Most wives and fiancees are suspicious, whatever stage a marriage is at and Ian the Tracker (as he was now known) would cost us all a severe telling-off when we got home. But when golf calls, wives get pushed to the back of the queue, so we eagerly hurried to the course. Seacroft itself is a magnificent links course with well manicured greens, rolling fairways and a picturesque setting. We didn't look, I have to say, like hairdressers. We wore caps of various kinds and managed to stay well out of the pro's way until the fees had been paid. Declan handled this very well, thanks to his omnipresent hairdryer, and was the only one who looked remotely like a professional crimper. As we had some 25 minutes before our allotted tee time, we all attacked the putting green with some gusto. In the middle of our practice the pro called Declan over. We watched in some alarm. Had one of our wives in a fit of pique rung the club and told them we weren't hairdressers at all? We were much relieved to find that the lady captain had just arrived and wanted to know if she could tee off before us.

We agreed with some degree of haste. The last thing we all wanted was the lady captain and her companion following us down the unfamiliar fairways. She thanked us and strode to the tee. Her lady companion had the honour and promptly lashed her drive straight down the fairway some 150 yards away. Now you must appreciate that Sam the Groom is probably the worst putter in the society, if not the world. He's been known to lie two feet from the cup and knock the ball six feet past. But he does concentrate very hard. He stands over the putt for ages, his eyebrows beetle, his knuckles whiten, oblivious to everything around him. Completely unaware of the lady captain, he attempted an ambitious 30 ft putt. As her elegant backswing began, his long putt rolled up sweetly, hit the stick and dropped in. The lady captain's 3- wood began its downward spiral just as Sam yelled " Jeee-sus, did you see that son of a bitch drop?"

The 3- wood swished past the lady captain's Pinnacle Gold, caught it on the side and trickled it 5 feet to the right. Sam, meantime, agog with the excitement of it all, threw his putter up in the air in ecstasy. We watched in horror as it spiralled its way back to earth. Sam's reputation for being a bit of a butter fingers was well known. Even in the pub we all had to be careful when handing him a pint. Jim Bob the Parcel was the first to react. Trying to save the situation, he pushed Sam out of the way, grabbed at the putter, missed and shrieked as it hit him on the ankle. Sam, meanwhile, lost his balance, tripped over hole no.2 and fell down in a heap. The putter rebounded off Jim Bob's ankle and hit him in the eye. The lady captain glowered, the watching pro bit his lip, Jim Bob hopped on one leg and Sam held both hands to his eye. The rest of us bent over our putts and studied the grass, the curves and the borrows. Declan the Muscle was wobbling uncontrollably, trying not to laugh. Hard stares from the rest of us ensured his self control.

To her eternal credit, the lady captain graciously accepted my strangled apology and marched silently to where her ball lay. This time, as she addressed the Pinnacle, not a soul stirred, not a muscle moved, not a single putter swung. Even Jim Bob's groans had subsided as she drove her second shot with some venom and a 5-wood into a deep bunker on the left side of the fairway some 150 yards away and marched off, still steaming. By now we were all conscious of the pro's unwavering stare from the door of his shop. "No pressure, boys," I said, "but we'd better be bloody good off the tee." There were a few worried, even ashen, faces. All this bloody way, we were thinking, to be ignominiously thrown off the course.

Now every golfer knows the importance of the first tee. Whichever writer described the first tee as the perfect laxative ought to be commended as much for his accuracy as his wit. Jim Bob the Parcel volunteered to go first. Swish. Miss. Swish. Miss." Hard bloody course" he said. His third (although his scorecard later confirmed it was his first) landed respectably 150 yards away on the fairway. Two of the better golfers went next and produced decent drives. That took the pressure off. The pro went back into his shop, apparently satisfied. The lady captain had long since disappeared, though a small black cloud 400 yards away in the sandhills suggested she was still not in the best of spirits.

Declan the Muscle was next to the tee. Three air shots later, he stood rooted to the spot in despair. "In God's name, what do I have to do to hit this frigging thing?" Mark the Teabag summed it all up for him."Whatever you die from, Declan, it won't be from a stroke!" That seemed to break the tension and we all went off quite competently. For the rest of the day noone got injured, threw putters, sank 18 footers or offended any more lady captains. We played slowly enough to keep her 3 or 4 holes ahead and plodded around over the sandhills, keeping a wary eye open for hostile members.

By the 15th, with nobody in sight behind us, we slowed to a crawl. The lady captain loomed large again in our thoughts. We figured that she'd go back to the clubhouse for a cup of tea, or more likely a gin. We decided to give her at least an hour there before we made our entrance. By the 18th we decided not to go anywhere near the clubhouse in case she had the lynching party ready.

Call us cowards if you will, but we slunk off the course, into our cars and back toward the A1 as quietly as we could. By now it was 5pm and our stomachs had made a recovery from the ravages of the night before and were rumbling again. An hour later we reached a Happy Eater on the A1 and considered it far enough away from the lady captain and the pro to be safe. We consumed yet another huge breakfast plus the obligatory plates of chips. Already we had almost forgotten the horrors and the hangovers and the shanked drives of the previous 24 hours. Our spirits returned as we munched and joked and laughed. We were soon the same happy bunch of stagnight kings and golfing no-hopers who had left Pitsfield the previous evening. Then there was a sudden silence. Simultaneously we'd remembered the one thing we were all trying to forget. We'd be home in an hour, and we'd better have the excuses good and ready.

Our wives would be waiting for us.

The Nostalgia Trail...

Have you ever noticed when you visit the United States and Canada that there are more than a few names that ring a bell, like Northampton, Cheltenham, Bath, Halifax, Dublin and Maidstone? There's also a Glasgow, Newcastle, Lincoln, (as you would expect), Manchester and London, but did you know there's a list of golf clubs that will also remind you of home? Well, sit back, fasten your seat belt and we'll take you on a tour of some famous golf courses many thousand miles away that might just make you wonder what country you're in...

Balmoral Woods Country Club
　　Crete, near Chicago, Illinois. 18 holes, 6700 yds, par 72, $35.
Bangor Golf Course
　　Maine. 27 holes, 3 loops of 3000 yds, par 35/36/36, $20.
Birkdale Golf Club
　　Chesterfield, Virginia. 18 holes, 6500 yds, par 71, $20-$49.
Bradford Country Club
　　near Boston, Massachusetts. 18 holes, 6500 yds, par 70, $ 35.
Broadmoor Golf Club
　　Colorado. 54 holes, 6700-7200 yds, all par 72, $50-$99.
Broadmoor Golf Course
　　Portland, Oregon. 18 holes, 6500 yds, par 72, $20.
Brookside Golf Club
　　Pasadena, California. 18 holes, 6880 yds, par 72, $20.
Dundee Golf Course
　　West Bay, near Halifax, Nova Scotia. 18 holes, 6475 yds, par 72, $25.
Dungeness Golf Club
　　Sequim, near Seattle, Washington. 18 holes, 6400 yds, par 72, $20-$49.
Edinburgh Golf Club
　　Brooklyn Park, Minneapolis, Minnesota. 18 holes, 6700 yds, par 72, $35.
Exeter Country Club
　　near Warwick, Rhode Island. 18 holes, 6900 yds, par 72, $35.
Gleneagles Golf Course
　　Manchester Village, Vermont. 18 holes, 6400 yds, par 71, $50-$99.
Hillsborough Country Club
　　Flemington, New Jersey. 18 holes, 5880 yds, par 70, $20-$49.
Inverness Golf Club
　　near Denver, Colorado. 18 holes, 6948n yds, par 70, $50.
Litchfield Country Club
　　Pawleys Island, South Carolina. 18 holes, 6750 yds, par 72, $40.

London Bridge Golf Club
> Lake Havasu, Arizona. 18 holes, 6618 yds, par 71, $25.

Mayfair Country Club
> Sanford, near Orlando, Florida. 18 holes, 6375 yds, par 72, $ 35.

Newport Country Club
> Newport, Vermont. 18 holes, 6110 yds, par 72, $20-449.

Northwood Golf Club
> Rhinelander, Wisconsin. 18 holes, 6700 yds, par 72, $35.

Norwich Golf Course
> near Hartford, Connecticut. 18 holes, 6100 yds, par 71, $35.

Olde Barnstable Golf Course
> near Hyannis, Massachusetts. 18 holes, 6500 yds, par 71, $20-$49.

Portsmouth Country Club
> near Manchester, New Hampshire. 18 holes, 7000 yds, par 72, $35.

Rutland Country Club
> Rutland, Vermont. 18 holes, 6060 yds, par 70, $35.

St. Andrews Golf & Country Club
> West Chicago, Illinois. 18 holes, 6700 yds, par 72, $20-$49.

Sevenoaks Golf Club
> Hamilton, New York. 18 holes, 6900 yds, par 72, $35

Southgate Golf Club
> St George, Utah. 18 holes, 6100 yds, par 70, $20.

Stowe Country Club
> Stowe, Vermont. 18 holes, 6200 yds, par 72, $35.

Troon North Golf Club
> Scottsdale, Arizona. 18 holes, 7000 yds, par 72, $100.

Turnberry Resort
> North Miami Beach, Florida. 36 holes, 6320-7000yds, par 70, 72, $50-$99.

Turnberry Golf Course
> Columbus, Ohio. 18 holes, 6600 yds, par 72, $20-$49.

Village Greens of Woodbridge Golf Club
> near Chicago, Illinois. 18 holes, 6650 yds, par 72, $35.

Wentworth Golf Club
> Portsmouth, New Hampshire. 18 holes, 6200 yds, par 70, $50-$99.

West Bolton Golf Club
> Jericho, Vermont. 18 holes, 5400 yds, par 70, $20.

Whitney Golf Course
> near Bridgeport, Connecticut. 18 holes, 6600 yds, par 72, $ 20-$49.

Windsor Golf Club
> Windsor, California. 18 holes, 6650 yds, par 72, $20.

Windsor Park Golf Club
> Jacksonville, Florida. 18 holes, 6740 yds, par 72, $50-$99.

Finally, the last stop on our tour is the phonetically wonderful **Kokanee Golf Resort** in British Columbia which would make any Londoner homesick! It was obviously named by a West Country exile from the old country.

A QUESTION OF ETHICS

They say that all of life is reflected in the game of Golf, more than any other sport. There's Greed, Cheating, Lust, Lies, every breach of the Charlton Heston Commandments that could possibly be breached. But unlike life in the business jungle, golf crime is far less obvious, and therefore far more sinister.

It all came to my attention one sunny afternoon at Corby when some poor harmless man collapsed on the course, on the nearby and parallel fairway to the one I was playing on with the guys. We're a pretty worldly bunch, Jim the Sales Manager, Mark the Teacher, Billy the nightclub owner and me, a doctor from Harvey Street.

The next hole was a long par 4, and we'd just gotten ready to play our approach shots to the green when we noticed this shape lying down on the next fairway, the one we'd just played. I've seen the odd golfer lying down on the putting green to line up a 4-footer, but never on a fairway to line up his shot.

"What's going on?" Jim muttered, in a foul mood. He'd shanked his tee shot into the trees, taken his penalty drop, then topped his next into a bunker, then chipped out. He'd had 4 strokes to our one, and wasn't a happy man.

The figure ignored his glower and continued to lie there, and his two playing partners had begun to realise that all was not well and were making their way toward him.

"Has anyone got a mobile phone?" called one of the worried figures.

Well, one does, doesn't one? An essential piece of kit these days on the links. The seductive ads in the Sunday magazines offering the latest designs for £99.99 had done their job and Jim and Billy had brought their Sonys, tucked into their Ping lightweight bags. Jim was the first to react. Battery dead. Billy reached for his with a flourish, dialled 999 with a glance of triumph at Jim's flushed face as he shook the phone, held it to his ear, still useless.

"Ambulance on its way. Let's see how he is."

Golf, meanwhile, had ground to a complete halt. Two holes behind us we could see a crowd of at least twelve on the tee. Even from 300 yards they looked angry and impatient, as golfers do when they witness slow play or another player in the woods dropping a ball down his trouser leg. Mark walked across to explain the delay, and immediately both fourballs cut across to the hole in front of us, a now-empty par three.

"Nice shoes. Gore-Tex, size nine" said Jim. "I saw Faldo advertising them in one of the magazines."

We were examining the prone figure. He was ashen faced and quite still.

"Hmm, they are nice and I've always wanted a set of Pings," said Billy.

"Let's get him into the recovery position and never mind his bloody Pings," I said, worried about the state of a fellow golfer. I took his pulse. Strong enough. It was just a faint, or a spot of food poisoning.

We manoeuvred him into the position, and stood about, helpless. "Are you a doctor?" one of his companions asked. I nodded briefly. I'm always careful who I tell about my medical ability, especially on the golf course. The last time I did so, I got a litany of complaints, including a false hip, a son's acne and a lecture about the state of the NHS.

"He's only had them since Christmas," said one of his companions.

"What?" I asked, wondering what on earth he was talking about.

"The golf clubs and the shoes. He was only saying a few holes ago that he was useless at the game and going to give it up."

"I'll give you two hundred for the Pings." Jim had bent down and spoke quietly in the poor man's ear.

"Three hundred for the bag, clubs and shoes," said Billy. "And another fifty for the wetsuit."

The prone figure groaned. "Will you take a cheque?" said Jim.

"God, you guys make me totally sick. He's lying there half dead and all you can think about is his clubs and his waterproof shoes. Don't you have any consideration for the way he feels? He might bloody die and you want to play Make a Deal. You disgust me." I was really mad by now. "Look you play through. I'll wait till the ambulance comes. Where does he live?" I asked his companions. They mentioned a village not far away. "Look, you play on. I'll wait till they arrive and catch you up. Just leave your phone, Billy" They accepted readily. They looked almost as pale as the victim, obviously not capable of dealing with the crisis, seeing it only as an unwelcome interruption to their golf match.

They played their shots and strolled on sheepishly. I rang 999 again to make sure they were somewhere on the way. As I did I could hear the siren in the distance. The victim, whose name turned out to be Bob, began to stir. "Stay still," I commanded, "You've had a nasty shock." I took his pulse again, and the colour came back to his cheeks, as the ambulancemen arrived, carrying a stretcher.

"Sorry, sir, some bloody fool locked the gates and went off to lunch with the key in his pocket. We had to trek the long way round. What happened?"

I gave them a rundown. "He's as comfortable as I could make him. Can you get his shoes off?" They covered him with a blanket, and the victim stirred and moaned again. I gave them my card. "Where are you taking him?" "Kettering General."

"Good. I'll look in afterwards to see if he's O.K. I'll bring his clubs with me. And the shoes."

They trooped off, the long way round again. I could see the ambulance on top of the hill. They had a fair way to carry the victim, at least a mile.

There wasn't much I could do, so I decided to finish my game. I tied the shoes together and slung them over my cart, his clubs over my shoulder. I went to the hospital several hours later. Poor old Bob had died. Heart attack. His two friends were there, crestfallen. "Has he got any family?" I asked. "Divorced, no children. Thank you for all you did, doctor."

I muttered condolences and left. The surgery was busy for the next two weeks, so no golf. It was only when I went to the garage a few Sundays later that I noticed the Gore-Tex shoes and the Pings...

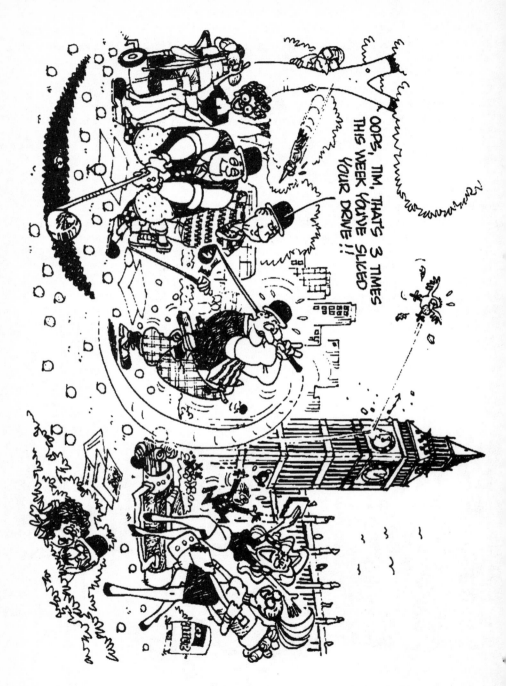

GOLF IN PARLIAMENT
Your honour, Milord

Golfing societies reach into every corner of our society. The desire to play the game crosses religious, social and even political boundaries. The Parliamentary Golfing Society is an all-party meeting of like souls who are either in the House of Commons or the Lords. The only bickering on the tee is likely to be over the choice of coloured balls. The increasingly common practice of using yellow golf balls is frowned upon because they could be construed as being supporters of the Liberal Democrats, so all members must play with white golf balls.

There are around 66 members and they have 16 tournaments a year between March and November, half of which are all day affairs, or should I say events. Tim Yeo is the present captain, and David Martin and Alan Maskell, a left hander who plays off 15, are co-secretaries. Active members include Gavin Partington of GMTV, Michael Morris, a past captain, Bryan Davies and Lord Weatherill, the former speaker, as well as Lord Deedes and Lord Geddes. Ex members include Lords Young and Parkinson. The society is open to members of either house, plus officers of the house, employees of the House of Commons Commission and members of the press gallery. The current president is Lord Whitelaw, and the vice-captain's job is shared by Andrew Mackay and John McFaul.

All the games are played on a Friday or Saturday and the highlight of the year is the 3-day tour, this year to Hoylake and Muirfield in August. Once a year in May, they play against the High Commissioners and Ambassadors at Swinley Forest, an event sponsored by Beefeater Gin! They also play one game a year against the Ladies Parliamentary Golfing Association, open to any lady who is related to a member of the Lords or Commons. The games are played all over the UK, from Rye to Woburn and from Sunningdale to Walton Heath.

Surprisingly, perhaps, few of the members are duffers. Most are in the mid-teen handicap range, the best of them being ex-captain Neil McFarlane off 7. Although he went out of Parliament at the election in April 1992, he remains a society member as a former captain. Tim Yeo plays off 12, Andrew Mackay 14, Gavin Partington also 14, Michael Morris 17, and Bryan Davies 16. Of the Lords, the former Cecil Parkinson plays off 13, Lord Weatherill is 18, Lord Geddes 22 and Lord Whitelaw, who was once a single figure handicapper, now plays in the mid teens. But the most startling golfer of them all is Lord Deedes, now in his eighties, who is still a useful player off a handicap of 19. He has played golf over many years with the equally fanatic Denis Thatcher and the link with the Thatchers was even more evident when he was reputed to be the Bill of the "Dear Bill" column in Private Eye, which ran for several years.

Two members of the Parliamentary Golfing Society, Lord Deedes and Lord Young, have been elected as honourary members of the new London Golf Club, designed by Jack Nicklaus. Other members of the elite band are Denis Thatcher, Lord Prior, Sir Paul Girolami and Jack Nicklaus as honourary captain. Lord Gnome's application, we understand, is still in the pending tray.

THERE WERE TWO ITALIAN LOOKING MEN IN THE FRONT . . .

Golf, the Yankee Clipper and
Marilyn Monroe

by Eddie McGraw

A very long time ago, or so it seems, my father asked me if I would like to caddy for him. It was late summer,1956, in south Connecticut and I was ten, almost. The night before he'd been with me at the baseball park when our Little League team had lost in the final to the Greenwich White Sox. He'd carried my kit, yelled and screamed at the umpire, shouted all the words of encouragement he could find as I faced the final batter in the bottom of the last inning. There were two outs, one on, and we led one-nil. The man on first base was a walk. I'd felt my arm tighten after the second out, and I just couldn't find the plate for a strike. It had been a long game.

I saw my father leaning on the fence behind home plate, watching intently, his favourite position at ball games, where he could best shout at the umpire. I leaned into the pitch and sent a fastball past their big slugger, Rick McKeown, for a strike. Yips and yells from the parents, "Waytago, Eddie", as I fooled him with a curve on the outside corner. Two strikes. McKeown was a big Irish kid, already almost five feet, and his uncle told everybody who'd listen that he was destined for the majors, if he didn't overdose on hamburgers. He was copying his favourite slugger, Mickey Mantle of the New York Yankees, even wore his number seven, and had a big wad of chewing tobacco in his cheek. He dug into the batters box and spat on the plate as I wound up and threw him another curve. The runner at first took off. I heard the crack and my heart sank as the ball soared toward right field. No problem, Mike Doyle was under it, then reached out, stumbled as the ball hit his glove and went past him into the corner. Joe Varadi came racing over from centre field, stopped to see if Doyle was O.K, then ran into the fence. By the time the ball was finally picked up and returned to home plate both runners were safe in the dugout, surrounded by coach, parents and school friends. We were beaten. I looked for my father. He was leaning on the fence, with his head in his hands. He came slowly across and put his arms around me, as the scorer announced the result. It was no consolation to know that the last at bat had been scored an error, or that I had given up only three hits and two walks. We had lost.

My father squeezed my shoulders. "I should have thrown the fastball," I said, close to tears. "No, you had him fooled. He only got a piece of the ball. Any other outfielder would have caught it. You did everything right." He had a way of hitting you with honest criticism when you goofed up, but he knew his baseball. Varadi and Doyle limped over.

"We're really sorry. I just turned my ankle," Doyle said.

"It's not your fault. Just an accident." I had to choke back the tears. All the way home after the presentation, my father and I talked through the game in detail. He could remember every play, every pitch. I'd listen sometimes when he had some of his golfing friends over, and it was the same thing. He could remember every shot he'd played, and all their shots as well. So when he asked me to caddy for him the next morning, I figured I owed him. Besides, I'd only ever been to a real course twice before, though we'd go to the driving range a few times a month. I'd read his golfing magazines and knew all about the equipment and the famous players like Sam Snead, Jackie Burke and Jerry Barber. Dad was best friends with Lloyd Mangrum, and had gone to see the Ryder Cup a few years before over in England to cover the story for the New York Times. When he came back he brought me a cut down set of clubs and a big net to practice with in the back garden.

It was one of those beautiful mornings in Connecticut with no clouds and only a little breeze. Dad said the boys were picking him up after nine, so we had a leisurely breakfast and read the papers. The Hartford Courant carried a report on our Little League game and Dad read it out to me. "They're very complimentary about your pitching," he said, "A real snapping fastball and an unhittable curve." He grinned. "And they called the final out a real comedy of errors." I laughed too. I was over the loss. Ten years later, I would go through the same thing again as a fan, and later a player, with the team that the whole of New York loved, the Mets. "There's a whole bunch of outfielders circling around a fly ball, taking it in turns to miss it, "Casey Stengel would say. The right fielder would run into the fence, the centre fielder would trip over the second baseman, Stengel would tear what was left of his hair out, the reporters would laugh, the crowd would laugh, but they'd come back for more. They stopped laughing and started cheering when Seaver, Koosman and Gentry pitched them to a World Series win over the Orioles in 1969, and the outfielders started catching all the balls. But that's another story.

A car horn honked, and my father got his clubs. We walked down the drive. It was a white Ford Thunderbird convertible, big fins and white-wall tyres. My dream car, every kid's dream. There were two Italian-looking men in the front, wearing sunglasses, a woman in a white dress in the back. "Joe, Dom, how are you?" my father said. "This is my son, Eddie, he's going to caddy for me."

"Hi, Eddie," they shook my hand.

"Hello, Eddie," said the woman in a low husky voice. She had very blonde hair and white teeth as she smiled. I couldn't see her eyes for the sunglasses.

"Hello, Marilyn, honey," said my father. "This is Joe's wife."

I sat in the back between the woman and Dad. She was very friendly, smiling at me in a nice way.

"I hear you were unlucky last night at the game," said the one called Joe. "I hear you pitched real well."

"Just an accident," I said, "I should have thrown another fastball instead of a curve."

They laughed. It wasn't far to the golf course, and the men bantered

about the game they'd had last week. They said Dad had taken five dol-
lars off them in bets because he'd chipped in the hole out of a bunker on
the eighteenth. Joe looked kinda familiar. When we arrived at the club,
he had an easy walk, nice and loose and full of confidence.

"Usual bets, guys?" said the one called Dom. I guessed it was short for
Dominic. I couldn't work it out, he looked so Italian, but he had an Irish
name. They all played off a 10 handicap, I discovered, and they always
played for a dollar a corner, whatever that was. Dad's two friends began
ribbing him about giving them a couple of shots because he had the
advantage of a caddy. My father said no way. When it came to sport and
bets, he was as hard as nails. Joe took a pair of flat walking shoes out of
the trunk and gave them to his wife. "The last time you wore high heels,
you left spike marks on the green and almost got us thrown off the
course," he grinned. They all laughed as Marilyn changed.

The game went quickly. They could all hit the ball a fair distance, especially Joe. He didn't seem to try, he just swung in a lazy way and the ball
went a mile. My father hit the ball with a fast, flat swing. It went as far
as Joe's, but hardly ever straight. Dom's drives were a lot shorter, but
straight. I carried Dad's clubs, and Marilyn pulled a trolley with Joe's
clubs in it. I didn't see much of her, because my father was always way
to the left or right of Joe's drive, but I'd see her on the tees and the
greens and in the distance. She didn't really look like a lady golfer. She
wore her shades and a white baseball hat with NY on it. Her white dress
looked a bit out of place, like a man playing golf in a tuxedo.

Once, when Dad managed to get the ball straight, near Joe's, she came
over and asked me about my Mom. She'd been gone a few years and was
living in California, near Los Angeles. "Do you miss her?"

I gulped, not used to being asked such a direct question.

"She came home for my birthday last year and took me out for dinner.
Dad was O.K, but he didn't really want to see her."

"I live in Los Angeles some of the year with Clipper. Do you want me to
call her and say Hi?"

I wasn't sure, my father might get upset, I told her. "Who's Clipper?"

"Clipper? Don't you know?" I shook my head. She looked at me in astonishment. " Never mind. I'll tell you later."

After Mom left, it was the only time I'd ever seen my father cry. She'd
called him at the office and told him she wanted to get away for a while.
She was an actress and wanted to try a new career in Hollywood, but
she needed to try it alone. That meant without my father and me. Dad
picked me up at school that day, which was unusual, and told me my
aunt in California was very ill, and Mom had gone out to the west coast
to help. A week or so later he told me the truth and we cried ourselves to
sleep. From then on, Dad did the cooking and ironed my school shirts
and all that stuff. It was O.K but I got tired sometimes of steak and
spaghetti. For a few years, any time my Mom's name was mentioned, he
would stiffen up and go all quiet. Our lives revolved around school,
baseball, golf and his job at the newspaper, the Hartford Courant, where
he was sports editor.

"I'll talk to your father, if you like." She took off her sunglasses and gave me a big hug. "I'm an actress too, so it might help." I gulped again, and nodded.

We had reached the eighteenth, a really evil par three, where you can't actually see the green from the tee. You have to drive up over a steep hill with trees on one side, a cliff hiding a ravine on the other. We were told to go on ahead to either side of the green to watch out for the balls. Father had won the previous hole, so he would drive off, and I couldn't remember whether Joe or Dom would drive off next. For once, Dad's drive was straight, sailed up over the hill, bounced just short of the green and rolled up six feet short. The next ball soared up, bounced on the back of the green and rolled into a steep bunker behind. The third ball went a little to the left, dangerously close to the ravine, but bent back sharply and landed near Marilyn on the edge of the apron. I watched open mouthed as she bent to pick up the ball, kicked off her flat shoes, raced over the green and popped the ball against the flag-stick, then hared back to her shoes. She held her finger to her lips and then started to yell, " You've done it, you've done it!"

She then ran across and hugged me. "It'll be our secret, please, please don't tell a soul."

I gulped and nodded in agreement. "Promise me," she demanded. I promised. "Cross your heart and hope to die." "Cross my heart and hope to die."

My father came over the hill with Joe and Dom. "What's all the yelling about?" Joe asked me.

"Somebody's got a hole in one," I lied.

"Which ball?"

"Well, the first was Dad's and it's near the pin. Who drove last?"

Dom's was the second ball. Joe went white. "But that was the worst teeshot I played all round. It went a bit left." He looked at me sharply.

"It came back pretty well, bounced on the edge and that's it, leaning against the flag."

Joe took his sunglasses off and his baseball hat. I'd never really noticed how big his nose was before. The guys surrounded him, pumping his hand, clapping his back. His wife gave him a huge hug and covered his face with kisses.

"It's amazing, I've never done it before," Joe gasped. He walked over to the hole. The ball was sitting gently against the stick. My father gingerly grasped the flag and the ball dropped quietly in. "Unbelievable, Joe. I've never even seen a hole in one," he said. As Joe's ball dropped, so did the penny with me. This was no ordinary friend of Dad's. This was the Yankee Clipper that his wife was talking about, Joe DiMaggio, the most amazing baseball player ever, and I hadn't recognised him. I'd read that he was married to an actress, but didn't really know much about that. It was his baseball stats that kids were interested in.

Dom splashed out of the bunker to three feet, and sank the putt for a par, Dad made his birdie putt and was highly delighted. The win for Joe had tied the game with my father, with Dom a few holes adrift of them.

After the game, we all had lunch at the club. Marilyn sat beside me. When the men went to the bar, she made me promise again never, ever to tell anyone what had really happened. I had to cross my heart and hope to die at least three times. They dropped us off at home that afternoon, and Joe's wife squeezed my hand as we said goodbye and gave me an extra special cuddle. My father told me that night that Joe had promised to take Marilyn on a world cruise if he ever got a hole in one, and that they'd be leaving soon after the World Series.

DiMaggio and his brothers stayed friends with Dad for a lot of years after. They've played a lot of golf together, but never once repeated that hole in one. Joe would send me tickets for Yankee Stadium all the way through school and college. When I finally got into the majors as a relief pitcher with the Mets, I was able to return the favours. Joe DiMaggio and his wife, Marilyn Monroe went off on the promised world cruise. It was in Europe that she met Arthur Miller, who didn't play baseball or golf, but wrote books and plays for a living. I often think that if it hadn't been for that damned hole in one she might still be married to the Clipper, and alive. The papers said later that she died with no clothes on, that she'd been sleeping with President Kennedy, and all that stuff. Joe was always very quiet and dignified about the whole thing, like Dad was about my mom. Men are sometimes like that when the sense of loss is too great to talk about without crying.

My career with the New York Mets didn't last too long. Maybe I threw too many curve balls, but at least my father lived long enough to see his own ambition to be a ball player realised in his son. He probably remembered every single pitch I ever threw, like he can remember every golf shot he ever hit. I went into newspapers, like Dad, but I never told anyone about that ghost hole in one, not even my father. Miss Monroe and I made a promise, and I've kept it to myself over the years. Till now.

SHE RACED OVER THE GREEN AND POPPED THE BALL AGAINST THE FLAGSTICK . . .

THE PROFESSIONALS
A year in Review

For Europe and the USA, it was the best of times, and the worst of times. The United States won the Ryder Cup in dramatic circumstances, though not as heart-stopping as in Kiawah Island. They also won the Dunhill Cup in October at St Andrews, Corey Pavin beat Nick Faldo in the Toyota World Matchplay Championship, and Fred Couples and Davis Love won the World Cup for their country at Lake Nona. Lee Janzen had won the US Open, Paul Azinger the USPGA. But the rest of the world seemed to be catching up. Greg Norman had won the 1993 British Open in masterful style from Faldo and Langer with hardly an American in sight. When he won the Players Championship at Sawgrass in March by four strokes from Fuzzy Zoeller, he looked unbeatable. European women, with the Solheim Cup won at a canter, were making an assault on US domination, as the European men had done.

When Jose-Maria Olazabal won the 1994 Masters from Tom Lehman to lose his title as the best golfer never to have won a Major, and Ernie Els took the 1994 US Open in a playoff with American Loren Roberts and Europe's Colin Montgomerie, the rest of the world was pressing American domination. By the middle of 1994, Laura Davies was at the top of the Ping leaderboard and there were only two American men in the Sony Top Ten, Fred Couples and the inactive Paul Azinger. Worse was to come in the British Open. Despite brave attempts by Tom Watson, Fuzzy Zoeller and Brad Faxon, Nick Price from Zimbabwe won in dramatic fashion from a Swede, Jesper Parnevick. Curtis Strange and Hale Irwin stayed home and Fred Couples was injured.

In Europe, Olazabal had taken over the Ballesteros mantle. Seve himself had become embroiled in an unsightly row with the Ryder Cup committee over the choice of venue for the contest in Spain in 1997. He lost. Nick Faldo and Peter Alliss were again at odds over the former's swing and verbal blows were traded. If John Buchan had been alive he would have renamed his book "The Fourteen Steps (to the Pressbox.)" A European (Ballesteros) credited an American (Mac O'Grady) for helping his return to form after a two year period in the loser's enclosure. He won the Benson and Hedges at St Mellion from a chasing Nick Faldo.

In the USA, there were some signs that the American star was rising. Ben Crenshaw beat Olazabal by three strokes at the Freeport McMoran Classic in April. Hale Irwin beat Greg Norman at the MCI Heritage Classic in May. John Daly won the Bell South Classic in May. But there was a general fear that the invading foreigners would clean up in the Majors. When Olazabal won the Masters, it was the sixth European in seven years. In the past twelve years, only four have been Americans. By contrast, from 1973 to 1982, seven Americans won the Green Jacket, with only Seve Ballesteros from Europe and Gary Player twice. When Els won the US Open, only a revitalised Curtis Strange and the ageless Tom Watson challenged the top three. When Loren Roberts blew his chance to go one shot up at the eighteenth, there was a feeling of inevitability about the eventual result. So in 1994, the US were 0-3 in Majors, finishing second twice. In 1993, they had finished the Majors winning two with Europe and Australia one each. The year was turning into a Major disaster.

The patrician New York Times has expressed worry about the long term state of the game in America. Part of the problem seemed to lie in the perception of golf as an elitist sport. Of the most recently opened golf courses in the USA, only one was public. The Times has now started a campaign to set golf on a more populist basis, campaigning for the opening of more municipal courses, and to make the game appeal to players from all socio-economic backgrounds. Americans rightly cite the examples of football, basketball and baseball players who come from a multitude of backgrounds. For some players, basketball and football have been career paths out of the ghetto.

The National Golf Foundation of America exists, with the prime objective of getting everyone playing the game. Based in Jupiter, Florida, they are concerned with improving facilities for all those who want to play the game and are trying to widen its appeal. They do devote a little time to developing junior golf, a sharp contrast with the work of the UK's Golf Foundation, where 100% of the time is devoted to junior golf. Newspapers like the Daily Telegraph and the Sunday Express also help the young British golfer with national competitions like the Junior Golfer of the Year and the Under-14 Golf Championship.

American feeling seems to be that the system which bred Palmer, Nicklaus, Watson and Trevino has been overtaken by the rest of the world, certainly Europe, Australia and South Africa. US golfers are not used to being beaten and team golf in the US made a fine recovery from the poor results of 1985 and 1987, but what the experts always said is spot on i.e, the gap between US and European golf hasn't really existed since the early eighties. Many sports journalists in America see it as a similar situation to England, which gave soccer to the world, not being at the 1994 World Cup Finals.

But the solution isn't simple, nor the road ahead easy. Private golf courses in the US propagate the elitist image by charging phenomenal joining fees and annual subscriptions. Public courses are crowded to the point where queuing begins, as in Japan, at dawn, and the six hour round is the norm. Clearly the US is worried that if something dramatic isn't done fairly quickly, the natural talent from the different socio-economic backgrounds that so enrich football and basketball and make the US unbeatable will be lost forever to American golf. That would be a tragedy, but good news for the rest of the world's golfers.

AZINGER

The Long Road Back

Soon after the Ryder Cup at The Belfry in 1993, and four short months after his dramatic win at the PGA championship, Paul Azinger was diagnosed with cancer in his shoulder, having suffered with back and shoulder trouble for some time. The news shocked the world of golf and floored the popular Azinger.

Once the diagnosis was made, there was a dramatic wait to see if the cancer had spread to the lymph nodes. To everyone's relief, it hadn't. The cancer is restricted to the bone, not in the marrow or the blood.

Azinger's distinctive boyish haircut is no more. He is bald due to the chemotherapy treatment he endures once a month, but he wears a bandana and jokes about his Kojak looks. His immediate aim is to defend the PGA Championship crown, and the whole world of golf wishes him a speedy comeback. Not just players like Nick Faldo, Seve Ballesteros, and his Ryder Cup team mates, not just his sponsors who, he says, have been very supportive, but golf followers around the world who see his present plight as one he faces in the same way he faced the almost impossible shot at The Belfry against Ballesteros in 1989 at the dreaded 18th.

Azinger had hit the water off the tee, dropped out behind a tree, then screamed a 3-wood to the bunker beside the green that many could not believe. Certainly Seve was so staggered he put his second shot into the water short of the green. The American halved the hole with the shaken Spaniard and preserved his one-hole advantage. If that's the way Azinger approaches life's great difficulties, he'll outstrip everyone's expectations, beat the dreaded cancer, and win the PGA again in August. Everyone here is rooting for him.

THE MASTERS
Olazabal maintains European domination of Green Jacket

Jose-Maria Olazabal came out of the deep depression that seemed to engulf him since he blew the 1991 Masters with a bogey on the 18th, and let Ian Woosnam in to win. He also lost the tag of being the best player never to have won a Major when he overcame Augusta, Tom Lehman and the chasing pack of Americans to take the title with some style. Apart from superb displays in the Ryder Cup, he'd been close in Majors, but never closer than in 1991. His vicious hook off the tee was threatening to unhinge his whole game, and his mental approach was sour. He returned from a three month rest to play in the Tenerife Open in February. When he sank a 25 foot putt at the second extra hole of sudden death to win the Mediterranean Open from Paul McGinley, he was flying again. He had slightly adjusted his swing and found a metal driver that suited him. He was also hungry again. At the age of 28 he has fourteen European Tour wins under his belt, and now the Masters, what some say is the greatest prize of all.

On the final day, it was Larry Mize who made all the early running with three birdies on the first nine holes. Tom Lehman and the pugnacious Tom Kite were both playing well. But Olazabal possessed a note from the legendary Ballesteros. He found it in his locker and kept it with him during the final round. The note advised him to wait for his opponents to crumble, that Olazabal was the best golfer in the world. And at the seventh hole, it seemed the gods were on his side. His drive ended up under a tree, his second struck a branch. He then put a wedge shot six feet from the pin and holed a difficult putt for an astonishing par. It was then you had the feeling that whatever Lehman and Kite did, the Ollie Green Giant, as he would come to be called, would go one better.

Mize had a great front nine, and led at the halfway point, but the back nine found ways to kick the local hero of 1987. Tom Kite needed his putter to get hot. It stayed cool. When Olazabal hit a five iron over the water at the 15th, hearts stopped as the ball thought about retreating to the water, then held. Not as dramatic as Couples at the 12th two years earlier, but Olazabal raised his eyes to the sky in a silent prayer, nevertheless. When he holed out for an eagle from 30 feet, and Lehman's eagle attempt from 15 feet stopped a hair short, the feeling strengthened. Lehman, the picture of impassivity all weekend, couldn't believe it. Had he been Japanese, he might have fallen on his putter. Yet twenty four hours earlier, he had sunk a curling 40 footer with a huge break on the very same green. But hearts beat faster in San Sebastian when Olazabal bogeyed the 17th, to lead Lehman by a single stroke. That was only his second bogey for 56 holes, a measure of his consistency. But he parred the 18th, and the Green Jacket was his, at last. The nearest European was seventeen places away, thirteen shots behind the winner, his great friend and note-writer, Seve Ballesteros. His win meant that Spain was the only country, apart from the US, to have produced more than one Masters winner.

American legends Jack Nicklaus and Arnold Palmer both missed the cut, so for the first time in forty years, neither of them played at the weekend. Fred Couples, Paul Azinger and Phil Mickelson were all absent through illness or injury. Only 13 players shot par or better, compared with 25 the previous year. Ernie Els finished tied with Raymond Floyd in eighth place, Nick Faldo failed to break par in any round and finished 32nd. Colin Montgomerie missed the cut. Defending champion Bernhard Langer was 14 shots behind Olazabal in 25th place. Pre-tournament favourite Nick Price finished tied for 35th, Ian Woosnam for 46th. Greg Norman, who had been 24 under at the Players Championship, ended tied with Ballesteros on 292, thirteen shots behind.

Eight Americans finished in the top ten, but none could match Olazabal, who overcame his erratic long game to reveal a magical short game, a steely nerve and a hot putter.

THE MASTERS ROLL OF HONOUR - THE WINNERS 1934 - 1994

1934	Horton Smith	1966	Jack Nicklaus*
1935	Gene Sarazen*	1967	Gay Brewer
1936	Horton Smith	1968	Bob Goalby
1937	Byron Nelson	1969	George Archer
1938	Henry Picard	1970	Billy Casper*
1939	Ralph Guldahl	1971	Charles Coody
1940	Jimmy Demaret	1972	Jack Nicklaus
1941	Craig Wood	1973	Tommy Aaron
1942	Byron Nelson*	1974	Gary Player
1946	Herman Keiser	1975	Jack Nicklaus
1947	Jimmy Demaret	1976	Raymond Floyd
1948	Claude Harmon	1977	Tom Watson
1949	Sam Snead	1978	Gary Player
1950	Jimmy Demaret	1979	Fuzzy Zoeller*
1951	Ben Hogan	1980	Seve Ballesteros
1952	Sam Snead	1981	Tom Watson
1953	Ben Hogan	1982	Craig Stadler*
1954	Sam Snead*	1983	Seve Ballesteros
1955	Cary Middlecoff	1984	Ben Crenshaw
1956	Jack Burke Jnr	1985	Bernhard Langer
1957	Doug Ford	1986	Jack Nicklaus
1958	Arnold Palmer	1987	Larry Mize*
1959	Art Wall Jnr	1988	Sandy Lyle
1960	Arnold Palmer	1989	Nick Faldo*
1961	Gary Player	1990	Nick Faldo*
1962	Arnold Palmer*	1991	Ian Woosnam
1963	Jack Nicklaus	1992	Fred Couples
1964	Arnold Palmer	1993	Bernhard Langer
1965	Jack Nicklaus	1994	Jose-Maria Olazabal

* Won after playoff.

THE UNITED STATES OPEN
...Els wins US Open and jolts US pride

Ernie Els won the United States Open at Oakmont, near Pittsburgh, Pennsylvania, in a Monday play-off with America's Loren Roberts and Scotland's Colin Montgomerie. The Scot was eliminated after 18 holes and the other two were left in a sudden death playoff. For the first time ever, foreigners won the Masters and the US Open in the same year. And Americans finished as runners up in both events. To make things worse for America, a different foreigner has won six of the last eight Majors. Nick Faldo won the British Open in 1992, Greg Norman in 1993, Bernhard Langer the 1993 Masters and Nick Price the PGA in 1992. Only Lee Janzen in the 1993 US Open and Paul Azinger in the 1993 PGA Championship have won for the United States.

Janzen missed the cut at Oakmont, and Azinger hopes to recover from lymphoma in the right shoulder and defend his title in August. Apart from Roberts, a 38 year old from Memphis, only Curtis Strange, who missed the playoff by a single stroke, John Cook and Tom Watson made any kind of challenge on Els. The glamour boy of American golf, Phil Mickelson, returning from a skiing injury, finished in a tie for 47th and shot a final round 79. Jack Nicklaus made the early running, but faded over the last two days and Arnold Palmer, at 64, made an emotional last appearance.

Had Roberts made a putt for par at the eighteenth, it would have been a different story. Montgomerie was already sitting in the clubhouse at five under when Els drove wildly to the left of the last green, then had to pitch out left, having had a lucky free drop. The best he could hope for was a five. Roberts three putted, Els nervelessly made his bogey and there was a three way tie. With Montgomerie eliminated after 18 playoff holes, Els and Roberts parred the first sudden death hole, the tenth. Then Roberts drove into the unforgiving rough at the next hole, found a bunker with his second, but came out to within 30 feet. Els meantime was less than 20 feet away in two, and ran his birdie putt a yard past. When Roberts lipped the hole in a brave attempt at a par, the 24 year old South African made his to become the third youngest player since the Second World War to win the US Open. Only Nicklaus at 22 (1962), and Jerry Pate at 23 (1976) were younger.

THE BRITISH OPEN AND PRICE IS RIGHT

It was a day of huge highs and lows in the world of sport. On the day when the boys from Brazil took the World Soccer Cup in a dramatic penalty shoot-out as the little old lady from Pasadena watched in awe; on the day when British tennis slumped to its lowest point in the 94-year history of the Davis Cup; on the day when Nick Faldo clowned with a banana, then threw the skin to the crowd; on the day when twenty wallets or credit cards were lost at Turnberry, and nineteen handed in to the police; on the day when Jesper Parnevik, whose father is a stand-up comic, wore a baseball hat that recalled the days of Norman Wisdom, and slipped on a banana skin on the final green; on the day when yet another American challenge in a Major tournament faded sadly away; and on the day the Fat Lady started humming her song on the eighteenth green, Nick Price won the Open with a display of relentless pursuit and a brilliant birdie on the 17th hole. Twice before, in 1982 and 1988, he had come very close. This time he almost finished runner up to the most dazzling of the crop of young Swedes.

But the last hole will be branded on Jesper Parnevik's soul as long as he lives. He blew it. Although Price's unbelievable putt would conceivably have taken the championship into a playoff, Parnevik knows it could have all ended differently. His drive on the last was perfect, on the right of the fairway. He could see the pin clearly. But he pulled his second, going for the pin, underhit his third from a fluffy hollow and took what was to prove a disastrous five.

Tom Watson, Fuzzy Zoeller and Brad Faxon led the American charge, with Tom Kite close behind. Watson looked almost as relaxed as the laid-back Zoeller on the Saturday. But he took 38 putts on Sunday and his attempt to equal Harry Vardon's record of six Open wins perished in the heat of the day and the cold of his putter. He fell back down the field and finished eighth behind Price. Zoeller played immaculately, but he also suffered from putts that did everything but drop, finishing third on nine under, while Faxon finished six under with a last round 73. Tom Lehman, Bob Estes, Mark Calcavecchia and Loren Roberts flattered early to deceive later, as did Craig Stadler and John Daly, who had a disastrous 80 on the final day and finished last, twelve over par. The only consolation for America was that a European hadn't won it either.

Nick Faldo, who had looked out of sorts on the first day, and played the wrong ball in a round of 75, went bananas and finished strongly with a 64, tied at five under with Kite and Colin Montgomerie. Mark James, David Feherty, Russell Claydon and Ronan Rafferty all played well without really getting close to winning. Claydon's magnicent 65 on the last day went almost unnoticed as he finished at four under. Masters winner Olazabal finished level par, as did Ballesteros, Bernhard Langer was well down the field, as were Peter Baker and Sandy Lyle.

But the real story was the relentless Price, who has now won four times this year, but finished 35th in the US Masters and missed the cut in the US Open. He finished at twelve under par, just one shot behind Greg Norman's Open record. He had dogged Parnevik all day, just hanging in, it seemed. He was two behind the Swede when he came to the seventeenth, and rarely have fortunes changed so much and so late. Parnevik had already accepted Tom Watson's congratulations at eleven under, and was signing his scorecard when a huge wave of applause told him the Fat Lady had started her song.

He looked at the screen and saw that Price was back on the seventeenth green, cavorting on the television screen. The horrified Parnevik, ice cool all day, went ice cold. Price's unlikely eagle putt put him twelve under, one ahead. He only needed a par at the last, and there was never any doubt now in the Swede's mind that the man who'd been at his shoulder all that day had caught him on the final bend and was sprinting for the claret jug. Price's unruffled par at the last ensured the Open and £110,000 for the "nearly man" from Zimbabwe, and another new name on the trophy. As the last notes of the Fat Lady's song echoed over Turnberry, Parnevik was overcome, Price elated.

Results:

N. Price	69	66	67	66	268
J. Parnevik	68	66	68	67	269
F. Zoeller	71	66	64	70	271
A. Forsbrand	72	71	66	64	273
M. James	72	67	66	68	273
D. Feherty	68	69	66	70	273
B. Faxon	69	65	67	73	274
N. Faldo	75	66	70	64	275
T. Kite	71	69	66	69	275
C. Montgomerie	72	69	65	69	275

THE BRITISH OPEN
WINNERS SINCE 1946

1946	Sam Snead	290	1971	Lee Trevino	278
1947	Fred Daly	293	1972	Lee Trevino	278
1948	Henry Cotton	284	1973	Tom Weiskopf	276
1949	Bobby Locke	283	1974	Gary Player	282
1950	Bobby Locke	279	1975	Tom Watson	279
1951	Max Faulkner	285	1976	Johnny Miller	278
1952	Bobby Locke	287	1977	Tom Watson	268
1953	Ben Hogan	282	1978	Jack Nicklaus	281
1954	Peter Thompson	283	1979	Seve Ballesteros	283
1955	Peter Thompson	281	1980	Tom Watson	271
1956	Peter Thompson	286	1981	Bill Rogers	276
1957	Bobby Locke	279	1982	Tom Watson	284
1958	Peter Thompson	278	1983	Tom Watson	275
1959	Gary Player	284	1984	Seve Ballesteros	276
1960	Kel Nagle	278	1985	Sandy Lyle	282
1961	Arnold Palmer	284	1986	Greg Norman	280
1962	Arnold Palmer	276	1987	Nick Faldo	279
1963	Bob Charles	277	1988	Seve Ballesteros	273
1964	Tony Lema	279	1989	Mark Calcavecchia	275
1965	Peter Thompson	285	1990	Nick Faldo	270
1966	Jack Nicklaus	282	1991	Ian Baker-Finch	272
1967	Roberto de Vicenzo	278	1992	Nick Faldo	272
1968	Gary Player	289	1993	Greg Norman	267
1969	Tony Jacklin	280	1994	Nick Price	268
1970	Jack Nicklaus	283			

The Return of Saint Jude

Saint Jude lives on. The patron of hopeless cases has been quiet, or so it has seemed, for a few years. But at the Peugeot French Open in June, Anders Forsbrand proved the old saint was still alive and mischievous as ever. Those of us who play golf off a handicap of 20 or so have been awash with self-pity since Sandy Lyle won the Masters with his near-impossible shot. Out of a bunker, too. That was the kind of shot no 20-handicapper would ever dream of playing. Should he do so, even once, he would carry the "bandit" label forever.

When Fred Couples' shot at Augusta hit the bank and rolled toward the lake, we all rubbed our hands. Here comes another fallible golfer, we thought. Then the ball defied the laws of gravity, stopped dead while still on terra firma, the rest is history, and we were left wondering what happened to the fallible golfers who used to give all the duffers hope.

I used to go and watch Arnold Palmer when he was at the mid-point of his fame in the late sixties. He had forearms like Popeye, but you knew he was fallible. The whole world saw him once take five out of a bunker. He would often say that if he didn't make it as a golfer, he would go digging ditches or driving trucks. To those of us in the gallery, he was one of us. The famous Palmer "charge" that so excited the galleries won him many tournaments. But he always seemed to have to come from behind, he had played a few bad shots early on, and there was none of the manicured succession of four sub-par rounds that are so common now. You'd watch Lee Trevino with his bad back, alimony problems and his "musical" swing. The New Yorkers called it so because it was flat. He never seemed to be out of trouble on the course. As for Gary Player, well, he never seemed to hit the ball far enough to win. Only Jack Nicklaus had an invincible aura. We New Yorkers called him the Fat Farmboy. He hit a few bad shots too. But when he did, he'd look at us in the gallery as if to say, "See, I'm only human." He might have been seething inside, but he'd never let you know. Some of the Palmer fans gathered on one hole near the trees and unfurled a banner which read, "Hit it here, fat boy!" Golf was fallible and fun in the days when Nicklaus, Palmer, Trevino and Player were swapping titles like we used to swap baseball cards.

Then came the new breed. Unsmiling, like drill sergeants. They'd turn in the succession of sub-par rounds. Some journalists said they had charisma by-pass ops, or tennis elbow of the personality. They'd hit a bad shot, grimace, roll their eyes toward heaven, throw the odd club, and never, ever talk to the press after a bad round. They seemed infallible, except for Ballesteros, who spent most of his golf life behind one tree or another. They'd snarl when they lost, smile only when they won. It was becoming the age of Robo-Golf. Gone were the days when you'd look forward to

Spiro Agnew hitting spectators. We'd ring up Jimmy the Greek in Las Vegas to get odds on which spectator he'd clunk with his Maxfli next. You had the feeling that, apart from Ian Woosnam who would have looked the part behind the wheel of a semi-truck, few of them would have made it in the factory or on the farm. Faced with such automation amongst the pros, we 20-handicappers began to lose all hope in fallibility.

Then one day, as the sun was going down on the 80's, Mark Calcavecchia's tee shot at the 18th in a crucial Ryder Cup singles hit the water. Another glimmer of hope when the gaudy Payne Stewart did the same. Knee-deep in water, he tried to play his second, failed, then, wet suit bottoms on, tried a third before giving up. Was fallibility making a come-back? Not quite. Christy O'Connor Jnr's miracle two iron shot at the same hole sent Saint Jude back to his pew. But then, the following year, Tom Kite's tee shot whistled off the tee about 35 yards and hit a fat woman from New Jersey. Saint Jude, where have you been for so long? By 1993 at the Open at Sandwich, I was convinced. Greg Norman's tee shot at the first on the opening day found the deep spinach. He hacked out, only to find more deep rough, hacked out, and took a six. Three days later, he was to be a spectacular winner. Saint Jude was still hovering somewhere, as Norman himself played some God-like shots down the home stretch. Later on, the amazingly fallible John Daly drove a 415-yard par four hole while the robo-golfers were still putting out. And I knew with some certainty that fallibility had returned. By June of 1994, there was no doubt. The news came in that some of the robo-golfers were consulting gurus, quacks, sports psychologists, and that the already fallible Ballesteros had taken on Mac O'Grady as a coach. A sure sign that robo-golf had had its day. As all we New Yorkers know, Mac and Saint Jude have been through a lot together.

Enter stage right the Swede Anders Forsbrand. The 33-year old had a 73 in the first round at the French Open. On Friday 25th June, he played golf of such fallibility that he ran out of balls. He just LOST NINE balls! By the time he reached the par five 18th tee, he had taken 93 shots and lost seven balls. Totally unnerved and with Saint Jude laughing his support hose off, he hit the water in front of the green twice. Had he dropped with a penalty, chipped on and, say three putted, he would have had a round of 102. Giving him a three putt hole is not being unkind. He had taken FIVE putts on the 12th. However, he was completely out of balls. He was then disqualified for failing to complete his round. When he hit his last shot into the lake, he was 27 over par.

Now as we all know, nine balls is not enough. I carry at least a dozen, as you just never know with trees and water around. It's academic, I know, but do the Tour rules not allow borrowing balls from an opponent? Club golfers do it all the time, and are pleased to do so, especially if there's a chance to palm off a sub-standard ball on your opponent at a critical stage. Forsbrand would have finished with 102, presumably, if he'd been allowed to carry on. To know that most of the 20-ish handicappers in the country would have beaten him is heady stuff indeed. Saint Jude is now at last alive and kicking, fallibility lives again and, as the admen at Peugeot say, it takes your breath away.

The Ryder Cup, 1995

The next Ryder Cup will be held at Oak Hill, Pittsford, near Rochester, New York, and the contest has been kept at the forefront of everyone's mind in the past twelve months. Bernard Gallacher was again chosen as Europe's captain, and the combative Lanny Wadkins as his US counterpart. But there was another row brewing through the winter of 1993/94, and the "disagreement" over the choice of venue for the 1997 Ryder Cup was finally ended when the Ryder Cup Committee announced in June that Valderrama had been chosen. But the weeks leading up to that decision had been marked by bitter argument and counter argument. Severiano Ballesteros had been instrumental in the original decision to hold the contest in Spain, but he challenged the Valderrama course, on the Costa del Sol and owned by Jaime Ortiz-Patino, the Bolivian tin millionaire. He called it the "Augusta of Europe", and claimed it was too elite to be a viable venue.

The Spaniard, who was thought by many to have saved the Ryder Cup from dying of boredom, was the favourite to be the European captain for the 1997 event. But press revelations of alleged bribery, and his own choice of Novo Sancti Petri, which he designed, as the venue, set Ballesteros and the Ryder Cup Committee on a collision course. He resigned from the committee, claiming that Valderrama had offered him $1 million to support their bid. Ballesteros was alleged to have hinted after the Spanish Open that other members of the Ryder Cup committee may have been offered inducements to choose the Valderrama club. This was angrily denied by the other five members of the committee, and at one time Valderrama were considering legal action against Ballesteros.

The issue was finally settled on June 25 when Valderrama was chosen, and for a while there was some doubt whether Ballesteros would captain the 1997 team, or even play in another Ryder Cup. The row simmered on through the summer months.

European Dream Sunk

at The Belfry 1993

If the titanic struggle at Kiawah Island stopped the golfing world in its tracks, the event at The Belfry last September was tame by comparison. Sure enough, there was drama every day but never the crescendo of excitement that marked the "war on the shore", when it all came down to the last match, the last hole, the last green and the final agony of Langer's missed putt. When Nick Faldo, playing last with Paul Azinger on Sunday, reached the last few holes, he knew all was lost, and whatever he did, the Ryder Cup would travel back to the US by Concorde. Tom Watson's team won by 15-13 and, more importantly, there was none of the jingoism that had spoiled the previous encounter. Both teams and the huge crowds played their parts in making the event as memorable as always. The crowds were polite and appreciative and the raucous yells of "get in the hole!" were hardly heard. The teams were close, too, and when Peter Baker had to rush off to hospital to be with his wife, the player most visibly upset was his American rival, Davis Love.

There were so many examples of this closeness between the teams -and the crowd- that all thoughts of the military hats and chants of Kiawah were long forgotten. When Faldo aced at the 14th, only the second hole-in-one in Ryder Cup history, Azinger rushed to shake him warmly by the hand. Woosnam needed a nervy putt on the eighteenth and Fred Couples admitted praying that he wouldn't miss. So intense was the pressure on the Welshman that Couples later said that he had considered offering him a halved game without either having to putt. Lanny Wadkins remembered the agony of David Gilford when he was left out at Kiawah. When Sam Torrance was forced to scratch from the Sunday singles, Wadkins, a wild card pick by Tom Watson, volunteered to be the "man in the envelope", not wanting one of his team mates, who had all been chosen on merit, to go through the same agony and frustration. He followed all the games, giving encouragement to his team. When spectators realised what he was going through and tried to console him, he wept unashamedly.

And the crowd, festooned with a sea of stars and stripes in their hair and in their hats, decked out smartly in their Brooks Brothers blazers, acted like it was an Allied Army reunion, as if it were a preview of the 50th anniversary of the forthcoming D-Day celebrations. They applauded both teams, swapped sandwiches and addresses in the bars, around the practice areas and on the course. Both sets of supporters warmly applauded the unbeaten rookie Peter Baker as he sank putt after putt.

The match itself was won and lost in the Sunday singles. After Friday's Foursomes and Fourballs, Europe had its nose in front by a point. By

Saturday lunchtime, the lead was three points, thanks to a 3-1 win in the Foursomes. Knowing that the Americans are always strong in the final day singles, all the experts were predicting that if Europe could halve the Saturday afternoon Fourballs and take a three point lead into Sunday, they ought to regain the Ryder Cup. It was later seen to be an astonishing piece of captaincy by Bernard Gallacher that tipped the balance back toward the US. Both Langer and Ballesteros asked to be rested for Saturday afternoon. Despite indifferent form, Ballesteros had still been seen as the inspiration of the Europeans. With Olazabal he had been the man at Kiawah that no American wanted to play, and he was still feared. In three matches at the Belfry, he had won two, and narrowly lost the other. Langer had a similar record, winning two of three. Both had won their Saturday morning matches.

Gallacher reasoned that his Langer-less and Ballesteros-less team could halve the Fourballs, and that both would be fresh for the following day's crucial singles. It was not to be.

Gallacher stressed later that the superstars had told him they were struggling and wanted to practice, rather than play. But he insisted that the final decision was his, and that if he had ordered them to play, they would have. One journalist compared Gallacher's situation to the Alf Ramsey decision to take off Bobby Charlton in the 1970 World Cup when England were leading 2-0, a game they eventually lost 3-2. "We all heard that Seve decided he wanted a rest, and there was no way Gallacher was going to make him play," he said. "Langer we thought was injured, then we saw him practising, so we wondered what was going on in the dressing room. Most of us agreed that the objective on the Saturday afternoon was to put the match out of the Americans' reach. They could have done that with a half and gone into Sunday three points ahead. He should have ordered them to play. And look at the four players involved. Ballesteros and Langer had the afternoon off, then both lost the singles and their games weren't even close. Haeggman and Rocca both lost on the Saturday afternoon, and Rocca lost on the Sunday. It's easy to be wise after the event, but many of us felt at the time that Gallacher was there to be the boss, not a nursemaid." In the post mortem that followed in the media, many felt that Ballesteros and Langer had let the team down, and that Gallacher had been far too soft with them.

Their replacements, Rocca and Haeggman, both rookies, lost in the Fourballs, as did the previously unbeaten Faldo and Montgomerie, very narrowly, by one hole to John Cook and Chip Beck. Only Peter Baker, paired with Woosnam, continued to dazzle, and the US won the Saturday afternoon 3-1. That still left Europe ahead by a single point. But the Americans were jubilant on the Saturday evening. From being on the ropes at lunchtime, they were now right back in it. "The news of the afternoon fourballs gave us a huge boost," recalls Floyd. "Instead of facing the Ballesteros-Olazabal nightmare, we saw two rookies. We figured we might win all four if we got some breaks against Faldo, and we didn't think Woosnam could carry on playing brilliantly. When we took three out of four, we were on a roll, and it gave us the momentum we needed desperately for Sunday."

Gallacher loaded his singles order for Sunday with the strength at the back. The last four players out would be Ballesteros, Olazabal, Langer and Faldo. All the significant drama had happened before their games were settled. Barry Lane was three up with five to play against Chip Beck, then lost the next three holes to go level. They halved the 17th, but Lane's drive found the bunker, then the lake and Beck won the match with a par. Woosnam had already halved with Couples, sinking his nerve-tingling putt at the last. So the contest was all-square. Then Montgomerie beat Lee Janzen by one hole, the brilliant Baker beat up the never-say-die Corey Pavin by two holes and rookie Haeggman shaded John Cook by a hole. Europe were a crucial three points ahead and, with the rested and reliable heavyweights to come, it looked, as the Americans say, a shoo-in.

But Payne Stewart beat Mark James 3 &2, Kite destroyed Langer 5 &3, and suddenly the whole match had turned. Rocca was up, Olazabal was playing a 51-year old, Faldo was still out there. And it still looked safe for the Europeans, although the main dish on The Belfry restaurant menu was bitten fingernails. Then came another rookie, Costantino Rocca. The battle with Davis Love had see-sawed from the third, neither player able to get more than one hole ahead. Rocca got a two on the 14th to level, then went one up when he birdied the fifteenth to the American's par. When Rocca took a six at the 17th, it was all square. The Italian had a putt to win by 3 &2, but he narrowly missed, then missed again from four feet coming back. It was a lucky break, a turning point the Americans could never have dreamed about.

The unhappy Ballesteros had already lost to Jim Gallagher Jnr when Rocca's drive at the 18th landed in the rough and his second just cleared the lake. His difficult chip ran past, he missed the putt and the chance fell to Love for an unexpected win. He sank a difficult putt amid the ominously silent European and wildly celebrating American supporters. The contest was now all square. Even in his moment of triumph, Love sought out his weeping opponent to try to console him.

The rest was a question of the experienced Azinger and Floyd holding their nerve. Langer had already been thrashed by the brilliant Tom Kite, so suddenly the worst that could happen to Watson's team was a tie. Floyd, casual yet relentless as ever, beat Olazabal by two holes and suddenly there was nothing Faldo could do. He halved with the gutsy Azinger and the US had retained the trophy they won amid such high drama at Kiawah. In the end it was not a bang but a whimper in excitement, but the watching millions will remember Rocca's missed putt as much as they'll remember Langer's two years before.

In the end, some of the players were unhinged by the thought that there was so much at stake. Barry Lane looked as exhausted as Hale Irwin had done at Kiawah, Rocca as overcome by his failure as Calcavecchia was two years before. Even the giant Montgomerie thought that it was a major achievement just to stand up amid the tension. Seve Ballesteros put it in perspective. "Rocca should not feel worse than anyone else. He was very close to being the hero." The Italian was philosophical eventually. "The moment I lost, I felt responsible for losing the Ryder Cup for the team. Then I realised that some of the best players in the world had not won either, that it wasn't just down to me."

US captain Tom Watson summed it up. "This is the finest experience I have ever had in the game of golf. We had the guts which is typical of all our teams. My feelings are a mixture of pride, relief and satisfaction." Apart from the Sam Torrance menu incident, he and his team didn't put a foot wrong, either in diplomacy, behaviour or golf. The watchers, both at The Belfry and millions around the world, shared, as they have in other Ryder Cup contests, memories they will never forget. The incidents, the crowd banter, the memories and the unbearable tension will be treasured for a long time, and by the players too. Many, like me, wished that the Sunday afternoon would never end, and that there could be a Ryder Cup every weekend.

Oak Hill 1995

It could be a very interesting 1995 for rookies and those who have never played in the Ryder Cup before. On the European side, Ian Woosnam and Seve Ballesteros are by no means certain of being selected. There could be three Swedes in the team including Cup rookies Anders Forsbrand and Peter Hedblom. Iain Pyman, who's just turned pro, could even make the team, along with the in-form Miguel Angel Jimenez.

The US team looks even more inexperienced, with Loren Roberts, Tom Lehman and John Huston in good form. Phil Mickelson is a possible, as is old warhorse Ben Crenshaw. The table of runners and riders which follows has of necessity, been compiled in mid 1994, but it does throw up some interesting possibilities, and several names virtually unknown, who are all well up in the US money list and Volvo Order of Merit.

So have a look, take a flutter and have a bit of fun guessing the next teams to do Ryder Cup battle in New York.

The Ryder Cup 1995
Runners & Riders as at 4/7/94

Definites

EUROPE	US
J. M. Olazabal	Fred Couples
Colin Montgomerie	Paul Azinger (if fit)
Nick Faldo	Tom Lehman
Bernhard Langer	Loren Roberts
Jesper Parnevik	Hale Irwin

Probables

EUROPE	US
Miguel Angel Jimenez	Jeff Maggert
David Gilford	Fuzzy Zoeller
Ian Woosnam	John Huston
Joakim Haeggman	Tom Kite
Seve Ballesteros	Corey Pavin

Possibles

EUROPE	US
David Feherty	Mike Springer
Iain Pyman	Phil Mickelson
Peter Hedblom	Ben Crenshaw
Jonathan Lomas	Mark Brooks
Barry Lane	Davis Love
Anders Forsbrand	Brad Faxon
Howard Clark	John Cook

Ryder Cup appearances
since 1921

Since the Ryder Cup was "first" contested in 1921, Billy Casper has played in more games than any other American with 37 games. He has achieved 20 victories with seven halves. But Arnold Palmer has been the more successful with 22 victories and two halves from 32 appearances between 1961-1973. Lanny Wadkins has 20 wins from 33 appearances, followed by Raymond Floyd's 32, then Lee Trevino has played on 30 occasions, winning 17 with six halves while Jack Nicklaus is fifth on this United States Ryder Cup list with 28 games, recording 17 wins and three halves - the most memorable of which was with Tony Jacklin at Royal Birkdale, in 1969. Tom Kite also has 28 appearances and Gene Littler is next with 27 appearances, winning 14 and halving eight.

Of the 152 players who have represented the United States in the Ryder Cup series since its institution, only 12 can boast a 100 percent record while competing for their country. Ben Hogan is perhaps the most celebrated having played three times in 1947 and 1951 but funny man Jimmy Demaret was the most successful having appeared on six occasions between 1947-1951 and won them all.

The others include Herman Barron (1) in 1947; Billy Burke (3) in 1931 and 1933; Wilfred 'Wiffy' Cox (1) in 1947; Johnny Golden (3) in 1927 and 1929; Ralph Guldahl (2) in 1937; Chick Harbert (2) in 1949 and 1955; Bill Maxwell (4) in 1963; Rob Rosburg (2) in 1959; Jim Turnesa (1) in 1953; and Lew Worsham (2) in 1947.

Neil Coles made his Ryder Cup debut in 1961 and during the next 16 years he played more games than any other Great Britain and Ireland professional. Although making 40 appearances Neil only won on 12 occasions and was on the receiving end no fewer than 21 times.

Nick Faldo has recorded the most victories with 19 from 36 starts while Peter Oosterhuis won 14 from 28 starts with 11 losses.

Christy O'Connor Senior has played in more consecutive matches than anyone in the history of the Ryder Cup. He played in every contest from 1955 - 1973 inclusive, representing Great Britain and Ireland no fewer than 36 times despite recording only 11 victories.

Of the 99 different players who represented Great Britain and Ireland & Europe since 1921 only eight have a 100% record with Harry Vardon, Josh Taylor, James Ockenden and James Sherlock playing two games in the inaugural international match against the United States at Gleneagles in 1921. John Jacobs, later to become captain of the "European" side in 1979 and again in 1981, won both his games at Palm Springs in 1955.

The other professionals to achieve this unique distinction include: Johnny Fallon (1) in 1955; George Gadd (2) in 1926; and Peter Mills (1) in 1957; and Paul Broadhurst (2) in 1991.

There were a number of players who were selected but, for various reasons, did not play in the Series and they include: Laurie Ayton in 1949; Stewart Burns (1929); Allan Dailey (1933); George Gadd (1927); Eric Green (1947) Jack Hargreaves (1951); and Reg Horne (1947).

Since the inaugural match between America and Great Britain in 1921, the two sides have played a total of 928 separate games of which the European side were successful in 325 with 115 games halved.

George Gadd, a non-playing member of the British team in 1927, was the first person to be presented with the Ryder Cup. While accepting it on behalf of the PGA, Gadd thanked the Ryder family for what they had done and were doing for British professional golf. Mrs Ryder did the honours prior to the Great Britain and Ireland side departing for Worcester, Massachusetts, in the summer of 1927. It was local solicitor and nephew of Ryder, Tom Anderson-David, who drew up the deed of gift which put the Cup in the possession of the PGA.

Had the gold cup been made in time for the match at Wentworth in 1926 perhaps the PGAs, on both sides of the Atlantic, would have agreed that this would be the inaugural contest. However, the authorities decided that the 1926 contest, which the home side won in convincing fashion 13-1 and one half, would not count.

It was not reported in the British press why this decision should have stood but it would appear that the answer is that the American team included many players who emigrated from Europe and were therefore not US citizens. In a sense, the 1926 US team represented the American Tour rather that the United States as a nation. This was amended for the "inaugural" match on June 3-4, 1927 when the hosts won 9-2 with one game halved. In those days when two players competed with each other it was known as a twosomes game whereas today, such games are referred to as singles.

The *New York Times* reported the 1927 contest in graphic detail and the complete score cards, for the individual games, were published in full.

The paper's correspondent, *William D. Richardson*, wrote, on June 4th:

"America's homebreds avenged the drubbing that the British professionals gave their pick-up team in England last year by swamping the British professionals in the international matches of the Ryder Cup.

The score was paid off with full interest when the Americans won six of the twosome matches at the Worcester Country Club today, halved another and lost only one out of the eight.

Starting with a lead of three points to one by virtue of their victory in yesterday's foursomes, the homebreds finished the series with a score of 9-2, with one halved. It was not quite as bad a drubbing as the British handed them last year when the score of the first match for the Cup stood 13-1 with one halved game. But last year

England put its full strength into the test while the US side was made up of a number of fill-ins."

It is also interesting to note that the newspaper referred to the match as being the second in the Series. This is in stark contrast to the decision made by the PGA when the international contest was staged on the Burma Road course, Wentworth, Surrey, the previous season. To this day the PGA refuse to recognise the 1926 as part of the Ryder Cup series yet Mrs Ryder presented the trophy prior to the "new inaugural" match staged in the US.

The Great Britain and Ireland team won the return match at Moortown in Leeds by 7-5 but since then the Americans have reigned supreme except for a few occasions when the Great Britain and Ireland side played inspired golf to win in 1933 and 1957, for example.

The Americans have now won 23 of the official matches to date while GB & I/Europe recorded five wins and two tied.

From 1921, GB & I/Europe have won 7, US 23, and two tied.

The emergence of Nick Faldo and Sandy Lyle on the world stage of golf coincided with the British PGA's decision to throw open the Ryder Cup selection to Europe for the 1979 match. Brian Huggett, who played on six occasions and captained the side once, argued that the decision to include European players was correct as only 50 percent of the Britain and Ireland professionals were good enough to take part.

The inclusion of the likes of Seve Ballesteros in 1979 and Bernhard Langer in 1981 did not produce an immediate effect for the European squad. It was not until the PGA National Golf and Country Club in Florida in 1983 did harmony emerge as the European side's greatest ally. Never before did the sporting public see a German, two Spaniards and British players fight for each other to over-power the opposition.

They were narrowly beaten following three day's of nail-biting golf. The final scoreline reads: US 14 Europe 13 with one game halved.

Since the "new-look" European side successfully defended the Ryder Cup for the first time on American soil in 1987, the US dominance has become much less pronounced. From now on, the golfing enthusiast can look forward, with relish, to a succession of thrilling contests.

Recently the partisan galleries showed little vocal restraint. When the European side were victorious at The Belfry in 1985 some members of the visiting side complained about the paying public who showed little regard for the traditions of the game. "They should all be gagged", retorted Hal Sutton as Langer hammered him by 5 & 4. Many Europeans at Kiawah Island felt that the combat hats and raucous galleries were too vocal. Tom Watson stressed the need for less chauvinistic behaviour in the lead-up to the 1993 event. The Belfry crowds returned golf gallery behaviour to some kind of sanity, and golf was all the better for it.

RYDER CUP PLAYING RECORDS

A **THE COMPLETE** - Z
since 1921

There have been 273 players involved in the Ryder Cup since the humble beginnings in 1921, 928 separate games in 32 events. In the following pages we analyse their playing performances, list their appearances, wins, losses and halves. It is the most complete record available on the Ryder Cup, but to save you reading every name, we have tried to summarise some of the best records of players old and new in the few tables that follow.

RYDER CUP
BEST and WORST

100% RECORDS

PERFECT — Minimum 2 games

Jimmy Demaret	USA	Appeared 1947-51	Played 6	Won 6
Billy Maxwell	USA	Appeared 1963	Played 4	Won 4
Billy Burke	USA	Appeared 1931-33	Played 3	Won 3
John Golden	USA	Appeared 1927-29	Played 3	Won 3
Ben Hogan	USA	Appeared 1947, 51	Played 3	Won 3
Melvin Harbert	USA	Appeared 1949, 55	Played 2	Won 2
John Jacobs	GB & I	Appeared 1955	Played 2	Won 2
Bob Rosburgh	USA	Appeared 1959	Played 2	Won 2
Lew Worsham	USA	Appeared 1947	Played 2	Won 2
Paul Broadhurst	EUR	Appeared 1991	Played 2	Won 2

CLOSE TO PERFECT — Minimum 6 games

Gardner Dickinson	USA	Appeared 1967, 71	P 10	W 9	L 1	H 0
Jack Burke	USA	Appeared 1951-59	P 8	W 7	L 1	H 0
Jesse Snead	USA	Appeared 1971-75	P 11	W 9	L 2	H 0
Tony Lema	USA	Appeared 1963-65	P 11	W 8	L 1	H 2
Walter Hagen	USA	Appeared 1927-35	P 9	W 7	L 1	H 1
Sam Snead	USA	Appeared 1939, 47-59	P 13	W 10	L 2	H 1
Lloyd Mangrum	USA	Appeared 1947-53	P 8	W 6	L 2	H 0

THE WORST — Minimum 4 games

Tom Haliburton	GB & I	Appeared 1961-63	P 6	W 0	L 6	H 0
Malcolm Gregson	GB & I	Appeared 1967	P 4	W 0	L 4	H 0
Eamonn Darcy	EUR	Appeared 1975-81, 87	P 11	W 1	L 8	H 2
Tommy Horton	GB & I	Appeared 1975-77	P 8	W 1	L 6	H 1
Max Faulkner	GB & I	Appeared 1947-53, 57	P 8	W 1	L 7	H 0
Miller Barber	USA	Appeared 1969-71	P 7	W 1	L 4	H 2
Tommy Aaron	USA	Appeared 1969, 73	P 6	W 1	L 4	H 1
Archie Compton	GB & I	Appeared 1927-31	P 6	W 1	L 4	H 1
Antonio Garrido	EUR	Appeared 1979	P 5	W 1	L 4	H 0
Jerry Barber	USA	Appeared 1955, 61	P 5	W 1	L 4	H 0
Sam Torrance	EUR	Appeared 1981-93	P 22	W 4	L 13	H 5

MOST WINS

22	Arnold Palmer	USA
20	Billy Casper	USA
20	Lanny Wadkins	USA
19	Seve Ballesteros	EUR
19	Nick Faldo	EUR
17	Lee Trevino	USA
17	Jack Nicklaus	USA
15	Tom Kite	USA

MOST LOSSES

21	Neil Coles	GB & I
21	Christy O'Connor	GB & I
16	Bernard Hunt	GB & I
16	Raymond Floyd	USA
15	Peter Alliss	GB & I

MOST HALVES

8	Tony Jacklin	EUR
8	Gene Littler	USA
7	Billy Casper	USA

MOST APPEARANCES

40	Neil Coles	GB & I	W 12	L 21	H 0
37	Billy Casper	USA	W 20	L 10	H 7
36	Nick Faldo	EUR	W 19	L 13	H 4
36	Christy O'Connor	GB & I	W 11	L 21	H 4
35	Tony Jacklin	EUR	W 13	L 14	H 8
34	Seve Ballesteros	EUR	W 19	L 10	H 5
33	Lanny Wadkins	USA	W 20	L 11	H 2
32	Arnold Palmer	USA	W 22	L 8	H 2
31	Raymond Floyd	USA	W 12	L 16	H 3
31	Bernard Gallacher	GB & I	W 13	L 13	H 5
30	Peter Alliss	GB & I	W 10	L 15	H 5
30	Lee Trevino	USA	W 17	L 7	H 6
29	Bernhard Langer	EUR	W 13	L 11	H 5
28	Bernard Hunt	GB & I	W 6	L 16	H 6
28	Tom Kite	USA	W 15	L 9	H 4
28	Jack Nicklaus	USA	W 17	L 8	H 3
28	Peter Oosterhuis	GB & I	W 14	L 11	H 3
27	Gene Littler	USA	W 14	L 5	H 8
26	Ian Woosnam	EUR	W 12	L 10	H 4
25	Brian Barnes	GB & I/EUR	W 10	L 14	H 1
25	Brian Huggett	GB & I	W 9	L 10	H 6
22	Mark James	EUR	W 7	L 14	H 1
22	Sam Torrance	EUR	W 4	L 13	H 5
20	Hale Irwin	USA	W 13	L 5	H 2

　　　　　　　　The Professionals

A

Tommy Aaron USA
1969-73　P6　W1　L4　H1
Jimmy Adams　GB & I
1947-53　P7　W2　L5　H0
Stewart Alexander USA
1949-51　P2　W1　L1　H0
Percy Alliss　GB & I
1929, 1933-37　P6　W3　L2　H1
Peter Alliss　GB & I
1953, 1957-69　P30　W10　L15　H5
Tommy Armour USA
1926　P2　W0　L2　H0
Lawrence Ayton　GB & I
1949　P0　W0　L0　H0
Paul Azinger USA
1989-93　P14　W5　L7　H2

B

Seve Ballesteros　EUR
1979, 1983-93　P34　W19　L10　H5
Peter Baker　EUR
1993　P4　W3　L1　H0
Harry Bannerman　GB & I
1971　P5　W2　L2　H1
Jerry Barber USA
1955, 1961　P5　W1　L4　H0
Miller Barber USA
1969, 1971　P7　W1　L4　H2
Brian Barnes　GB & I/EUR
1969-79　P25　W10　L14　H1
Jim Barnes USA
1926　P2　W0　L2　H0
Herman Barron USA
1947　P1　W1　L0　H0
Andy Bean USA
1979, 1987　P6　W4　L2　H0
Frank Beard USA
1969, 1971　P8　W2　L3　H3
Chip Beck USA
1989-93　P9　W6　L2　H1
Maurice Bembridge　GB & I
1969-75　P16　W5　L8　H3
Homero Blancas USA
1973　P4　W2　L1　H1
Tommy Bolt USA
1955-57　P4　W3　L1　H0
Aubrey Boomer　GB & I

1926, 1927-29　P6　W4　L2　H0
Julius Boros USA
1959, 1963-67　P16　W9　L3　H4
Ken Bousfield　GB & I
1949-51,1955-61　P10　W5　L5　H0
Hugh Boyle　GB & I
1967　P3　W0　L3　H0
Harry Bradshaw　GB & I
1953-57　P5　W2　L2　H1
James Braid　GB & I
1921　P2　W2　L0　H0
Gordon Brand Jnr　EUR
1987-89　P7　W2　L4　H1
Gordon J. Brand　EUR
1983　P1　W0　L1　H0
Gay Brewer USA
1967, 1973　P9　W5　L3　H1
Paul Broadhurst　EUR
1991　P2　W2　L0　H0
Eric Brown　GB & I
1953-59　P8　W4　L4　H0
Ken Brown　GB & I/EUR
1977-79, 1983-87　P13　W4　L9　H0
Billy Burke USA
1931-33　P3　W3　L0　H0
Jack Burke USA
1951-59　P8　W7　L1　H0
Walter Burkemo USA
1953　P1　W0　L1　H0
Stewart Burns　GB & I
1929　P0　W0　L0　H0
Richard Burton　GB & I
1935, 1937, 1949　P5　W2　L3　H0
Jack Busson　GB & I
1935　P2　W0　L2　H0
Peter Butler　GB & I
1965-69, 1973　P14　W3　L9　H2

C

Mark Calcavecchia USA
1987-91　P11　W5　L5　H1
José-Maria Canizares　EUR
1981-89　P11　W5　L4　H2
Billy Casper USA
1961-75　P37　W20　L10　H7
Alex Caygill　GB & I
1969　P1　W0　L0　H1
Clive Clark　GB & I
1973　P1　W0　L1　H0
Howard Clark　GB & I/EUR
1977, 81, 87, 89　P13　W6　L6　H1

Neil Coles	GB & I			
1961-77	P40	W12	L21	H7
Bill Collins	**USA**			
1961	P3	W1	L2	H0
Archie Compston	GB & I			
1926-31	P8	W2	L5	H1
Charles Coody	**USA**			
1971	P3	W0	L2	H1
John Cook	**USA**			
1993	P2	W1	L1	H0
Henry Cotton	GB & I			
1929, 1937, 1947	P6	W2	L4	H0
Fred Couples	**USA**			
1989-93	P12	W3	L6	H3
Bill Cox	GB & I			
1935-37	P3	W0	L2	H1
Wilfred Cox	**USA**			
1931	P2	W2	L0	H0
Ben Crenshaw	**USA**			
1981-83, 87	P9	W3	L5	H1

D

Allan Dailey	GB & I			
1933	P0	W0	L0	H0
Fred Daly	GB & I			
1947-53	P8	W3	L4	H1
Eamonn Darcy	GB & I/EUR			
1975-77, 81, 87	P11	W1	L8	H2
William Davies	GB & I			
1931, 1933	P4	W2	L2	H0
Peter Dawson	GB & I			
1977	P3	W1	L2	H0
Jimmy Demaret	**USA**			
1947-51	P6	W6	L0	H0
Gardner Dickinson	**USA**			
1967, 1971	P10	W9	L1	H0
Leo Diegel	**USA**			
1927-33	P6	W3	L3	H0
Dave Douglas	**USA**			
1953	P2	W1	L0	H0
Dale Douglass	**USA**			
1969	P2	W0	L2	H0
Norman Drew	GB & I			
1959	P1	W0	L0	H1
Ed Dudley	**USA**			
1929, 33, 37	P4	W3	L1	H0
George Duncan	GB & I			
1927-31	P9	W5	L3	H1
Olin Dutra	**USA**			
1933-35	P4	W1	L3	H0

E

Syd Easterbrook	GB & I			
1931-33	P3	W2	L1	H0
Lee Elder	**USA**			
1979	P4	W1	L3	H0
Al Espinosa	**USA**			
1927-31	P4	W2	L1	H1

F

Nick Faldo	GB & I/EUR			
1977-93	P36	W19	L13	H4
John Fallon	GB & I			
1955	P1	W1	L0	H0
Johnny Farrell	**USA**			
1927-31	P6	W3	L2	H1
Max Faulkner	GB & I			
1947-57	P8	W1	L7	H0
David Feherty	EUR			
1991	P3	W1	L1	H1
Dow Finsterwald	**USA**			
1957-63	P13	W9	L3	H1
Raymond Floyd	**USA**			
1969, 75-77, 81-85	P31	W12	L16	H3
Doug Ford	**USA**			
1955-61	P9	W4	L4	H1
Emmett French	**USA**			
1921, 1926	P4	W1	L2	H1
Ed Furgol	**USA**			
1957	P1	W0	L1	H0
Marty Furgol	**USA**			
1955	P1	W0	L1	H0

G

George Gadd	GB & I (Did not play in			
	1927)			
1926-27	P2	W2	L0	H0
Bernard Gallacher	GB & I/EUR			
1969-83	P31	W13	L13	H5
Jim Gallagher Jnr.	**USA**			
1993	P3	W2	L1	H0
John Garner	GB & I			
1971, 73	P1	W0	L1	H0
Antonio Garrido	EUR			
1979	P5	W1	L4	H0
Al Geiberger	**USA**			
1967, 75	P9	W5	L1	H3

Bob Gilder	USA			
1983	P4	W2	L2	H0
David Gilford	EUR			
1991	P2	W0	L2	H0
Bob Goalby	USA			
1963	P5	W3	L1	H1
John Golden	USA			
1927-29	P3	W3	L0	H0
Lou Graham	USA			
1973-77	P9	W5	L3	H1
Eric Green	GB & I			
1947	P0	W0	L0	H0
Hubert Green	USA			
1977-79, 85	P7	W4	L3	H0
Ken Green	USA			
1989	P4	W2	L2	H0
Malcolm Gregson	GB & I			
1967	P4	W0	L4	H0
Ralph Guldahl	USA			
1937	P2	W2	L0	H0

H

Fred Haas	USA			
1953	P1	W0	L1	H0
Jay Haas	USA			
1983	P4	W2	L1	H1
Clarence Hackney	USA			
1921	P2	W0	L1	H1
Walter Hagen	USA			
1921-26, 1927-35	P13	W7	L3	H3
Tom Haliburton	GB & I			
1961,63	P6	W0	L6	H0
Bob Hamilton	USA			
1949	P2	W0	L2	H0
Melvin Harbert	USA			
1949, 55	P2	W2	L0	H0
Jack Hargreaves	GB & I			
1951	P0	W0	L0	H0
Joakim Haeggman	EUR			
1991	P2	W1	L1	H0
Chandler Harper	USA			
1955	P1	W0	L1	H0
'Dutch' Harrison	USA			
1947-51	P3	W2	L1	H0
Arthur Havers	GB & I			
1921, 26, 27-33	P10	W6	L4	H0
Fred Hawkins	USA			
1957	P2	W1	L1	H0
Mark Hayes	USA			
1979	P3	W1	L2	H0
Clayton Heafner	USA			
1949-51	P4	W3	L0	H1
Jay Hebert	USA			
1959-61	P4	W2	L1	H1

Lionel Hebert	USA			
1957	P1	W0	L1	H0
Dave Hill	USA			
1969, 73, 77	P9	W6	L3	H0
Jimmy Hitchcock	GB & I			
1965	P3	W0	L3	H0
Bert Hodson	GB & I			
1931	P1	W0	L1	H0
Charles Hoffner	USA			
1921	P2	W0	L2	H0
Ben Hogan	USA			
1947, 51	P3	W3	L0	H0
Reg Horne	GB & I			
1947	P0	W0	L0	H0
Tommy Horton	GB & I			
1975-77	P8	W1	L6	H1
Brian Huggett	GB & I			
1963, 67-75	P25	W9	L10	H6
Bernard Hunt	GB & I			
1953, 57-69	P28	W6	L16	H6
Geoffrey Hunt	GB & I			
1963	P3	W0	L3	H0
Guy Hunt	GB & I			
1975	P3	W0	L2	H1
Jock Hutchinson	USA			
1921	P2	W0	L1	H1

I

Hale Irwin	USA			
1975-81, 91	P20	W13	L5	H2

J

Tony Jacklin	GB & I/EUR			
1967-79	P35	W13	L14	H8
John Jacobs	GB & I			
1955	P2	W2	L0	H0
Tommy Jacobs	USA			
1965	P4	W3	L1	H0
Peter Jacobsen	USA			
1985	P3	W1	L2	H0
Mark James	GB & I/EUR			
1977-81, 89-93	P22	W7	L14	H1
Don January	USA			
1965, 77	P7	W2	L3	H2
Lee Janzen	USA			
1993	P2	W0	L2	H0
Edward Jarman	GB & I			
1935	P1	W0	L1	H0
Herbert Jolly	GB & I			
1926, 27	P4	W2	L2	H0

K

Herman Keiser	USA			
1947	P1	W0	L1	H0
Tommy Kerrigan	USA			
1921	P2	W0	L2	H0
Michael King	EUR			
1979	P1	W0	L1	H0
Joe Kirkwood	USA			
1926	P2	W0	L2	H0
Tom Kite	USA			
1979-89, 93	P28	W15	L9	H4
Ted Kroll	USA			
1953-57	P4	W3	L1	H0

L

Arthur Lacey	GB & I			
1933, 37	P3	W0	L3	H0
Ky Laffoon	USA			
1935	P1	W0	L1	H0
Barry Lane	EUR			
1993	P3	W0	L3	H0
Bernhard Langer	EUR			
1981-93	P29	W13	L11	H5
Arthur Lees	GB & I			
1947-51, 55	P8	W4	L4	H0
Tony Lema	USA			
1963-65	P11	W8	L1	H2
Wayne Levi	USA			
1991	P2	W0	L2	H0
Bruce Lietzke	USA			
1981	P3	W0	L2	H1
Gene Littler	USA			
1961-71, 75	P27	W14	L5	H8
Davis Love III	USA			
1933	P4	W2	L2	H0
Sandy Lyle	EUR			
1979-87	P18	W7	L9	H2

M

Mark McCumber	USA			
1989	P3	W2	L1	H0
Jerry McGee	USA			
1977	P2	W1	L1	H0

George McLean	USA			
1921	P2	W0	L2	H0
Freddie McLeod	USA			
1926	P2	W0	L2	H0
John Mahaffey	USA			
1979	P3	W1	L2	H0
Tony Manero	USA			
1937	P2	W1	L1	H0
Lloyd Mangrum	USA			
1947-53	P8	W6	L2	H0
Dave Marr	USA			
1965	P6	W4	L2	H0
Jimmy Martin	GB & I			
1965	P1	W0	L1	H0
Billy Maxwell	USA			
1963	P4	W4	L0	H0
Dick Mayer	USA			
1957	P2	W1	L0	H1
William Mehlhorn	USA			
1921, 26, 27	P6	W2	L4	H0
Cary Middlecoff	USA			
1953-59	P6	W2	L3	H1
Johnny Miller	USA			
1975, 81	P6	W2	L2	H2
Peter Mills	GB & I			
1957-59	P1	W1	L0	H0
Abe Mitchell	GB & I			
1921, 26, 29-33	P10	W6	L2	H2
Larry Mize	USA			
1987	P4	W1	L1	H2
Ralph Moffitt	GB & I			
1961	P1	W0	L1	H0
Colin Montgomerie	EUR			
1991-93	P8	W4	L2	H2
Gil Morgan	USA			
1979, 83	P6	W1	L2	H3
Bob Murphy	USA			
1975	P4	W2	L1	H1

N

Byron Nelson	USA			
1937, 47	P4	W3	L1	H0
Larry Nelson	USA			
1979-81, 87	P13	W9	L3	H1
Bobby Nichols	USA			
1967	P5	W4	L1	H0
Jack Nicklaus	USA			
1969-77, 81	P28	W17	L8	H3
Andy North	USA			
1985	P3	W0	L3	H0

O

Christy O'Connor	GB & I			
1955-73	P36	W11	L21	H4
Christy O'Connor Jnr.	GB & I/EUR			
1975, 89	P4	W1	L3	H0
John O'Leary	GB & I			
1975	P4	W0	L4	H0
Mark O'Meara	**USA**			
1985, 89-91	P8	W2	L5	H1
James Ockenden	GB & I			
1921	P2	W2	L0	H0
José-Maria Olazabal	EUR			
1987-93	P20	W12	L6	H2
Ed Oliver	**USA**			
1947, 51, 53	P5	W3	L2	H0
Peter Oosterhuis	GB & I/EUR			
1971-81	P28	W14	L11	H3

P

Alf Padgham	GB & I			
1933-37	P6	W0	L6	H0
Arnold Palmer	**USA**			
1961-67, 71-73	P32	W22	L8	H2
Johnny Palmer	**USA**			
1949	P2	W0	L2	H0
John Panton	GB & I			
1951-53, 61	P5	W0	L5	H0
Sam Parks	**USA**			
1935	P1	W0	L0	H1
Jerry Pate	**USA**			
1981	P4	W2	L2	H0
Steve Pate	**USA**			
1991	P1	W0	L1	H0
Corey Pavin	**USA**			
1991-93	P8	W4	L4	H0
Calvin Peete	**USA**			
1983-85	P7	W4	L2	H1
Alf Perry	GB & I			
1933-37	P4	W0	L3	H1
Henry Picard	**USA**			
1935-37	P4	W3	L1	H0
Manuel Pinero	EUR			
1981, 85	P9	W6	L3	H0
Lionel Platts	GB & I			
1965	P5	W1	L2	H2
Dan Pohl	**USA**			
1987	P3	W1	L2	H0
Eddie Polland	GB & I			
1973	P2	W0	L2	H0
Johnny Pott	**USA**			
1963-67	P7	W5	L2	H0

R

Ronan Rafferty	EUR			
1989	P3	W1	L2	H0
Dave Ragan	**USA**			
1963	P4	W2	L1	H1
Henry Ransom	**USA**			
1951	P1	W0	L1	H0
Ted Ray	GB & I			
1921, 26, 27	P6	W3	L3	H0
Dai Rees	GB & I			
1937, 47-61	P18	W7	L10	H1
Wilf Reid	**USA**			
1921	P2	W1	L1	H0
John Revolta	**USA**			
1935-37	P3	W2	L1	H0
Steven Richardson	EUR			
1991	P4	W2	L2	H0
Jose Rivero	EUR			
1985-87	P5	W2	L3	H0
Fred Robson	GB & I			
1926, 27-31	P8	W4	L4	H0
Costantino Rocca	EUR			
1993	P2	W0	L2	H0
Juan Rodriguez	**USA**			
1973	P2	W0	L1	H1
Bill Rogers	**USA**			
1981	P4	W1	L2	H1
Bob Rosburg	**USA**			
1959	P2	W2	L0	H0
Mason Rudolph	**USA**			
1971	P3	W1	L1	H1
Paul Runyan	**USA**			
1933-35	P4	W2	L2	H0

S

Doug Sanders	**USA**			
1967	P5	W2	L3	H0
Gene Sarazen	**USA**			
1927-37	P12	W7	L2	H3
Syd Scott	GB & I			
1955	P2	W0	L2	H0
James Sherlock	GB & I			
1921	P2	W2	L0	H0
Denny Shute	**USA**			
1931-33, 37	P6	W2	L2	H2
Dan Sikes	**USA**			
1969	P3	W2	L1	H0
Scott Simpson	**USA**			
1987	P2	W1	L1	H0

Horton Smith	USA			
1929-37	P4	W3	L0	H1
Des Smyth	EUR			
1979-81	P7	W2	L5	H0
Jesse Snead	USA			
1971-75	P11	W9	L2	H0
Sam Snead	USA			
1939, 47-55, 59	P13	W10	L2	H1
Ed Sneed	USA			
1977	P2	W1	L0	H1
Mike Souchak	USA			
1959-61	P6	W5	L1	H0
Craig Stadler	USA			
1983-85	P8	W4	L2	H2
Joe Stein	USA			
1926	P2	W0	L2	H0
Payne Stewart	USA			
1987-93	P16	W8	L7	H1
Ken Still	USA			
1969	P3	W0	L2	H1
Dave Stockton	USA			
1971, 77	P5	W3	L1	H1
Curtis Strange	USA			
1983-89	P17	W6	L9	H2
Hal Sutton	USA			
1985-87	P9	W3	L3	H3

T

J. H. Taylor	GB & I			
1921	P2	W0	L1	H1
Josh Taylor	GB & I			
1921	P2	W2	L0	H0
David Thomas	GB & I			
1959, 63-67	P18	W3	L10	H5
Sam Torrance	EUR			
1981-93	P22	W4	L13	H5
Peter Townsend	GB & I			
1969-71	P11	W3	L8	H0
Lee Trevino	USA			
1969-75, 79-81	P30	W17	L7	H6
Jim Turnesa	USA			
1953	P1	W1	L0	H0
Joe Turnesa	USA			
1927-29	P4	W1	L2	H1

V

Harry Vardon	GB & I			
1921	P2	W2	L0	H0
Ken Venturi	USA			
1965	P4	W1	L3	H0

W

Lanny Wadkins	USA			
1977-79, 83-93	P33	W20	L11	H2
Brian Waites	EUR			
1983	P4	W1	L3	H0
Art Wall	USA			
1957-61	P6	W4	L2	H0
Cyril Walker	USA			
1926	P2	W0	L2	H0
Charles Ward	GB & I			
1947-51	P6	W1	L5	H0
Al Watrous	USA			
1926, 27-29	P5	W2	L3	H0
Tom Watson	USA			
1977, 81-83	P15	W10	L4	H1
Paul Way	EUR			
1983-85	P9	W6	L2	H1
Harry Weetman	GB & I			
1951-63	P15	W2	L11	H2
Tom Weiskopf	USA			
1973-753	P10	W7	L2	H1
Charles Whitcombe	GB & I			
1927-37	P9	W3	L2	H4
Ernest Whitcombe	GB & I			
1926, 29-31, 35	P8	W2	L4	H2
Reg Whitcombe	GB & I			
1935	P1	W0	L1	H0
George Will	GB & I			
1963-67	P15	W2	L11	H2
Craig Wood	USA			
1931-35	P4	W1	L3	H0
Norman Wood	GB & I			
1975	P3	W1	L2	H0
Lew Worsham	USA			
1947	P2	W2	L0	H0
Ian Woosnam	EUR			
1983-93	P26	W12	L10	H4

Z

Frank 'Fuzzy' Zoeller	USA			
1979, 83-85	P10	W1	L8	H1

1993 teams' Sony rankings

Despite media reports claiming that US captain, Tom Watson, said that he could not accept Nick Faldo as the world's No I golfer following his team's victory over Europe at The Belfry in 1993, the Sony rankings clearly show the Englishman in pole position before the contest and he set a record of 63 successive weeks as No I. Greg Norman held the previous record of 62 weeks between September 1986 and November 1987. The European team had higher rankings than their opponents with an average points difference of 0.26 i.e. 9.02 pts to 8.76 pts.

	Europe			USA	
1.	Faldo	21.40	5.	Azinger	15.43
2.	Langer	18.08	6.	Couples	14.39
7.	Woosnam	12.90	8.	Kite	10.08
9.	Olazabal	9.76	11.	Stewart	9.48
16.	Montgomerie	8.04	12.	Love III	9.43
21.	Ballesteros	7.18	13.	Cook	9.20
31.	James	5.70	15.	Pavin	8.93
35.	Lane	5.59	22.	Janzen	7.08
37.	Torrance	5.58	23.	Floyd	6.45
40.	Rocca	5.40	26.	Beck	6.10
59.	Haeggman	4.40	53.	Gallagher Jnr	4.54
64.	Baker	4.30	74.	Wadkins	3.99

Cup records prior to the 1993 contest

Each side selected four rookies for The Belfry in 1993. But the Europeans had more Cup experience with an average 20.6 games per player against an average 14.87 games per player for the visiting Americans.

Player	P	W	L	H	Player	P	W	L	H
Faldo	31	17	12	2	Azinger	9	5	4	0
Ballesteros	30	17	8	5	Beck	7	4	2	1
James	19	7	11	1	Couples	7	3	3	1
Langer	25	11	9	5	Floyd	27	9	15	3
Montgomerie	3	1	1	1	Kite	24	13	7	4
Olazabal	15	10	3	2	Pavin	3	1	2	0
Torrance	21	4	12	5	Stewart	12	5	6	1
Woosnam	21	8	10	3	Wadkins	30	18	10	2
Totals	**165**	**75**	**66**	**24**	**Totals**	**119**	**58**	**49**	**12**

The Ryder Cup Results
1921-1993

Year	Winners	Result		Course
1921	GB & Ireland	$10\frac{1}{2}$	- $4\frac{1}{2}$	Gleneagles, Scotland
19261	GB & Ireland	$13\frac{1}{2}$	- $1\frac{1}{2}$	Wentworth, Surrey
1927	America	$9\frac{1}{2}$	- $2\frac{1}{2}$	Worcester, Mass
1929	GB & Ireland	7	- 5	Moortown, Leeds, Yorks
1931	America	9	- 3	Scioto, Columbus, Ohio
1933	America	$6\frac{1}{2}$	- $5\frac{1}{2}$	Southport & Ainsdale, Lancs
1935	America	9	- 3	Ridgewood, New Jersey
1937	America	8	- 4	Southport & Ainsdale, Lancs
1939 - 1945	Not played due to outbreak of Second World War			
1947	America	11	- 1	Portland, Oregon
1949	America	7	- 5	Ganton, Scarborough, Yorks
1951	America	$9\frac{1}{2}$	- $2\frac{1}{2}$	Pinehurst, N.Carolina
1953	America	$6\frac{1}{2}$	- $5\frac{1}{2}$	Wentworth, Surrey
1955	America	8	- 4	Palm Springs, Cal.
1957	GB & Ireland	$7\frac{1}{2}$	- $4\frac{1}{2}$	Lindrick, nr Sheffield, Yorks
1959	America	$8\frac{1}{2}$	- $3\frac{1}{2}$	Palm Desert, Ca
1961	America	$14\frac{1}{2}$	- $9\frac{1}{2}$	Lytham & St. Anne's, Lancs
1963	America	23	- 9	East Lake, Atlanta, Georgia
1965	America	$19\frac{1}{2}$	- $12\frac{1}{2}$	Royal Birkdale, Lancs
1967	America	$23\frac{1}{2}$	- $8\frac{1}{2}$	Champion, Houston, Texas
1969	Match Tied	16	- 16	Royal Birkdale, Lancs
1971	America	$18\frac{1}{2}$	- $13\frac{1}{2}$	Old Warson, St Louis, Mo
1973	America	19	- 13	Muirfield, Scotland
1975	America	21	- 11	Laurel Valley, Pa.
1977	America	$12\frac{1}{2}$	- $7\frac{1}{2}$	Lytham & St. Anne's, Lancs

The Continent of Europe players joined the GB & Ireland squad in 1979 to compete against the Americans.

Year	Winners	Result		Course
1979	America	17	- 11	The Greenbrier, W.Virginia
1981	America	$18\frac{1}{2}$	- $9\frac{1}{2}$	Walton Heath, Surrey
1983	America	$14\frac{1}{2}$	- $13\frac{1}{2}$	PGA National, Florida
1985	Europe	$16\frac{1}{2}$	- $11\frac{1}{2}$	The Belfry, Warwicks
1987	Europe	15	- 13	Muirfield Village, Ohio
1989	Match Tied	14	- 14	The Belfry, Warwicks
1991	America	14	- 13	Kiawah Island, S. Carolina
1993	America	15	- 13	The Belfry, Warwicks

THE SOLHEIM CUP

The Greenbrier, Virginia will be the venue for the Solheim Cup from October 21 to 23. A fundamental change to the rules was decided in March in Phoenix when the Ryder Cup's " Player in an envelope" system for dealing with illness or injury was rejected for the Solheim Cup, currently held by Europe.

Each team is now allowed a travelling reserve who will fill in for any injured member of either team. The European team will consist of the first five on the money list, plus five wild cards. The travelling reserve will be another captain's choice. The Americans will take the first nine from the money list, plus one wild card. Their travelling reserve will be the 10th player on the money list.

The trophy is named after Karsten Solheim, founder of Karsten Manufacturing Corporation, the makers of Ping. In 1990, as interest in a Ryder Cup type match for ladies was developing, LPGA and WPGET approached Karsten about becoming involved as a sponsor. Because Ping had been long and avid supporters of ladies golf, and felt the Tours needed the support, the company agreed to sponsor the event and that the name would somehow reflect that involvement. The Ping Cup and the Karsten Cup were discarded as being too commercial, and eventually the Solheim Cup was chosen because it would serve as a legacy to the Solheim family and all they have done for women's professional golf. Once this was decided, Karsten signed for 20 years, thus guaranteeing 10 events until 2010.

Karsten Solheim is still a keen golfer at the age of 83, playing to about a 20 handicap and hitting balls almost every day. At his best he played off five. His sons all are in the business and all play golf, son Allan being the most avid. Solheim is another story of the American dream come true, being the son of a shoemaker who brought his family to the United States from Norway in 1913, when Karsten was two.

In the Depression years, he had to drop out of his mechanical engineering studies at Washington University and started a shoe repair business in Seattle. Later, thanks to a University of California extension course, he resumed his training and eventually joined GEC in 1953, working on radar. He started making his putters in 1958 in California in his garage. With a loan of $1000, he began by making the mould for the putter that he named "Ping", after the sound it made, a putter that, after several frustrating years, would become the sensation of the pro tour. By 1967, the demand for Ping putters was so great that Solheim left GEC and started making them full-time. Now the garage has been replaced by the Karsten Manufacturing Corporation, a series of air conditioned buildings set against a backdrop of mountains in Phoenix, Arizona.

Solheim has been a fixture at major golf tournaments since the early 1960's, and is easily recognisable with his steel grey goatee, bushy eyebrows and steel rim spectacles. He spent long hours on tournament practice grounds, trying to persuade the pros to try his putter, and his biggest break came in 1967 when Julius Boros, Gary Player, Jack Nicklaus and George Archer started using them. The rest, as they say, is history, and 36 of 57 majors since 1980 have been won with a Ping putter, including Jose-Maria Olazabal at the last Masters. Today Solheim

Karsten Solheim

spends a lot of time in airplanes, usually with his wife Louise, whom he married in 1935, travelling the world, opening up new markets and visiting old friends. Sons John, Allan and Louis are all in the business as vice presidents, and the company owns two golf courses, one in Moon Valley, Arizona and the Thonock course near Karsten's factory in Gainsborough, Lincolnshire.

So, with Ping now being sold in 87 countries, is there anything left to achieve? "I used to shoot in the seventies," he chuckles. "Now I struggle to break 90. But there's not much you can do when you can only play two or three times a month. Still, with golf design changing, there's no end to it. You think you've reached the ultimate and you find you've just scratched the surface. But I think I'm a better putter these days." The familiar twinkle comes into his eyes, and then he is off to open another market in China, Russia or Japan. "People write to me from all over the world, telling me that we've made their golfing lives more enjoyable. Now that's real satisfaction."

He made no mention of fulfiling the American dream, a poor immigrant made good, who became a household name throughout the world. He made no reference to his long time support for ladies golf which remains constant and which, some say, helped save both major ladies' tours. He refused to gloat over his legal triumph over the USGA when they banned his Pings a few years ago. He wouldn't talk about his legendary generosity to his staff, just remarking that he preferred to work hand in hand with his employees. All he really wanted to talk about was getting his handicap down again. He waved as he boarded the plane, and the man who built a legend was off to conquer another market in another country.

The Women's Game

It was a magnicent year for women's golf. The Ford Classic at Woburn broke all attendance records and there were almost 20,000 on the last day alone. Compare that with the previous year's Weetabix British Open where there were 30,000 spectators for the whole event. Then Sky Television announced that their coverage of the 1994 event had attracted more viewers than for the men's event at Cannes! Sky have been repaid for their faith in women's golf and they will cover the Solheim Cup live, with the BBC chipping in with highlights. All those in the media are aware that there is a turnaround in interest in ladies golf, with sponsors now trying to climb on the bandwagon. Mazda have recently joined Skoda in providing cars for the ladies, and the list of sponsors is growing dramatically. The Weetabix prize fund for the British Open now stands at £335,000, the richest prize in European women's golf. Skoda themselves are sponsoring the Women's Scottish Open.

Three factors seem to be in play in the dramatic rise in interest. Laura Davies is by far the outstanding personality in the game. Her magnificent start to the season saw her at the top of the Ping leaderboard by over 100 points at the end of June. She headed the table then with 321 points with Patty Sheehan her closest rival on 210. Dottie Mochrie, Donna Andrews, Brandie Burton and Betsy King, all certain to play for America in the Solheim Cup, are on her heels, but probably too far away to catch her.

Another factor is the Solheim Cup itself. After the way Mickie Walker's team dismembered the Americans last time, the contest has become almost of equal importance as Samuel Ryder's trophy. When Catrin Nilsmark's putt went down, the reaction from the team and the spectators told its own story. Europe just loves beating the United States. The last factor seems to be the fresh crop of exciting women professional golfers that the crowds like to follow. Annika Sorenstam, Helen Alfredsson, Trish Johnson, Joanne Morley, Lora Fairclough and Lisa Hackney lead a new wave of superb players from Europe, and, as with the men's game in the late seventies, European women are now determined to challenge American supremacy in numbers. With charismatic golfers like Laura Davies leading the world, it is no wonder that sponsors are now attracted by the women's game.

Cup fever is also evident on the women's amateur scene, with the Curtis Cup contest at Chattanooga, Tennessee. Despite the controversy surrounding the public announcement of the Great Britain and Ireland team, Liz Boatman thinks that her team, with Julie Hall and Catriona Matthews two of the best amateurs in the world at the moment, is certainly good enough to win. Lisa Walton, Mhairi McKay and Janice

Moodie, all at colloeg in the US, have won ten titles between them in America. It may well be the last Curtis Cup for Catriona Matthews, as she is now contemplating joining the European tour.

** A second edition of the Ping Women's Golf Year was launched at the Evian Masters in France in June. Published by Kensington West at £12.99, it provides an analysis in 160 pages of the world of women's golf. With over 150 colour photographs, it charts the season as it unfolds in Europe, the United States, and also covers the amateur scene.

SOLHEIM CUP STANDINGS
After 19-6-94

The Top Five on the WPGET after the English Open qualify automatically. The remaining five are wild cards. The top nine Americans qualify with one wild card.

Europeans	Points	Americans	Points
1. Laura Davies	482	1. Betsy King	225
2. Annika Sorenstam	427	2. Donna Andrews	213
3. Lora Fairclough	424	3. D ottie Mochrie	193
4. Catrin Nilsmark	354	4. Brandie Burton	180
5. M-L. de Lorenzi	324	5. Sherri Steinhauer	156
6. Trish Johnson	309	6. Patty Sheehan	154
7. Frederica Dassu	299	7. Beth Daniel	141
8. Florence Descampe	284	8. Tammie Green	139
9. Sandrine Mendiburu	254	9. Lauri Merten	137
10. Helen Alfredsson	253	10. Nancy Lopez	125
11. Lisa Hackney	216	11. Michelle McGann	114
12. Helen Wadsworth	210	12. Meg Mallon	103
13. Joanne Morley	186	13. Kelly Robbins	102

PING LEADERBOARD
After 19-6-94
Position and Points

1.	Laura Davies	321
2.	Dottie Mochrie	206
3.	Betsy King	199
4.	Patty Sheehan	199
5.	Donna Andrews	197
6.	Brandie Burton	186
7.	Helen Alfredsson	166
8.	Sherri Steinhauer	139
9.	Beth daniel	135
10.	Tammie Green	127

FORD ORDER OF MERIT
After the OVB Damen Open
Position and Winnings

1.	Helen Alfredsson	£34875
2.	Florence Descampe	£27555
3.	Lora fairclough	£26627
4.	Sarah Gautrey	£21162
5.	Catrin Nilsmark	£20104
6.	Trish Johnson	£18543
7.	Tracy Hanson	£16149
8.	Sandrine Mendiburu	£15597
9.	Joanne Morley	£13437
10.	Loraine Lambert	£11309

RENTON LAIDLAW
Around the World in 260 Days

Like the wicked, there's no rest for the golf writer and broadcaster. From Georgia to Pennsylvania to Turnberry to Oaklahoma and back in five months is a piece of cake for Ewen Murray, Alex Hay, Peter Alliss and Dave Marr. If you're based in London, it's a mere 19000 miles round trip. But that's just the Majors. If you add the Ryder Cup, the World Cup of Golf, the Dunhill Masters and the Toyota World Matchplay, put another 18,000 miles on your clock, for a total of 37000 miles. At the speed of modern airplanes, you're travelling for 74 hours. Add four hours for each event at airports in taxis, limos and waiting, plus 28 hours on the M25, the New York Thruway, the Pennsylvania Turnpike and the Beeline Expressway etc and you're travelling for at least 134 hours. That's over six days. Add six days for each event including practice and you're tied up for 54 days, almost two months for eight events!

For Renton Laidlaw, the schedule is even more punishing. There are 45 events worldwide in the space of 49 weeks, plus Walker Cup matches, Curtis Cup, Ryder and Solheim Cups, key Amateur events, a total of almost sixty events spanning almost 300 days. Laidlaw is the Golf Correspondent of the London Evening Standard, and also does the "colour" for television. He's based in London, covering the Volvo tour events, plus the Majors as well as Dubai and Jamaica. He covers well over 100,000 miles in the year and has almost 300 deadlines to hit, and half a million words to type. So if your average golf journalist looks permanently jet-lagged, has stubby fingers, an even stubbier temper, a well-groomed five o' clock shadow and a wrinkled brow, you've got an accurate picture. You never see too many press journalists on television. They look too haggard to pass the screen test.

But has Renton Laidlaw got a picture of Dorian Gray hidden away in his attic? He surely must. He travels all those miles, types all those words but still smiles and looks under 40 when he's closer to 50. The little Scot cut his teeth on local newspapers in Edinburgh, then Newcastle with Thomson Regional newspapers. He's been with the Evening Standard for 20 years. Along the way he covered every kind of sports story from skittles to polo. " You get to know the Superstars while they're still human," he smiles. "A lot of them stay that way despite their success. Some of them go the other way, they want to win so much they introvert. Some of them come across as cold, when they're just shy."

He was always interested in golf. "The game is 90% mental. A player in a jam has got to think how best to get his ball back into play. Viewers and listeners enjoy thinking along with him. For me, it's fun trying to get inside his mind. It's great if it's someone like Seve. He's got such a range of shots and options, and he'll always go for broke. So if the commentator can explain the problem and the solution, it makes for enjoyable watching."

He cites Peter Alliss as the most successful. "He doesn't try to compete with the camera, but adds depth and knowledge to what the viewer is seeing." Alliss is the son of a pro, so is Sky's Ewen Murray. Laidlaw's own lifelong passion for golf helps him add to the listeners' enjoyment. "You don't talk when the players are swinging. I also try to bring some humour into a game that wasn't meant to be taken seriously all the time,"he says.

Then he's off to cover the US Open, to Pittsburg via New York, another few thousand miles, more deadlines, more words. "Does he ever get tired of the constant travel?"

The game's a drug, he says. And he's totally hooked on the game, the drama and the sometimes unbearable tension. The most dramatic moment?

"Unquestionably, the Langer putt at Kiawah Island. The eyes of most of the world were focussed on that six feet between the ball and the hole. We were all like wet rags afterward. Those hard bitten boys in the press tent were all in tears. When I got home, someone sent me a book they'd written on the Ryder Cup. In it was a poem about the missed putt. They'd put me in it, and summed me up: "If Renton Laidlaw hadn't been bald, his hair would have stood on end." That encapsuled the whole moment. The drama, the excitement and the great emotions of the winners and losers. That's why I like what I do, that's why I'm hooked."

Malcolm Campbell took this picture of Laidlaw in Dubai -
before the course was built!

THE CLOWN PRINCE OF GOLF

It's been said that Noel Hunt could hit a golf ball over 200 yards with a broomstick. He probably could hit it almost that distance with an umbrella if he put his mind to it. The quiet Manchunian may not be as famous as Sir Bobby Charlton, but he is now as well known in golf circles as anyone. His claim to fame is his Golf Show, which has thrilled and amused golf fans all over the world. Men of such stature as Gary Player, Peter Alliss, Colin Montgomerie, Sandy Lyle and David Leadbetter think he is the best in the world. If you catch the Noel Hunt Golf Show, you'll soon agree. He swung his way into the Guinness Book of Records recently when he hit 1536 golf balls over 100 yards in an hour at Shrigley Hall in Cheshire.

Noel Hunt was a professional golfer who couldn't make the putts drop. He gave up the Tour in 1982, having failed to win a tournament anywhere except one in Africa. Then he saw the legendary American showman, the late Paul Hahn, who did amazing tricks with golf balls. Hunt decided to try to develop a similar golf act. "I spent over two years perfecting the routine," he says. "It took me at least 6000 hours of practice." He went on the road with it in 1986, and developed the routine with a slick array of trick shots and comedy patter that has led to invitations to perform all over the world, including opening the proceedings at the Ryder Cup at The Belfry, most recently in 1993 in front of 25000 gasping spectators.

Matthew Barr makes the astonishing range of clubs used in the act, while Hunt is constantly on the lookout for new ideas. Few of the clubs are custom made, but shortened, or lengthened with other bits added. And for all the trick artistry, Hunt is keen to stress the basics of the game. The whole performance is aimed at the four fundamentals of the game: clubhead control, set-up, rhythm and turn. His act has been described as the World's Best. That description came from Greg Norman, who saw his Show for the first time recently in Singapore at a special event attended by fifteen of the top professionals on the tour, including Ian Woosnam, Bernhard Langer and Nick Price.

"That was awesome," Norman told Hunt afterward. Nick Faldo has watched the show a dozen times, and never gets tired of seeing it. He is, in fact, usually the first to take his seat. Hunt astonishes watchers with his amazing ability to put the ball exactly where he wants it, using some of the oddest clubs you've ever seen. He hams it up with floppy hats, impersonations, a funny walk, stripey plus fours, coloured balls and barber-pole tees plus a list of one-liners and a stream of snappy comments. The audience alternately gasp, laugh and shake their heads in wonder. The question they all ask is: "How on earth does he do that?" But the real core of the show is the skill and expertise, unlike many of the "trick shot" shows in the United States. That skill is what keeps the world's top professionals coming back for more.

Noel Hunt has played with the greats of golf, Palmer, Nicklaus, Trevino and Player, but he has no regrets about his change of direction a lucky thirteen years ago. "I have none of the grinding pressure of having to win all the time," he says. "But I enjoy my life and I get a lot of time to spend with my family, wife Pamela and children Laura Jane (10) and Jenny (8)." He loves living in the Manchester area, and is a big fan of football legends, Manchester United. "It's the best place in the world. I have played the odd round with Sir Bobby Charlton and Kenny Dalglish. I get to Old Trafford whenever I can. I've played to audiences in the USA, Hong Kong and all over Europe, but I can't wait to get home."

For all this, he longs to conquer new markets. They're golf mad in Japan and he's been offered a chance to perform there. What they all seem to want to see is Hunt driving a golf ball 200 yards with a putter. It's a strange twist from the days when the unsteady putter was Noel's enemy, now it's his piece de resistance. Life for Noel has come full circle. He takes his shows all over the globe and his unique golf show is especially suited to corporate days and special events. See it and you'll agree with Greg Norman that it's "awesome". If you would like more information about the world's No.1 Golf Show, telephone 061-370-1917, or fax 061-371-8748.

A "BETA" DEAL FOR GOLFERS?
Daly calls for drug tests

The golf world was rocked in April when American professional Mac O'Grady, who was coaching the out of form Seve Ballesteros, accused the European Tour players of using Beta-Blockers. He refused to name the offenders, but claimed that at least seven of the world's top 30 pros, mainly European players, were using the drug to improve their putting.

Taken to reduce blood pressure, slow the heart rate and reduce anxiety, beta-blockers can only be obtained on prescription, and O'Grady admitted he had used the drug in the 1980's to improve his putting, but had stopped because the decided it was unethical. He claimed the use of the drug was widespread and called for random urine testing on the PGA Tour.

Nick Faldo was accused by an American magazine of using them constantly on tour, and learned of the rumours during the Players Championship in Florida. He denied it strongly, insisted that he restricted himself to vitamins, and commented, " I don't use any drugs, hard or soft. The only grass I've seen is the stuff on my golf shoes."

Two players, however, did admit using beta-blockers, Zimbabwe's Nick Price and Scotland's Sam Torrance. Price said he had used them over a seven year period to lower his blood pressure since 1982, but had switched away from them in 1989. Torrance had consulted Tour officials in 1992, before using the drug for a year. He won three events in 1993 after coming off the drug.

In July, the American John Daly accused some tour players of snorting cocaine, in an exclusive interview with Ben Bacon of "The Sun". Daly, who spent some time in an alcohol rehabilitation clinic after the collapse of his stormy marriage to Bettye, and was banned from the US Tour for walking out of a tournament in Hawaii, claimed that some of the tour players were taking drugs, especially cocaine. He called for a system of random testing, as they have in American Football and the NBA.

The Sports Council and the International Olympic committee have banned beta-blockers, but R and A and USGA have no such ban. But if golf does become an olympic sport, it will have to observe a drugs ban.

PROFESSIONAL STANDINGS

SONY RANKINGS
After 19-6-94

1.	Greg Norman	22.34
2.	Nick Faldo	19.36
3.	Nick Price	17.77
4.	Bernhard Langer	15.64
5.	Fred Couples	14.11
6.	Jose-Maria Olazabal	12.39
7.	Ernie Els	11.88
8.	Paul Azinger	10.77
9.	Colin Montgomerie	10.67
10.	David Frost	10.49

US MONEY LIST
After US Open

1.	Greg Norman	$988,898
2.	Tom Lehman	$748,628
3.	Loren Roberts	$725,169
4.	Hale Irwin	$693,250
5.	Jeff Maggert	$638,733
6.	Nick Price	$564,721
7.	Jose-Maria Olazabal	$532,100
8.	Ernie Els	$529,130
9.	Fuzzy Zoeller	$514,561
10.	John Huston	$508,260

VOLVO ORDER OF MERIT
After Jersey European Airways Open

1.	Jose-Maria Olazabal	£241,402
2.	Colin Montgomerie	£193,741
3.	Ernie Els	£188,230
4.	Nick Faldo	£180,730
5.	Bernhard Langer	£169,975
6.	Severiano Ballesteros	£149,608
7.	Miguel Angel Jiminez	£148,638
8.	Robert Allenby	£123,719
9.	David Gilford	£120,165
10.	Peter Hedblom	£120,139

WORLDWIDE

**R
E
S
U
L
T
S**

How did Colin Montgomerie fare in the Players Championship in March?

Who won the Indonesian Open?

Who did Ernie Els beat into second place in the Dubai Desert Clasic?

Who won the Australian Masters?

Which event did John Daly win in May in Georgia?

Which two events did Beth Daniel win in a week?

Where does Laura Davies stand on the Ping leader-board?

We tell all . . . and more!

**1
9
9
3
-
9
4**

WORLD WIDE RESULTS

123rd OPEN GOLF CHAMPIONSHIP.

Turnberry, Scotland   14-17 July, 1994
Winner: Nick Price
Results:

N. Price	69	66	67	66	268
J. Parnevik	68	66	68	67	269
F. Zoeller	71	66	64	70	271
A. Forsbrand	72	71	66	64	273
M. James	72	67	66	68	273
D. Feherty	68	69	66	70	273

ANHEUSER-BUSCH CLASSIC. US PGA TOUR

Kingsmill, Williamsburg, Virginia   7-10 July, 1994
Results:

M.McCumber	67	69	65	66	267
G. Day	64	68	72	66	270
J. Leonard	67	69	67	69	272

LPGA CLASSIC. US WOMEN'S TOUR

Toledo, Ohio.   7-9 July, 1994
Results:

K. Robbins	69	70	65	204
T. Green	66	71	67	204

(Robbins won at the first playoff hole.)

BELL'S SCOTTISH OPEN. VOLVO EUROPEAN TOUR

Gleneagles, Perthshire, Scotland   7-9 July, 1994
Winner Carl Mason struck a blow for the over-forties when he won for only the second time in his twenty years on tour. He took the £100,000 first prize by one stroke from Peter Mitchell, both of whom grabbed an exemption place in the British Open. Early leader Howard Twitty finished as joint 16th.
Results:

C. Mason	265
P. Mitchell	266
J. Parnevik	267
C. Montgomerie	268
J. Lomas	270
D. Clarke	270

US SENIORS OPEN. US SENIOR TOUR

Pinehurst, N. Carolina   30 June - 3 July, 1994

South African Simon Hobday weathered storms and a last round 75 to win the title by two strokes from Jim Albus and Australian Graham Marsh. Hobday had tied the Senior Open 36-hole scoring record of 133 for the first two rounds.

Results:

S. Hobday	66	67	66	75	274
J. Albus	66	69	66	74	275
G. Marsh	68	68	69	70	275
T.Weiskopf	72	66	72	67	277
T. Wargo	69	70	68	70	277
D. Stockton	74	67	68	68	277

MURPHY'S IRISH OPEN. VOLVO EUROPEAN TOUR

Mount Juliet, Kilkenny   30 June- 3 July, 1994

Bernhard Langer won his third Irish Open, but his first victory of the year with a final round 67 to hold off the charging John Daly by one stroke. Langer's golf was like snow on a Christmas card in the heat - cool and crisp and even. while the big-hitting American equalled the record with a last round 65, having started seven shots behind the overnight leader, Australian Robert Allenby. Nick Faldo, joint second overnight, never recovered from disaster at the third, where his tee shot hit a rock in the river and he took a double bogey five. Masters champion Jose-Maria Olazabal suffered from a cold putter to finish joint fourth.

Results:

B. Langer	70	68	70	67	275
J. Daly	70	68	73	65	276
R. Allenby	68	68	68	72	276
G. Turner	73	70	69	66	278
J-M Olazabal	68	68	71	71	278
S. Richardson	71	70	69	69	279
P. Baker	70	68	71	70	279
S. Torrance	65	73	73	69	280
E. Els	71	73	67	69	280
C. Parry	70	69	70	71	280
A. Binaghi	69	70	70	71	280
M. Harwood	69	69	70	72	280
P. Moloney	71	70	67	72	280
N. Faldo	69	71	67	73	280

YOUNGSTOWN-WARREN LPGA CLASSIC. US WOMEN'S TOUR

Warren, Ohio   1-3 July, 1994

Results:

T. Green	67	69	70	206
C. Walker	68	69	71	208
K. Shipman	69	69	71	209
D. Mochrie	68	70	71	209

TANDEM SENIORS OPEN. EUROPEAN SENIORS TOUR
Stockley Park, Heathrow.   1-3 July, 1994
Results:

M. Gregson	69	67	69		205
J. Morgan	71	70	65		206
L. Higgins	70	67	69		206

PHILANTHROPY GOLF TOURNAMENT
Nishiwaki, Japan   30 June - 3 July, 1994
Results:

T. Hamilton (US)	74	69	68	67	278
E. Mizoguchi (Japan)	70	69	72	67	278

Hamilton won at the first hole of sudden death.

CENTEL WESTERN OPEN. US PGA TOUR
Cog Hill, Lemont, Illinois   30 June - 3 July, 1994
Winner: Nick Price
Results:

N. Price	67	67	72	71	277
G. Kraft	67	70	68	73	278
S. Hoch	67	69	73	70	279
M. Calcavecchia	67	70	72	70	279
B. Glasson	66	70	72	71	279
K. Gibson	69	72	72	67	280
J. Sluman	68	69	69	74	280

HENNESSY CUP. WPGA TOUR
Cologne, Germany   30 June - 3 July, 1994
Winner Liselotte Neumann of Sweden smashed the course record at
Refath with a last round 65 to win by a stroke from Britain's Alison
Nicholas and American Kristal Parker.
Results:

L. Neumann	69	71	72	65	277
A. Nicholas	69	71	67	71	278
K. Parker	70	72	68	69	279
A. Sorenstam	71	73	69	68	281
H. Alfredsson	71	70	69	71	281
P. Wright	70	69	70	74	283
S. Waugh	73	72	71	69	285
K. Lunn	67	71	72	75	285

MEMORIAL OLIVER BARRAS
Crans-sur-Sierre, Switzerland.   24-26 June, 1994
Winner: Michael Campbell (NZ)

NORTHERN ELECTRIC SENIORS. EUROPEAN SENIORS TOUR

Slaley Hall, Northumberland   24-26 June, 1994

Winner John Morgan scored his first Senior tour win when he beat Bernard Hunt, the 64-year old former Ryder Cup captain at the sixth hole of sudden death.

Results:

J. Morgan	74	71	74	219
B. Hunt	70	76	73	219
T. Horton	76	72	72	220
L. Higgins	73	71	76	220
J. Fourie	72	74	76	222

GREATER HARTFORD OPEN. US PGA TOUR

Cromwell, Connecticut   23-26 June, 1994

David Frost held off the challenge from Greg Norman to win the title by a single stroke, thanks to a final round 69. He set a tournament record with his four round total of 12 under par.

Results:

D. Frost	65	68	66	69	268
G. Norman	69	65	66	69	269
S. Stricker	70	67	67	67	271
C. Pavin	65	73	66	67	271
D. Stockton Jnr	66	66	67	72	271
D. Barr	68	70	68	65	271
K. Triplett	71	66	69	67	273
W. Levi	68	66	71	68	273

PEUGEOT OPEN de FRANCE. VOLVO EUROPEAN TOUR

National Club, Paris   23-26 June, 1994

Mark Roe had a final round 66 to take the title, coming from three strokes behind to finish 14 under par, and one shot ahead of the nearest challenger, Swede Gabriel Hjerstedt, and four ahead of Masters Champion Jose-Maria Olazabal.

Results:

M. Roe	70	71	67	66	274
G. Hjerstedt	67	70	68	70	275
J-M. Olazabal	68	72	69	69	278
L. Westwood	66	74	68	71	279
R. Allenby	71	71	71	67	280
A. Coltart	68	60	71	71	280
P. McGinley	70	72	67	71	280

BMW EUROPEAN MASTERS. WPGA TOUR

Bercuit, Brussels   23-26 June, 1994

Former Curtis Cup player Helen Wadsworth had a three stroke margin over American Tracy Hanson to score her first tour win. She finished with a tournament record of 14 under par, despite a nervous start to the final day, dropping three shots on the first three holes.

Results:

H. Wadsworth	69	66	70	73	278
T. Hanson	69	69	70	73	281
L. Davies	69	70	72	72	283
A. Sorenstam	71	70	71	71	283
S. Prosser	70	73	72	70	285
K. Orum	65	75	73	71	285
S. Hodge	73	71	70	72	286

SENIOR PLAYERS CLASSIC. US SENIOR TOUR

Dearborn, Michigan   23-26 June, 1994

Winner: Dave Stockton

Results:

D. Stockton	66	66	71	68	271
J. Albus	67	69	72	69	277
I. Aoki	67	70	73	68	278
R. Floyd	72	68	71	67	278
L. Trevino	68	69	74	69	278
J. Nicklaus	68	72	73	67	280
H. Henning	69	67	74	70	280
J. Dent	72	67	70	71	280

MIZUNO OPEN. AUSTRALASIAN TOUR

Hakui, Japan   23-26 June, 1994

Winner: B. Watts (US) won at the first sudden death playoff hole.

Results:

B.Watts	68	68	73	71	280
E. Herrera	69	70	70	71	280
Y. Kaneko	67	75	70	68	280
K. Suzuki	66	70	74	70	280

NEDCAR OPEN

G.C.Hoenshuis, Netherlands.   21-25 June, 1994

Winner: Rolf Muntz (Holland)

CHAMPIONNAT DE FRANCE PRO

Golf d'Annonay, Gourdan, France.   16-19 June, 1994

Winner: Jean Charles Cambon

ANDALUCIAN & PGA SPANISH CHAMPIONSHIP

Alcaidesa Links, Spain.   16-19 June, 1994

Winner: Juan Pinero

UNITED STATES OPEN. US PGA TOUR

Oakmont, Pittsburg, Pennsylvania   16-19 June, 1994

The course was described by the pros as "Oak Monster" before a serious ball was struck. It was here that Johnny Miller won with a totally outrageous round of 63, and where little Larry Nelson beat Tom Watson after holing three crucial putts in a row. And the surprises continued with Jack Nicklaus leading the way early on at the age of 54. Colin Montgomerie, just back at the top of the European Order of Merit, was another early surprise, leading by two at six under after the second day's play. The big Scot, Ernie Els, Loren Roberts, Curtis Strange and Frank Nobilo plus a revitalised Tom Watson hanging in, led the way in the intense heat. An emotional Arnold Palmer, a Pennsylvania native son, missed the cut, as did Ian Woosnam and Nick Faldo. Palmer received a standing ovation in his final US Open, an event he graced since the late 1950's.

Strange made the early running on the Sunday but fell away to end on 4 under. But it was Loren Roberts' brilliant putting which kept him in it on the last day, yet it let him down when it most counted on the 18th. Colin Montgomerie ended the competition on 5 under and had to endure a nail-biting 30 minutes as Roberts dropped a crucial shot on the last, then Ernie Els struck two wayward drives on 17 and 18. He got away with a par on the seventeenth, thanks to a lucky free drop, then ballooned his drive way to the left and had to chip out sideways. But he sank a nervy putt to leave a three way tie on 5 under and a Monday play-off over 18 holes. Only eight of the field ended the competition under par. The Monday playoff saw Montgomerie run out of steam and all three played scrappy golf. The Scot was eliminated after 18 holes and Roberts and Els began their sudden death contest which Els won at the second hole when Roberts hooked his drive, and put his second into a bunker.

Winner: Ernie Els

Results:

Playoff:

E. Els	74
L. Roberts	74
C. Montgomerie	78

Scores:

E. Els	69	71	66	73	279
L. Roberts	76	69	64	70	279
C. Montgomerie	71	65	73	70	279
C. Strange	70	70	70	70	280
J. Cook	73	65	73	71	282

JERSEY EUROPEAN AIRWAYS OPEN.
VOLVO EUROPEAN TOUR

La Moye, Jersey   16-19 June, 1994

Winner Paul Curry shot a final round of 63 after his second round course-equalling 62 to take the title, his first in fifteen years on the tour, and the eighth so far this season to complete a maiden victory on the

Volvo Tour. He finished 22 under par, three strokes ahead of Mark James.

Results:

P. Curry	73	62	68	63	266
M. James	69	63	68	69	269
I. Pyman	66	67	68	70	271
R. Davis	69	66	66	72	273
J. Payne	70	69	67	67	273
P. Mitchell	70	68	66	69	273
T. Horton	71	65	70	67	273

OVB DAMEN OPEN. EUROPEAN WOMEN'S TOUR

Salzburg, Austria   16-19 June, 1994

Winner Florence Descampe took her sixth European title, but her first since 1991, after sudden death against American Tracy Hanson.

Results:

F. Descampe	277
T. Hanson	277
L. Lambert	279

BUICK CLASSIC. US PGA TOUR

Westchester, Rye, New York   9-12 June, 1994

Winner Lee Janzen registered his first win since the 1993 US open with a three shot win over the chasing Ernie Els.

Results:

L. Janzen	69	69	64	66	268
E. Els	68	66	69	68	271
B. Faxon	70	68	70	66	274
J. Haas	68	70	69	67	274

HONDA OPEN. VOLVO EUROPEAN TOUR

Gut Kaden G.C

Alveslohe, Germany   9-12 June 1994

Robert Allenby won the title after a playoff with Miguel Angel Jimenez

Results:

Robert Allenby	72	67	68	69	276
Miguel Jimenez	70	71	65	70	276
Rodger Davis	66	68	76	68	278
David Gilford	70	70	68	71	279
Bernhard Langer	70	72	72-	66	280
Paul Lawrie	68	71	72	69	280
Andrew Coltart	69	69	69	73	280
Gabriel Hjertstedt	69	71-73		67	280
Russell Claydon	73	70	63	75	281
Barry Lane	73	72	70	66	281

NATIONWIDE SENIORS CHAMPIONSHIP.
US SENIOR TOUR

6-12 June, 1994

Winner: Dave Stockton

MINNESOTA LPGA CLASSIC. US WOMEN'S TOUR

Brooklyn Park, Minnesota   10-12 June, 1994

Results:

L. Neumann	68	71	66	205
H. Kobayashi	72	70	65	207
S. Steinhauer	72	70	66	208

EVIAN MASTERS. EUROPEAN WOMEN'S TOUR

Evian, France   9-12 June, 1994

Winner Helen Alfredsson took the title by three strokes from Sarah Gautrey and Lora Fairclough.

Results:

H. Alfredsson	71	73	73	70	287
S. Gautrey	73	71	77	69	290
L. Fairclough	68	62	77	73	290
F. Descampe	73	74	72	72	291

D-DAY SENIORS OPEN. EUROPEAN SENIORS TOUR

Omaha Beach, Bayeux, France. 8-10 June, 1994
Winner: Brian Waites

OLDSMOBILE CLASSIC. US WOMEN'S TOUR

Walnut Hills, East Lansing, Michigan   2-5 June, 1994

Winner Beth Daniel took her second title in a week, by four strokes from Lisa Kiggens.

Results:

B. Daniel	67	63	70	69	268
L. Kiggens	68	69	67	68	272
A. Benz	68	67	70	68	273
M. Mallon	68	66	72	69	275

BRUNO'S MEMORIAL CLASSIC. US SENIOR TOUR

Greystone, Birmingham, Alabama   30 May - 5June, 1994

Results:

J. Dent	66	68	67	201
G. Gilbert	67	66	70	203
B. Charles	66	66	71	203
K. Zarley	67	68	68	203

ALFRED DUNHILL OPEN. VOLVO EUROPEAN TOUR

Royal Zoute, Knokke, Belgium   2-5 June, 1994

Nick Faldo pulled back from well behind to force a playoff, in which he beat Joakim Haeggman.

Results:

N. Faldo	67	74	67	71	279
J. Haeggman	73	68	66	72	279
P. Hedblom	69	73	65	73	280
B. Langer	69	68	68	75	280
C. Montgomerie	67	70	66	77	280
I. Garrido	67	70	71	73	281
P. Walton	73	67	69	72	281

KEMPER OPEN. US PGA TOUR

TPC at Avenel, Potomac, Maryland   2-5 June, 1994

Winner Mark Brooks took the title with a last round 69, to overtake leader Bobby Wadkins, and win by three strokes.

Results:

M. Brooks	65	68	69	69	271
D.A. Weibring	70	68	68	68	274
B. Wadkins	68	67	65	74	274
P. Mickelson	70	69	67	69	275
L. Janzen	70	71	68	66	275

BELL ATLANTIC CLASSIC. US SENIOR TOUR

Verdae Greens, Greenville, S. Carolina   26-29 May, 1994

Lee Trevino won his second title in two weeks, by two strokes over Mike Hill.

Results:

L. Trevino	71	67	68	206
M. Hill	69	71	68	208
T. Aaron	71	68	71	210

SOUTHWESTERN BELL COLONIAL. US PGA TOUR

Colonial CC, Fort Worth, Texas   26-29 May, 1994

Nick Price took the title after a playoff with Scott Simpson, after a final day charge of 64.

Results:

N. Price	65	70	67	64	266
S. Simpson	66	65	64	71	266
H. Irwin	64	70	68	65	267
P. Jordan	68	70	66	66	270

LPGA CORNING CLASSIC. US WOMEN'S TOUR

Corning, New York　　　　　　　　　　　　　26-29 May, 1994

Beth Daniel won with a last round 69 to pip Stephanie Farwig and Nancy Ramsbottom by a single stroke.

Results:

B. Daniel	67	71	71	69	278
S. Farwig	68	61	69	71	279
N. Ramsbottom	64	71	71	73	279

VOLVO PGA CHAMPIONSHIP. VOLVO EUROPEAN TOUR

Wentworth, Surrey　　　　　　　　　　　　27-30 May, 1994

Winner Jose-Maria Olazabal took the title with a narrow one shot victory over Ernie Els, thanks to a brilliant final round of 65.

Results:

J-M Olazabal	67	68	71	65	271
E. Els	66	66	71	69	272
B. Langer	69	70	67	68	274
J. Haeggman	69	69	70	68	276
M.A. Jimenez	68	66	72	70	276
S. Ballesteros	73	66	70	68	277
M. James	68	72	71	67	278

MITSUBISHI GALANT CHAMPIONSHIP.
JAPANESE PGA TOUR

26-29 May, 1994

Winner: Katsuyoshi Tomori

LA MANGA SPANISH SENIORS OPEN.
EUROPEAN SENIORS TOUR

La Manga, Spain　　　　　　　　　　　　　20-21 May, 1994

Winner Brian Huggett took the title after a playoff.

Results:

B. Huggett	72	74	69	215
D. Snell	69	78	68	215
M. Gregson	73	77	65	215

PEPSI UBE-KOSAN CHAMPIONSHIP.
JAPANESE PGA TOUR

19-22 May, 1994

Winner: Tommy Nakajima

IRISH PROFESSIONAL CHAMPIONSHIP

Galway Bay, Eire   19-22 May, 1994

Results:

D. Clarke	285
R. Burns	288
C. O'Connor	289
S. Hamill	290
P. McGinley	290

LADIES OPEN COSTA AZUL. EUROPEAN WOMEN'S TOUR

Montado and Aroeira Golf CC, Lisbon   19-22 May, 1994

Results:

S. Mendiburu	70	70	140*
L. Fairclough	70	71	141
F. Dassu	69	74	143
T. Hammond	72	71	143

* Two days were lost due to rain.

MEMORIAL TOURNAMENT. US PGA TOUR

Muirfield Village, Dublin, Ohio   19-22 May, 1994

Winner Tom Lehman took his first US Tour title by five strokes, despite Greg Norman's late charge, with four consistent rounds of 67. He also smashed the course record by three shots and ended 20 under par.

Results:

T. Lehman	67	67	67	67	268
G. Norman	70	69	70	64	273
J. Cook	67	69	69	71	276
D. Hammond	69	69	70	69	277
D. Edwards	69	67	72	70	278
R. Gamez	77	69	66	67	279

TISETTANTA ITALIAN OPEN. PGA EUROPEAN TOUR

Marco Simone, Rome   19-22 May, 1994

Eduardo Romero sank a seven foot putt on the last green to take his first title in three years, despite a final 65 by New Zealander Greg Turner.

Results:

E. Romero	69	67	69	67	272
G. Turner	69	69	70	65	273
F. Lingren	71	64	69	71	273

LADY KEYSTONE OPEN. US WOMEN'S TOUR

Hershey CC, Hershey, PA   20-22 May, 1994

Elaine Crosby beat Laura Davies by a single stroke, thanks to a final round 70.

Results:

E. Crosby	69	72	70	211
L. Davies	70	71	71	212
V. Skinner	70	71	72	213
B. King	70	70	73	213

CADILLAC NFL GOLF CLASSIC. US SENIOR TOUR

Upper Montclair, Clifton, New Jersey　　　　　　19-22 May, 1994
Results:

R. Floyd	64	68	74	206
B. Murphy	70	69	68	207
G. Player	71	67	69	207
D. Stockton	72	70	68	210
L. Trevino	70	69	71	210

ST PIERRE SENIORS CLASSIC, EUROPEAN SENIORS TOUR

St Pierre, Chepstow　　　　　　13-15 May, 1994
Winner: Tommy Horton
Results:

T. Horton	71	71	70	212
B. Huggett	73	70	72	215
N. Coles	71	71	74	216

GTE BYRON NELSON CLASSIC. US PGA TOUR

TPC at Los Colinas, Irving, Texas　　　　　　12-15 May, 1994

Another first-time winner, this time five-year man Neal Lancaster. Horrendous weather conditions shortened the tournament to 36 holes over two rounds. A record six players were tied for the title, but Lancaster holed a birdie putt at the first extra hole to win.
Results:

N. Lancaster	67	65	132
T. Byrum	68	64	132
M. Carnevale	65	67	132
D. Edwards	67	65	132
Y. Mizumaki	66	66	132
D. Ogrin	64	68	132
B. Bryant	66	67	133
R. Black	70	64	134
M. Brooks	67	67	134
B. Crenshaw	66	68	134
B. Gilder	67	67	134
G. Norman	66	68	134
J. Woodland	69	65	134

SCOTTISH PROFESSIONAL CHAMPIONSHIP

Dalmahoy　　　　　　12-15 May, 1994
Winner: Andrew Coltart*
Results:

A. Coltart	73	71	69	68	281
G. Orr	74	66	68	73	281

*Coltart won at the second extra hole

JAPAN PGA CHAMPIONSHIP. JAPANESE PGA TOUR
12-15 May, 1994

Winner: Hiroshi Gode

McDONALDS LPGA CHAMPIONSHIP. US WOMEN'S TOUR
Du Pont CC, Wilmington, Delaware   12-15 May, 1994

It was two wins in a week for Laura Davies as she shot a final round 68 to win by three shots over Alice Ritzman. Elaine Crosby, Pat Bradley, Hiromi Kobayashi and Lotte Neumann all tied for third on 283.
Results:

L. Davies	70	72	69	68	279
A. Ritzman	68	73	71	70	282
E. Crosby	76	71	69	67	283
P. Bradley	73	73	70	67	283
H. Kobayashi	72	73	71	67	283
L. Neumann	74	73	67	69	283

PEUGEOT SPANISH OPEN. VOLVO EUROPEAN TOUR
Club de Campo, Madrid, Spain   12-15 May 1994

A birdie at the final hole gave Colin Montgomerie his fifth European title by one shot from Mark Roe in a rain-soaked tournament. So bad was the disruption from the freak storms that rounds two and three had to be played on Saturday. The big Scot returned to the top of the Order of Merit.

Colin Montgomerie	70	71	66	70	277
Mark Roe	70	68	69	71	278
Richard Boxall	69	69	70	70	278
Mark McNulty	68	69	70	71	278
Bernhard Langer	70	69	69	71	279
J. Lomas	74	73	67	67	281
Ernie Els	67	74	73	67	281
Phillip Price	72	72	67	71	282
S. Tinning	74	69	71	68	282
Seve Ballesteros	72	71	73	66	282
J-M Olazabal	71	70	69	72	282
G. Brand Jnr	69	72	71	70	282
F. Regard	69	71	71	71	282

SENIOR PAINE WEBBER INVITATIONAL. US SENIOR TOUR
TPC at Piper Glen, Charlotte, N. Carolina   9-15 May, 1994
Winner: Lee Trevino
Results:

L. Trevino	70	65	68	203
J. Colbert	68	70	66	204
J. Powell	69	66	69	204

SARA LEE CLASSIC. US WOMEN'S TOUR

Hermitage, Old Hickory, Tennessee   6-8 May, 1994

Winner Laura Davies took her second US title this year in a narrow win over Meg Mallon, who missed a six foot putt at the last, and the chance to force a playoff.

Results:

L. Davies	65	70	68	203
M. Mallon	65	70	69	204
D. Richard	71	71	64	206

BELL SOUTH CLASSIC. US PGA TOUR

Atlanta Country Club, Marietta, Georgia   5-8 May, 1994

Big John Daly claimed that this was his first win whilst sober with some classic bunker shots and fine putting. Four under par rounds left him with a first prize of $216000, and he beat defending champion Nolan Henke by one shot.

J. Daly	69	64	69	72	274
N. Henke	70	67	69	69	275
B. Henninger	68	67	69	71	275
B. Estes	71	69	68	68	276
D. Peoples	73	65	68	70	276
L. Clements	68	69	72	68	277
R. Cochran	69	69	69	70	277
B. McCallister	69	68	69	71	277
T. Kite	66	72	68	71	277
C. Dennis	71	66	72	69	278

FUJI SANKEI. JAPANESE PGA TOUR

5-8 May, 1994

Winner: Kiyoshi Murota

BENSON and HEDGES INTERNATIONAL OPEN.
VOLVO EUROPEAN TOUR

St Mellion, Plymouth, England   5-8 May, 1994

Seve Ballesteros came out of his tailspin and won by three strokes from Nick Faldo, for his first title in over two years. The ever popular Spaniard went into the last day trailing by one, but shot a final round without a bogey and two under par to hold off a late challenge from Nick Faldo.

Seve Ballesteros	69	70	72	70	281
Nick Faldo	75	69	70	70	284
J. Lomas	74	70	69	72	285
Gary Orr	70	70	70	75	285
Wayne Westner	70	74	69	74	287
Phillip Price	69	73	71	74	287
Robert Karlsson	73	72	70	72	287
Sam Torrance	75	68	69	75	287
Paul Curry	76	69	70	72	287

LIBERTY MUTUAL LEGENDS OF GOLF, US SENIOR TOUR

Barton Creek, Austin, Texas   2-8 May, 1994
Winners: Charles Coody & Dale Douglass by one stroke over Chi-Chi
Rodriguez and Jim Dent

SPRINT CHALLENGE, LPGA TOUR

Indigo Lakes, Daytona, Florida   28 April- 1 May, 1994
Winner Sherri Steinhauer started the final day with a three shot lead
over Kelly robbins, then almost threw it away. But she bravely birdied
the last to win by a single stroke.
Results:

S. Steinhauer	68	68	67	70	273
K. Robbins	68	68	70	68	274
B. Bunkowsky	68	72	68	70	278
B. Daniel	71	71	72	67	281

CHUNICHI CROWNS, JAPANESE PGA TOUR

                                              29 April-1 May, 1994
Winner: Roger MacKay

SHELL HOUSTON OPEN. US PGA TOUR

TPC at the Woodlands, Texas   28 April - 1 May, 1994
Mike Hennen became the fifth first time winner at this event in five successive years. The virtually unknown tour rookie had four rounds under
par, birdied five of the first nine holes on the third day and finished
three strokes ahead of three big names, Hal Sutton, Jeff Maggert and
Tom Kite.

M. Heinen	67	68	69	68	272
J. Maggert	70	66	68	71	275
H. Sutton	68	70	68	69	275
T. Kite	68	65	71	71	275
B. Gilder	66	76	69	67	278
V. Singh	72	67	69	70	278
J. Daly	68	74	70	67	279
G. Morgan	70	71	72	66	279
P. Jacobsen	68	73	69	69	279

AIR FRANCE CANNES OPEN. VOLVO EUROPEAN TOUR

Cannes-Mougins, France   28 April - 1 May, 1994
Ian Woosnam charged to a five-shot victory over Colin Montgomerie in
only his second appearance on the European tour this year. It was his
24th title on the tour and his staggering blast of birdies - 19 plus one
eagle in the last 47 holes - won him the £50000 first prize.

Ian Woosnam	72	70	63	66	271
C. Montgomerie	70	69	67	70	276

Jean Van de Velde	73	71	68	65	277
Wayne Riley	69	69	73	66	277
P. Fulke	68	69	69	72	278
T. Price	69	71	70	71	281
S. Luna	69	69	76	67	281
T. Johnstone	69	69	74	69	281
Russell Claydon	72	67	73	69	281
Darren Clarke	69	69	72	71	281
Sam Torrance	65	68	76	72	281
P-U. Johansson	73	70	69	69	281

LAS VEGAS CLASSIC, US SENIOR TOUR

TPC Summerlin, Las Vegas   29 April-1 May, 1994
Winner Raymond Floyd had a three shot cushion over Jim Wargo, helped by birdies on the last five holes and a final round of 65.
Results:

R. Floyd	67	70	65	203
J. Wargo	71	67	68	206
J. Dent	70	66	71	209
L. Gilbert	66	73	70	209

DALLAS REUNION PRO-AM, US SENIOR TOUR

Oak Cliff, Dallas, Texas   22-24 April, 1994
Winner Larry Gilbert squeezed home by one shot over George Archer and Rocky Thompson, thanks to a last round 65.
Results:

L. Gilbert	67	68	67	202
G. Archer	67	68	68	203
R. Thompson	68	67	68	203

DUNLOP OPEN. ASIAN TOUR

Ibaraki, Inamachi, Japan   21-24 April, 1994
Winner: Jumbo Ozaki
Results:

J. Ozaki	67	68	70	69	274
H. Chin-Seng	72	67	69	67	275
F. Minoza	69	69	66	74	278

K-MART GREATER GREENSBORO OPEN. US PGA TOUR

Forest Oaks, Greensboro, N. Carolina   21-24 April, 1994
Mike Springer won his first title since joining the tour in 1990. A birdie at the last and a rub of the green when his tee shot with two holes to go rebounded off a tree and dropped within bounds gave him a three stroke win over the streaking Hale Irwin. John Daly made a sensational appearance with his new "Kojak" look.

M. Springer	64	69	70	72	275
E. Humenik	72	65	73	68	278
H. Irwin	65	73	71	69	278
B. Bryant	68	71	68	71	278
B. Lohr	69	71	69	70	279
D. Hammond	70	71	69	70	280
J. Morse	72	68	67	73	280
D. Edwards	71	74	68	68	281
J. Edwards	69	69	73	70	281
M. Smith	69	73	69	70	281
D. Hart	75	69	67	70	281

HEINEKEN OPEN CATALONIA. VOLVO EUROPEAN TOUR

Girona, Pals, Spain   21-24 April 1994

Jose Coceres from Argentina had a remarkable three shot win over the virtually unknown Jean Louis Guepy from the New Hebrides to gain his first ever European tour win, becoming the sixth first-time winner on the tour this year. It was his fifth win in eight years as a pro, four of the victories coming in South America.

Jose Coceres	70	69	67	69	275
Jean-Louis Guepy	67	68	72	71	278
Russell Claydon	72	73	70	67	279
Sam Torrance	70	73	70	67	280
Wayne Riley	68	69	74	70	281
A. Hunter	70	72	69	70	281
P.Fulke	71	71	69	70	281
Gordon Brand Jnr	70	72	69	70	281
Mark Mouland	70	72	71	69	282
I. Garrido	74	73	70	66	283
Frank Nobilo	71	68	71	73	283
Retief Goosen	74	65	69	75	283

FORD GOLF CLASSIC. EUROPEAN WOMEN'S TOUR

Woburn, Bedfordshire   21-24 April, 1994

Winner Catrin Nilsmark beat world number One, Laura Davies into fourth place. In a year of so many first-time winners amongst the men, Catrin birdied the last two holes for a sizzling four shot margin over Trish Johnson and Joanne Morley. It was her first title in six years on the tour. Results:

C. Nilsmark	73	68	73	70	284
T. Johnson	74	70	73	71	288
J. Morley	73	69	77	69	288
L. Davies	74	73	71	71	289
S. Strudwick	74	72	72	72	290
A. Arruti	75	71	72	72	290
A. Sorenstam	73	71	73	73	290
M. Lunn	72	70	75	74	291
S. Prosser	73	73	74	71	291
J. Bartholemew	70	78	71	72	291

ATLANTA WOMEN'S CHAMPIONSHIP. US WOMEN'S TOUR

Stockbridge, Georgia   15-17 April,1994

Val Skinner, a 33 year old from Nebraska, won her fourth LPGA event by the narrowest of margins, with a last round 68.

V. Skinner	70	68	68		206
L. Neumann	69	67	71		207
B. Daniel	69	70	70		209
J. Dickinson	67	70	73		210
H. Alfredsson	68	74	69		211
D. Massey	72	72	67		211
D. Mochrie	71	69	71		211

PGA SENIORS CHAMPIONSHIP. US SENIOR TOUR

PGA National, Palm Beach Gardens, Florida   14-17 April, 1994

Lee Trevino joked his way round the course in four sub-par rounds, holding off a late charge by Jim Colbert to scramble home by one shot.

L. Trevino	70	69	70	70	279
J. Colbert	68	71	74	67	280
D. Stockton	70	69	71	72	282
R. Floyd	69	69	69	75	282

TOURNOI PERRIER de PARIS. VOLVO EUROPEAN TOUR
(Pairs)

Golf de Saint Cloud, Paris   14-17 April, 1994

This new and unusual event on the tour was won in the closest of finishes by Peter Baker and David J. Russell. The pairs event, which started with a fourball, then greensomes, foursomes and finally a fourball, does not count toward the Order of Merit.

Baker and Russell destroyed the field with an opening round 58 and led at the start of the final round by six. They had to hold off a late charge by second place Mouland and Spence who carded a 64.

P. Baker/ D.J. Russell	58	68	65	69	260
M. Mouland/ J. Spence	62	69	66	64	261
S. Ballesteros/J. Olazabal	63	67	67	66	263
R. Claydon/ P. Eales	60	66	71	66	263
M. Jiminez/ J. Rivero	66	70	64	64	264
M. Davis/ D.R. Jones	66	68	67	64	265

MCI HERITAGE CLASSIC. US PGA TOUR

Harbour Town, Hilton Head, S. Carolina   14-17 April, 1994

23 years after his first win, ironically also in the Heritage, Hale Irwin won by two strokes, thanks mainly to two middle round 65's, with Greg Norman breathing down his neck with a late charge. Despite a second round record breaking 61, David Frost ran out of steam and finished joint fourth.

H. Irwin	68	65	65	68	266
G. Norman	67	66	67	68	268

L. Roberts	69	70	68	62	269
D. Edwards	70	71	65	64	270
D. Frost	70	61	72	67	270
N. Henke	69	69	66	66	270
B. Estes	65	70	68	68	271
R. Cochran	67	67	66	71	271

THE US MASTERS. US PGA TOUR

Augusta National, Georgia   7-10 April, 1994

Results:

J-M Olazabal	74	67	69	69	279
T. Lehman	70	70	69	72	281
L. Mize	68	71	72	71	282
T. Kite	69	72	71	71	283
J. Haas	72	72	72	69	285
J. McGovern	72	70	71	72	285
L. Roberts	75	68	72	70	285
E. Els	74	67	74	71	286
C. Pavin	71	72	73	70	286
I. Baker-Finch	71	71	71	74	287
R. Floyd	70	74	71	72	287
J. Huston	72	72	74	69	287
T. Watson	70	71	73	74	288
D. Forsman	74	66	76	73	289
C. Beck	71	71	75	74	291
B. Faxon	71	73	73	74	291
M. O'Meara	75	70	78	70	291
S. Ballesteros	70	76	75	71	292
B. Crenshaw	74	73	73	72	292
D. Edwards	73	72	73	72	292
B. Glasson	72	73	75	72	292
H. Irwin	73	68	79	72	292
G. Norman	70	70	75	77	292
L. Wadkins	73	74	73	72	292
B. Langer	74	74	72	73	293
J. Sluman	74	75	71	73	293
S. Simpson	74	74	73	73	294
V. Singh	70	75	74	75	294
C. Strange	74	70	75	75	294
L. Janzen	75	71	76	73	295
C. Parry	75	74	73	73	295
N. Faldo	76	73	74	74	296
R. Cochran	71	74	74	78	297
S. Torrance	76	73	74	74	297
D. Frost	74	71	75	78	298
N. Price	74	73	74	77	298
F. Zoeller	74	72	74	78	298
F. Allem	69	77	76	76	299

F. Funk	79	70	75	75	299
S. Lyle	75	73	78	73	299
W. Grady	74	73	73	80	300
A. Magee	74	47	76	76	300
H. Meshiai	71	71	80	78	300
C. Rocca	79	70	78	73	300
M. Standly	77	69	79	75	300
J. Cook	77	72	77	75	301
I. Woosnam	76	73	77	75	301
J. Daly	76	73	77	78	304
H. Twitty	73	76	74	81	304
J. Maggert	75	73	82	75	305
J. Harris*	72	76	80	77	305

Cut set at 149. Players who missed were; M. Calcavecchia, 75,75; R. Fehr, 77,73; N. Henke, 77,73; J. Miller, 77,73; C. Montgomerie, 77,73; G. Morgan, 74,76; J. Ozaki, 76,74; G. Player, 71,79; C. Stadler, 76,74; J. Gallagher Jnr, 74,77; D. Hart, 76,75; B. Mayfair, 74,77; B. Ogle, 74,77; D. Ellis*, 78,74; J. Inman, 76,76; J. Nicklaus, 78,74; G. Waite, 74,78; P. Baker, 78,75; B. Estes,77,76; J. Adams, 76,78; B. Casper, 77,77; C. Coody, 80,74; A. Forsbrand, 80,74; S. Hoch, 75,79; D. Love III, 76,78; S. Elkington, 81,74; A. Palmer, 78,77; T. Aaron, 76,80; P. Stewart, 78,78; J. Thomas*,78,78; B. McCallister, 79,78; B. Lane,76,82; I. Pyman*, 82,79; G. Brewer, 84,79; D. Ford, 85,WD.
*denotes Amateur.

V33 du GRAND LYON OPEN. VOLVO EUROPEAN TOUR

Golf de Villette d'Anthon, Lyon, France   1-4 April, 1994

Despite the wind and rain, Stephen Ames from Trinidad & Tobago won his first title on the tour. Early leaders Gabriel Hjertstedt and Wayne Riley blew up on the final round and Ames coasted home, despite a two over par last eighteen.

S. Ames	70	67	71	74	282
G. Hjertstedt	68	68	71	77	284
P. Linhart	72	68	72	72	284
W. Riley	69	68	69	79	285
G. Orr	69	66	76	75	286
D. Gilford	70	73	71	73	287
M. Besanceney	69	75	68	75	287
M. Tunnicliff	72	68	75	73	288
P. Walton	72	71	72	73	288
Gordon J. Brand	70	69	73	76	288

FREEPORT McMORAN CLASSIC. US PGA TOUR

English Turn, New Orleans   31 March-3 April, 1994

A sizzling display of putting from Ben Crenshaw brought him a three stroke victory and his 18th tour victory. Sam Torrance blew a chance to challenge with a one over par final round, while Crenshaw had four sub-par rounds.

B. Crenshaw	69	68	68	68	273
J-M Olazabal	63	74	70	69	276
S. Torrance	67	71	67	73	278
D. Paulson	74	62	75	68	279
M. Springer	73	69	69	68	279
K. Perry	69	72	68	70	279
D. Mast	71	69	74	67	281
C. DiMarco	76	70	66	69	281
S. Brodie	71	67	72	71	281
B. Clampett	70	68	72	71	281

SABAH MASTERS. ASIAN TOUR

Kota Kinabalu, Malaysia   31 March - 3 April, 1994

Craig McCellan scorched around the final 18 holes in 67 to gain five shots on leader Kyi Hla Han, and then won at the second extra hole.

C. McClellan	67	71	71	67	284
Kyi Hla Han	73	70	69	72	284
R. Ponce	72	73	69	71	285
C. Franco	72	74	66	73	285

THE TRADITION. US SENIOR TOUR

Desert Mountain, Scottsdale, Arizona   31 March- 3 April, 1994

One of the "spring chickens" on the Seniors tour, Ray Floyd, was none too accurate in the last round, but scrambled a 68 and a 271 total. This took him into a playoff with Dale Douglass. A birdie at the first extra hole gave Floyd the title.

R. Floyd*	65	70	68	68	271
D. Douglass	68	68	69	66	271
J. Colbert	70	66	68	70	274
J. Nicklaus	70	71	69	68	278
J. Powell	67	69	72	70	278
T. Weiskopf	68	70	70	70	278

*Floyd won the playoff at the first extra hole, the 18th.

THE PLAYERS CHAMPIONSHIP. US PGA TOUR

TPC at Sawgrass, Ponte Vedra, Florida   24-27 March, 1994

Greg Norman broke all records with an astonishing 24 under par to win by four shots from Fuzzy Zoeller, leading from day one all through the tournament.

G. Norman	63	67	67	67	264
F. Zoeller	66	67	67	67	268
J. Maggert	65	69	69	68	271
H. Irwin	67	70	70	69	276
N. Faldo	67	69	68	73	277
S. Lowery	68	74	69	67	278
B. Faxon	68	68	70	72	278

Davis Love III	68	66	70	74	278
N. Henke	73	69	69	68	279
C. Montgomerie	65	73	71	70	279
T. Kite	65	71	70	73	279
G. Hallberg	68	69	69	73	279

INDONESIAN OPEN. ASIAN TOUR

Kapuk Indah, Jakarta   23-26 March, 1994

Frank Nobilo won with four sub-par rounds, and took the title by three shots despite a last-round charge by Jerry Smith.

F. Nobilo	69	67	68	69	273
J. Smith	68	72	70	66	276
P. Jonas	68	71	70	68	277
G. Webb	69	69	67	75	280

NABISCO DINAH SHORE. US WOMEN'S TOUR

Mission Hills, Rancho Mirage, California   24-27 March, 1994

Britain's Laura Davies bogeyed the 18th, while her nearest rival, Donna Andrews, holed a birdie putt to win the title in dramatic fashion.

D. Andrews	70	69	67	70	276
Laura Davies	70	68	69	70	277
T. Green	70	72	69	68	279
J. Stephenson	70	69	70	71	280
M. McGann	70	68	70	73	281

DOUG SANDERS CELEBRITY CLASSIC. US SENIOR TOUR

25-27 March, 1994

Tom Wargo won by a shot from Bob Murphy and Isao Aoki was disqualified when he dropped a plugged ball in a bunker after he had raked it, thus illegally improving his lie.

T. Wargo	71	66	72	209
B. Murphy	75	69	66	210
C.C. Rodriguez	69	69	73	211
J. Powell	72	70	70	212
M. Hill	74	70	69	213

BENSON & HEDGES MALASIAN OPEN. ASIAN TOUR

Royal Selangor, Kuala Lumpur   17-20 March, 1994

Ryder Cup player Joackim Haeggman won the title after a three-way playoff at the eighth extra hole.

J. Haeggman	71	67	72	69	279
P. Gunasegaran	68	69	72	70	279
F. Nobilo	72	70	69	68	279
B. Mattiace	70	69	72	69	280
J. Rutledge	72	69	69	70	280

STANDARD REGISTER PING.
US WOMEN'S TOUR

Moon Valley, Phoenix, Arizona   10-13 March, 1994

Big-hitting Laura Davies destroyed the field to win her seventh US tour title.

L. Davies	69	72	66	70	277
B. Daniel	71	71	70	69	281
E. Crosby	73	69	66	73	281
A. Ritzman	70	72	71	70	283
H. Kobayashi	70	70	72	71	283
K. Robbins	68	70	71	74	283

TURESPANA OPEN DE BALEARES.
VOLVO EUROPEAN TOUR

Son Vida, Majorca   10-13 March, 1994

Despite a determined attack from defending champion Jim Payne, Barry Lane led the field from start to finish and won his fourth title on the tour. His 19 under par tally tied the record for the tournament.

B. Lane	64	70	66	69	269
J. Payne	67	68	70	66	271
W. Westner	68	70	67	68	273
P. Lawrie	74	65	69	64	275
L. Westwood	69	67	71	68	275
S. Struver	71	67	72	67	277
A. Coltart	73	69	67	68	277
J. Rivero	72	67	66	72	277

THAILAND OPEN. ASIAN TOUR
10-13 March, 1994

Winner: Brandt Jobe

PING WELCH'S CHAMPIONSHIP. US WOMEN'S TOUR

Randolph North Golf Course, Tucson, Arizona   10-13 March, 1994

Donna Andrews coasted home by three shots over nearest rivals Judy Dickinson and Brandie Burton despite a last round 73.

D. Andrews	66	68	69	73	276
J. Dickinson	71	71	69	68	279
B. Burton	69	68	69	73	279
M. McGann	72	70	69	69	280
S. Steinhauer	66	70	72	72	280

VANTAGE AT THE DOMINION. US SENIOR TOUR
10-13 March, 1994

Winner: Jim Albus

HONDA CLASSIC. US PGA TOUR

Weston Hills, Ft. Lauderdale, Florida   10-13 March, 1994

John Daly returned to the tour after a four month suspension and finished joint fourth in a four player tie with Bernhard Langer, Curtis Strange and Davis Love. But Nick Price stole the show, winning by a single stroke, thanks to a last round 66. Nick Faldo and Ian Woosnam both had final rounds of 76.

N. Price	70	67	73	66	276
C. Parry	68	73	72	71	277
B. Chamblee	67	68	72	71	278
J. Daly	69	70	73	68	280
B. Langer	67	72	72	70	280
C. Strange	71	67	72	70	280
D. Love	68	71	70	71	280
D. Edwards	70	72	69	71	282

TURESPANA OPEN MEDITERRANIA.
VOLVO EUROPEAN TOUR

Villa Martin, Torrevieja, Spain   3-6 March, 1994

Paul Mc Ginley blew a three shot lead when he finished with a double bogey and bogey and was beaten at the second extra hole when Jose-Maria Olazabal sank a 25 foot putt. It was the Spaniard's first win in two years. Peter Baker finished third, and his third round 65 was the best of the tournament.

J-M. Olazabal*	70	65	71	70	276
P. McGinley	70	68	68	70	276
P. Baker	73	71	65	69	278
G. J. Brand	68	66	70	74	278
K. Eriksson	67	72	70	70	279
R. Allenby	70	68	71	70	279
T. Johnstone	68	68	68	75	279
P. Golding	68	73	70	69	280
J. Quiros	67	67	71	75	280

*Olazabal won at the second extra hole.

CHRYSLER TOURNAMENT OF CHAMPIONS.
US WOMEN'S TOUR

Grand Cypress Resort, Orlando, Florida   2-5 March, 1994

Winner: Dottie Mochrie

CLASSIC INDIAN OPEN. ASIAN TOUR

       3-6 March, 1994

Winner: Emlyn Aubrey

GTE WEST SENIOR CLASSIC. US SENIOR TOUR

Ojai Valley Inn, California   4-6 March, 1994
Winner: Jay Sigel.
Career amateur Sigel created a sensation when he won his first event on the US Seniors tour. He caused a stir when he announced in the autumn of 1993 that he would leave the amateur scene, turn professional and join the Seniors at the age of fifty. Ten shots behind at the start of the final round, Sigel shot an eight under par 62 to overhaul Jim Colbert, then beat him in a sudden death playoff.

DORAL - RYDER OPEN. US PGA TOUR

Doral, Miami, Florida   3-6 March 1994
Fred Couples had to retire with a worrying back injury on the final day, but his playing partner John Huston, a native Floridian, coasted to his third tour win by three strokes over Billy Andrade and Brad Bryant, thanks to a final round 66.

J. Huston	70	68	70	66	274
B. Andrade	70	68	66	73	277
B. Bryant	70	69	69	69	277
J. Thorpe	68	72	68	71	279
D. A. Weibring	74	69	65	71	279
L. Clements	72	70	66	71	279
B. Lietzke	74	69	71	67	281
G. Norman	71	74	69	67	281
L. Roberts	73	70	69	69	281

TURESPANA OPEN DE ANDALUCIA.
VOLVO EUROPEAN TOUR

Montecastillo, Jerez, Spain   24-27 February, 1994
Favourite Jose-Maria Olazabal was beaten into second place by a 21-year tour veteran who had never won a title. 40 year old Carl Mason, with six runner-up places to his name, held his nerve and shot a last round 70 to take the championship.

C. Mason	67	70	71	70	278
J-M Olazabal	69	68	71	72	280
G. Brand Jnr	71	69	69	72	281
P-U Johansson	69	72	71	70	282
M.A Jiminez	70	73	72	68	283
I. Palmer	69	71	72	72	284
J. Townsend	67	74	71	72	284
P. Teravainen	70	73	68	73	284
R. Drummond	69	69	73	73	284

BUICK INVITATIONAL OF GOLF. US PGA TOUR

Torrey Pines, San Diego, California   24-27 February, 1994
San Diego native Craig Stadler was a popular home town winner with a final round 66 to grab his first victory in almost two years, and his 11th

on the tour. He held off the challenge from defending champion Phil
Mickelson's 64 to win by one from overnight leader Steve Lowery.

C. Stadler	67	67	68	66	268
S. Lowery	67	68	66	68	269
P. Mickelson	68	69	69	64	270
H. Sutton	68	68	67	69	272
M. Carnevale	67	69	70	67	273
R. Freeman	68	67	71	68	274
B. Estes	70	67	67	70	274
K. Triplett	71	63	68	72	274

CANON CHALLENGE. AUSTRALIAN PGA TOUR

Castle Hill, Sydney, Australia   24-27 February, 1994

Peter Senior won the title after a playoff with C. Gray.

KENT HONG KONG OPEN. ASIAN TOUR

24-27 February, 1994

Winner: David Frost

CHRYSLER CUP. US SENIOR TOUR

TPC at Prestancia, Sarasota, Florida   25-27 February, 1994

Winner: George Archer (in a sudden death playoff with Simon Hobday.)

OPEN DE EXTREMADURA. VOLVO EUROPEAN TOUR

Golf de Guadiana, Spain   17-20 February, 1994

Paul Eales had a narrow one shot victory over Sweden's Peter Hedblom,
in only his second season on the tour. Although he three putted the final
green, his one shot cushion was just enough.

P. Eales	72	69	69	71	281
P. Hedblom	72	69	71	70	282
A. Coltart	68	74	71	70	283
J-M. Canizares	70	73	68	72	283
I. Spencer	74	71	68	71	284
L. Westwood	68	72	72	72	284
P. Mitchell	69	69	74	72	284
J. Payne	72	70	70	72	284
M.A. Jiminez	67	73	69	75	284
N. Henning	72	71	66	75	284

HAWAIIAN LADIES OPEN. US WOMEN'S TOUR

Ko Olina, Hawaii   17-19 February, 1994

Winner: Marta Figueras-Dotti

MICROSOFT AUSTRALIAN MASTERS.
AUSTRALIAN PGA TOUR

Huntingdale, Melbourne, Victoria   17-20 February, 1994

A final round 68 took Craig Parry three shots clear of Ernie Els and first prize of $A135000.

C. Parry	74	70	70	68	282
E. Els	70	70	72	73	285
P. Senior	73	71	74	68	286
P. Teravainen	71	70	75	70	286
W. Smith	71	74	72	70	287

THE INTELLINET CHALLENGE. US SENIOR TOUR

The Vineyards, Naples, Florida   18-20 February, 1994

Winner: Mike Hill

BOB HOPE CHRYSLER CLASSIC. US PGA TOUR

Indian Wells, California   16-20 February, 1994

Scott Hoch took the title by three shots in a five-round 334, from Fuzzy Zoeller, Lennie Clements and Jim Gallagher Jnr. An unspectacular final round of 70 saw him home, at 26 under par, and he was unruffled by a 63 from Payne Stewart and a mild charge of 66 from Zoeller. It was Hoch's first title since 1989

S. Hoch	66	62	70	66	70	334
F. Zoeller	70	67	66	68	66	337
L. Clements	67	69	61	72	68	337
J. Gallagher Jnr	66	67	74	62	68	337
P. Stewart	67	69	71	68	63	337
G. Boros	66	67	68	69	69	339
K. Clearwater	67	64	70	68	70	339
P. Stankowski	67	66	69	68	69	339

GTE SUNCOAST CLASSIC. US SENIOR TOUR

TPC of Tampa Bay, Lutz, Florida   11-13 February, 1994

Winner Rocky Thompson overcame a 73 in the first round to shoot a 61 on the last day and steal the title from under the noses of Mike Hill, who blew it with a 73 and Lee Trevino, whose final round of 66 failed to force a playoff by a single stroke.

R. Thompson	73	67	61	201
R. Floyd	70	66	66	202
L. Trevino	69	68	66	203
O. Moody	66	69	70	205
M. Hill	69	64	73	206
R. Rhyan	70	70	66	206
J. Colbert	68	74	65	207
G. Archer	66	70	72	208
B. Charles	71	70	67	208
S. Hobday	71	66	71	208
J.C. Snead	71	71	66	208

NISSAN LOS ANGELES OPEN. US PGA TOUR

Riviera C.C., Pacific Pallisades, California   10-13 February, 1994

Corey Pavin took himself to second place on the US money list with a two shot win at Los Angeles over Fred Couples and six ahead of third place Chip Beck. In an emotional acceptance speech, Pavin dedicated the win, his first since the 1992 Honda Classic, to his good friend Paul Azinger, currently under treatment for cancer.

C. Pavin	67	64	72	68	271
F. Couples	67	67	68	71	273
C. Beck	66	71	72	68	277
B. Faxon	70	71	68	69	278
D. Frost	67	74	71	67	279
P. Jacobsen	69	71	68	72	280
T. Watson	69	71	71	69	280

TURESPANA IBERIA - OPEN DE CANARIAS.
EUROPEAN VOLVO TOUR

Golf del Sur, Tenerife   10-13 February, 1994

It was a significant milestone for David Gilford as his win took him past the £1 million earnings mark and gave him his fifth European title in five years. Brian Barnes briefly enjoyed the spotlight with a third round 64, then fell down the list with a final 77.

D. Gilford	72	70	66	70	278
W. Riley	68	71	70	71	280
A. Murray	73	67	68	72	280
J. Quiros	70	68	67	75	280
B. Malley	69	76	69	67	281
J-M Canizares	67	70	73	71	281
D. Ray	70	70	69	72	281
B. Barnes	73	67	64	77	281

AUTOPAGE MOUNT EDGECOMBE TROPHY. S.A TOUR

Mount Edgecombe CC, Natal   10-13 February, 1994

Winner: Bruce Vaughan (at second hole of sudden death playoff)

Results:

B. Vaughan	72	70	70	63	275
T. Johnstone	68	71	68	68	275
H. Baiocchi	67	71	74	69	281

SENIOR GRAND SLAM. US SENIOR TOUR

Queretaro, Mexico   7-8 February, 1994

Tom Shaw won the title, two ahead of Jim Colbert and six in front of fourth place Jack Nicklaus.

T. Shaw	70	69	139
J. Colbert	70	71	141
T. Wargo	70	72	142
J. Nicklaus	75	70	145

AT&T PEBBLE BEACH NATIONAL PRO-AM.
US PGA TOUR

Pebble Beach, California   3-6 February, 1994

Johnny Miller, who is nowadays more of a course designer than active player, and had only played a handful of toue events since 1989, delighted the crowd by beating Tom Watson, neither of whom had won in ten years. Helped by Watson's cold putter, Miller held off the charging Jeff Maggert and Corey Pavin to take the title.

J. Miller	68	72	67	74	281
T. Watson	69	67	72	74	282
J. Maggert	68	72	72	70	282
C. Pavin	69	71	71	71	282
K. Triplett	69	74	67	72	282
T. Lehman	69	68	73	73	283
K. Clearwater	70	70	71	73	284
J. Delsing	66	75	70	73	284
D. Hart	65	71	72	73	284
B. McCallister	68	71	72	73	284
T. Tryba	70	70	70	74	284

JOHNNIE WALKER CLASSIC. VOLVO EUROPEAN TOUR

Blue Canyon, Phuket, Thailand   3-6 February, 1994

Greg Norman took the place of Nick Faldo at the top of the Sony Rankings with a dramatic ten-foot putt that robbed Fred Couples of a play-off. He had broken the course record with a 64 on the third day and was one behind Couples on the final session. The Briton had been at the top of the rankings for 81 unbroken weeks.

G. Norman	75	70	64	68	277
F. Couples	66	72	70	70	278
B. Langer	68	70	71	70	279
I. Woosnam	68	72	68	73	281
M. Harwood	71	72	69	70	282
C. Montgomerie	70	72	71	70	283
H. Chin-Sheng	70	69	70	74	283
F. Minoza	72	74	67	71	285
D. Feherty	69	71	73	71	284

ROYAL CARIBBEAN SENIORS CLASSIC. US SENIOR TOUR

The Links, Key Biscayne, Florida   3-6 February, 1994

Winner Lee Trevino needed four playoff holes to beat Kermit Zarley at Key Biscayne. Trevino started with a 66, then faltered to 73, but charged home with a 66 to tie Zarley on 205.

L. Trevino	66	73	66	205
K. Zarley	71	66	68	205
B. Charles	70	67	70	207
J C Snead	71	66	70	207
G. Archer	69	68	71	208

HEATHSOUTH PALM BEACH CLASSIC. US WOMEN'S TOUR
Wycliffe G &C Club, Lake Worth, Florida   4-6 February, 1994
Winner Dawn Coe-Jones had a narrow win over Lauri Merten and Laura Davies at Lake Worth. Trailing Lisa Walters and Davies by two at the start of the final round, she shot a 65, while the other two faded, and won by a single stroke.

D. Coe-Jones	67	69	65		201
L. Merten	71	67	64		202
L. Davies	69	65	69		203
L. Walters	66	68	70		204
D. Mochrie	70	67	69		206
J. Stephenson	71	69	68		207

ROYAL SWAZI SUN CLASSIC. S.A TOUR
Royal Swazi Sun, Mbabane, Swaziland   3-6 February, 1994
Winner: Omar Uresti
Results:

O. Uresti	65	73	68	68	274
A. Pitts	69	68	72	67	276
W. Westner	72	66	68	71	277

STANDARD CHARTERED KENYA OPEN.
Muthiago, Nairobi   3-6 February, 1994
Winner: Paul Carman (at the fourth hole of sudden death playoff with Glenn Ralph)
Results:

P. Carman	67	70	68	71	276
G. Ralph	69	67	69	71	276
M. Litton	67	73	71	68	279

INLAND EMPIRE OPEN. NIKE TOUR
Moreno Valley, California   4-6 February, 1994
Winner: Skip Kendall
Results:

S. Kendall	65	67	65		197
E. Aubrey	67	67	69		203
B. Murchison	66	68	71		205

SOUTH AFRICAN MASTERS. S.A.TOUR
Lost City, Sun City, S.A   27-30 January, 1994
Winner: Chris Davison
Results:

C. Davison	69	74	68	70	281
B. Vaughan	69	70	71	73	283
J. Becker	71	67	77	71	286
J. Kingston	75	69	69	73	286

DUBAI DESERT CLASSIC. VOLVO EUROPEAN TOUR

Emirates Golf Club, Dubai   27-30 January, 1994

Ernie Els started the tournament as he meat to go on, breaking the course record by three strokes with a 61. He finished 20 under par and six shots ahead of his nearest challenger, Greg Norman.

E. Els	61	69	67	71	268
G. Norman	68	69	68	69	274
W. Westner	70	68	69	68	275
J. Lomas	66	73	70	67	276
I. Aoki	67	72	70	67	276
T. Watanabe	70	70	67	69	276
P-U Johansson	70	71	69	67	277
G. Evans	67	69	71	70	277

PHOENIX OPEN. US PGA TOUR

TPC of Scottsdale, Arizona   27-30 January, 1994

Bill Glasson's ten year career on tour has been plagued by injury. His first three holes on the final day were birdies, and he coasted home in 64 for a three shot win and his sixth title on the tour.

B. Glasson	68	68	68	64	268
B. Estes	66	68	69	68	271
J. Maggert	70	68	69	65	272
B. McCallister	67	69	69	67	272
M. Springer	68	68	69	67	272
R. Fehr	66	67	69	71	273
T. Lehman	67	68	73	65	273
F. Funk	69	69	70	66	274
S. Hoch	72	66	67	69	274
P. Mickelson	64	70	71	66	274
S. Pate	68	69	69	68	274
C. Strange	71	70	69	64	274

HEINEKEN CLASSIC. AUSTRALASIAN TOUR

The Vines, Perth   27-30 January, 1994

Winner: Mike Clayton

Results:

M. Clayton	67	71	71	70	279
W. Smith	69	67	73	73	282
P. Burke	68	68	78	69	283
R. Allenby	70	69	71	73	283

SENIOR SKINS GAME. US SENIOR TOUR

Mauna Lani Resort, Hawaii   24-30 January, 1994

Winner: Raymond Floyd, 8 Skins

Arnold Palmer	5 Skins
Lee Trevino	4 Skins

MOROCCAN OPEN. VOLVO EUROPEAN TOUR

Golf Royal de Agadir   20-23 January, 1994

Anders Forsbrand played consistent golf with four under par rounds to beat Howard Clark by four strokes.

A. Forsbrand	70	68	69	69	276
H. Clark	68	67	72	73	280
R. Karlsson	68	72	70	71	281
P. Hedblom	68	72	73	69	282
F. Nobilo	72	72	68	70	282
J. Sewell	68	72	74	69	283
S. Watson	73	72	68	70	283
J. Van de Velde	72	68	71	72	283
A. Coltart	74	69	75	66	284
P. Fluke	75	68	73	69	285
G. Brand Jnr	70	68	75	72	285

OPTUS PLAYERS CHAMPIONSHIP. AUSTRALASIAN TOUR

Kingston Heath   20-23 January, 1994

Winner: Patrick Burke

Results:

P. Burke	69	67	72	72	280
B. Hughes	68	73	70	70	281
O. Moore	73	70	69	70	282
P. Senior	70	73	69	70	283
C. Parry	72	70	72	69	283

NORTHERN TELECOM OPEN. US PGA TOUR

Tucson National, Arizona   20-23 January, 1994

Andrew Magee took the $198000 first prize with a consistent display of under par golf, beating Jay Don Blake, Vijay Singh, Steve Stricker and Loren Roberts by two strokes. Phil Mickelson became the youngest (23) and fastest (19 months) golfer to earn a million dollars when he finished ninth.

A. Magee	69	67	67	67	270
J.D Blake	68	68	67	68	272
L. Roberts	68	68	72	64	272
V. Singh	67	68	72	65	272
S. Stricker	68	69	68	67	272
O. Browne	70	70	66	67	273
J. Furyk	68	68	67	71	274
R. Gamez	66	71	71	66	274

LEXINGTON PGA CHAMPIONSHIP. S.A TOUR

Wanderers G.C, Johannesberg   13-16 January, 1994

David Frost shot 65, 64 and a brilliant final round 63 to crush the chasing pack by seven shots.

D. Frost	64	67	65	63	259

N. Price	66	66	66	68	266
W. Westner	65	68	71	63	267
E. Els	68	67	66	67	268

UNITED AIRLINES HAWAIIAN OPEN. US PGA TOUR

Waialae Country Club, Honolulu, Hawaii   13-16 January, 1994
Brett Ogle shot a last round 68 to edge out challenger Davis Love, with John Huston, despite a 67, three shots behind.

B. Ogle	66	66	69	68	269
D. Love	68	60	71	71	270
J. Huston	70	68	67	67	272
C. Pavin	68	70	70	65	273
J. Parnevik	71	66	74	63	274
C. Parry	66	70	72	67	275
T. Tryba	69	71	68	67	275

MADEIRA ISLAND OPEN. VOLVO EUROPEAN TOUR

Campo de Golfe da Madeira   13-16 January, 1994
A Strong Swedish contingent finished with four of them in the top six, but Mats Lanner took the title by two shots, thanks to a final day 69.

M. Lanner	70	67	69	206
M. Gronberg	69	70	69	208
P. Hedblom	69	69	70	208
H. Clark	68	67	73	208
M. A. Martin	71	69	71	211
G. Hjerstedt	71	67	73	211
J. Robinson	71	66	74	211
P. Eales	69	73	70	212
D. Borrego	69	70	73	212
P. Broadhurst	70	67	75	212

THAILAND OPEN. ASIAN LADIES TOUR

Thana City, Bangkok   13-15 January, 1994
Winner: Laura Davies
Results:

L. Davies	66	70	70	206
M. Lunn	70	71	72	213
Y-M. Lee	70	71	74	215

BELL'S CUP. S.A. TOUR

Fancourt, Cape Province   6-9 January, 1994
Winner: Tony Johnstone
Results:

T. Johnstone	65	68	68	70	271
E. Els	65	65	72	71	274
D. Frost	68	67	72	67	274

MERCEDES CHAMPIONSHIP. US SENIOR TOUR

La Costa, Carlsbad, California   6-9 January, 1994

Dave Stockton and Bob Murphy blew three shot leads after the third round and were caught by a streaking Jack Nicklaus who shot a final 68 to Murphy's 72 and Stockton's 75.

J. Nicklaus	73	69	69	68	279
B. Murphy	71	70	67	72	280
D. Stockton	67	72	69	75	283
R. Floyd	73	72	70	69	284
L. Trevino	71	71	73	70	285
J. Colbert	71	74	70	70	285

MERCEDES CHAMPIONSHIP. US PGA TOUR

La Costa, Carlsbad, California   6-9 January, 1994

A neck and neck tussle between one of the established world stars and the man tipped to be the new Nicklaus ended in a sudden-death playoff, when Phil Mickelson beat Fred Couples at the second hole. The pair had been locked in combat over the four days, never separated by more than one shot.

P. Mickelson	70	68	70	68	276
F. Couples	69	70	69	68	276
T. Kite	73	68	69	68	278
D. Love	71	69	72	68	280
S. Simpson	70	72	70	68	280
J. Haas	71	71	69	69	280
J. Maggert	72	74	65	69	280
H. Twitty	72	73	67	69	281
D. Edwards	75	68	66	72	281
G. Norman	70	73	69	70	282

AMO NEW ZEALAND OPEN. AUSTRALIAN TOUR

Remuera, Auckland   6-9 January, 1994

Winner: Craig Jones

Results:

C. Jones	69	71	65	72	277
F. Nobilo	68	68	72	70	278
S. Conran	70	69	70	71	280

GREG NORMAN HOLDEN CLASSIC

The Lakes, New South Wales   2 - 5 December 1993

Winner: Curtis Strange

Results:

C. Strange	68	67	69	70	274
J. Wade	70	69	66	71	276
V. Singh	72	71	68	66	277
S. Elkington	67	70	71	72	280
R. Floyd	76	72	67	66	281
P. Senior	72	71	68	70	281

SUN CITY $1M CHALLENGE
Gary Player Country Club, Sun City, Bophuthatswana

2 - 5 December 1993

Winner: Nick Price

Results:

N. Price	67	66	66	65	264
M. McNulty	71	70	68	67	276
B. Langer	72	69	70	68	279
F. Allem	72	70	72	66	280
N. Faldo	67	73	72	69	281
C. Pavin	71	70	71	73	285

AUSTRALIAN OPEN. AUSTRALASIAN TOUR
Metropolitan Club, Melbourne   25-28 November 1993

Winner: Brad Faxon

Results:

B. Faxon	65	74	66	70	275
J. Woodland	71	68	68	70	277
M. Clayton	69	71	71	66	277
P. Senior	67	73	69	69	278
W. Grady	68	69	70	71	278

AUSTRALIAN PGA CHAMPIONSHIP.
AUSTRALASIAN TOUR
Sydney, Australia   18-21 November, 1993

Winner: Ian Baker-Finch (at the second playoff hole, after a three way tie with Grant Waite and Peter Fowler)

Results:

I. Baker-Finch	69	69	73	64	275
G. Waite	66	69	73	67	275
P. Fowler	71	64	67	73	275
J. Payne	71	67	73	66	277
J. Morse	68	67	70	72	277

CASIO WORLD OPEN
Kaimon Course, Ibusuki, Japan   25 - 28 November 1993

Winner: Tom Lehman

Results:

T. Lehman	69	69	67	69	274
P. Mickelson	69	71	65	70	275
S. Higashi	67	72	68	70	277
J. Haeggman	67	67	73	71	278

ZIMBABWE OPEN

Chapman GC, Harare, Zimbabwe   25 - 28 November 1993
Winner: Tony Johnstone
Results:

T. Johnstone	71	68	65	68	273
N. Henning	70	71	72	68	281
J. Kingston	70	70	73	68	281
M. McNulty	70	71	73	68	282
I. Leggatt	71	66	74	71	282

WORLD CUP OF GOLF BY HEINEKEN

Lake Nona, Orlando, Florida   11-14 November, 1993
Winners: United States
Results:

USA - 556 Winners get $ 130000 each

F. Couples	66	71	70	68	275
D. Love	71	69	71	70	281

ZIMBABWE 561 Runners-up get $ 75000 each

N. Price	70	69	71	68	278
M. McNulty	71	68	72	72	283

SCOTLAND 565 Third place gets $50000 each

S. Torrance	68	69	71	73	281
C. Montgomerie	75	70	69	70	284

AUSTRALIA   566

R. Allenby	280
R. Davis	286

SPAIN   567

M. A. Jimenez	282
J. Rivero	285

SOUTH AFRICA   567

E. Els	278
R. Goosen	290

NEW ZEALAND   568

F. Nobilo	283
G. Turner	285

GERMANY   571

B. Langer	272
S. Struver	299

IRELAND		573
R. Rafferty	284	
P. McGinley	289	

ITALY		573
C. Rocca	283	
S. Grappasonni	290	

ENGLAND		574
D. Gilford	286	
M. James	288	

CANADA		574
D. Barr	285	
R. Zokol	289	

SWEDEN		575
A. Forsbrand	282	
J. Haeggman	293	

FRANCE		575
J. Van de Velde	279	
M. Farry	296	

PARAGUAY		579
P.R. Martinez	287	
F.R. Franco	292	

WALES		582
M. Mouland	286	
I. Woosnam	296	

OTHER SCORES:
Brazil 583; Japan 588; Argentina 592; Hong Kong 592; Mexico 597;
Netherlands 602; Greece 603; Taiwan 609; Bermuda 617;
Puerto Rico 629; Fiji 646; Jamaica 652; Israel 682

EAGLE BLUE OPEN. AUSTRALASIAN TOUR

Royal Adelaide, Australia   11-14 November, 1993

Winner: Wayne Smith (at the third extra hole after a three way tie on
210 with Jim Kennedy and K. Miskimins.)
Results:

W. Smith	67	68	75	210
J. Kennedy	72	69	69	210
K. Miskimins	70	70	70	210

SUMITOMO VISA TAIHEIYO MASTERS

Gotemba, Japan　　　　　　　　　　　　11-14 November, 1993
Winner: Greg Norman
Results:

G. Norman	70	67	67	68	272
Y. Mizumaki	67	68	68	70	273
D. Frost	68	71	70	65	274
B. Lane	68	70	68	68	274
J. Ozaki	66	69	67	72	274
T. Nakajima	70	68	69	69	276

TORAY QUEEN'S CLASSIC. US WOMEN'S TOUR

Lions CC, Japan　　　　　　　　　　　　5-7 November, 1993
Winner: Betsy King
Results:

B. King	68	70	67	205
J. Geddes	70	70	66	206
T. Johnson	70	68	69	207
D. L. Dorman	69	68	70	207
D. Eggeling	70	66	71	207

LINCOLN MERCURY KAPALUA INTERNATIONAL.
US PGA TOUR

Kapalua, Maui, Hawaii　　　　　　　　　　4-7 November, 1993
US Ryder Cup stars Fred Couples and Davis Love maintained their recent good form, but Couples took the title despite a last round 70 to win by four shots.
Results:

F. Couples	69	68	67	70	274
B. McAllister	74	66	70	68	278
D. Love	70	72	69	68	279
P. Jacobsen	67	74	67	73	281

VOLVO MASTERS. VOLVO EUROPEAN TOUR

Valderrama, Sotogrande, Spain　　　　　　4-7 November, 1993
Colin Montgomerie maintained his slender one stroke lead on the final day, and finished strongly with a 68 to take the title.
Results:

C. Montgomerie	69	70	67	68	274
D. Clarke	69	73	65	68	275
D. Gilford	68	72	67	69	276
V. Singh	72	72	67	70	281
I. Woosnam	71	67	71	73	282
M. McNulty	73	73	67	71	284

VICTORIA OPEN. AUSTRALASIAN TOUR

Woodlands, Australia   4-7 November, 1993
Winner: Lucas Parsons
Results:

L. Parsons	72	69	65	70	276
B. Hughes	64	69	73	73	279
W. Riley	68	72	68	72	280

HASSAN II TROPHY

Royal Dar-es-Salaam Red Course, Rabat, Morocco

10 - 13 November 1993

Winner: Payne Stewart
Results:

P. Stewart	69	70	71	67	277
W. Westner	68	72	74	71	285
B. Claar	71	73	71	70	285
D. Pruitt	70	72	71	72	285

PRINCESS LALLA MERIE CUP

Royal Dar-es-Salaam Blue Course, Rabat, Morocco

11 - 13 November 1993

Winner: Marie Laure de Lorenzi
Results:

M.L de Lorenzi	73	66	70	209
H. Wadsworth	71	68	72	211
S. G Whitmore	68	71	73	212
C. Nilsmark	74	73	68	215

MADRID OPEN.
VOLVO EUROPEAN TOUR

Puerta de Hierro, Madrid   28 October - 1 November, 1993
Winner: Des Smyth
Results:

D. Smith	65	68	68	71	272
M. Roe	69	66	71	69	275
J. Rivero	68	72	66	69	275
D. Hospital	68	69	68	70	275
W. Westner	70	65	68	72	275
D. Feherty	68	72	70	66	276
D. J. Russell	74	67	68	67	276
E. Romero	73	66	68	69	276
S. Luna	70	70	67	69	276

TOUR CHAMPIONSHIP. US PGA TOUR

The Olympic Club, San Francisco, California   28-31 October, 1993
Another Ryder Cup hero, Jim Gallagher Jnr, won the title with a last round 69, holding off four cnallengers, Greg Norman, David Frost, John Huston and Scott Simpson by a single shot.
Results:

J. Gallagher Jnr	63	73	72	69		277
S. Simpson	68	70	70	70		278
J. Huston	72	68	68	70		278
D. Frost	68	68	69	73		278
G. Norman	72	67	68	71		278

KAANAPALI CLASSIC. US SENIOR TOUR

Kaanapali, Hawaii   29-31 October, 1993
Winner: George Archer (at the first extra hole after a three way tie with Dave Stockton and Lee Trevino)
Results:

G. Archer	67	69	63	199
L. Trevino	68	67	64	199
D. Stockton	66	66	67	199

TOYOTA WORLD MATCHPLAY CHAMPIONSHIP

West Course, Wentworth, Surrey   21-24 October, 1993
Winner: Corey Pavin (US)
Result: Final- Corey Pavin beat Nick Faldo 1 hole.

VAR OPEN DE FRANCE. EUROPEAN WOMEN'S TOUR

Ste Maxime et St Endreol, The Var, France   21-24th October, 1993
Winner: Marie Laure de Lorenzi
Results:

M.L. de Lorenzi	79	72	69	220
F. Dassu	78	70	73	221
K. Orum	73	79	69	221

LAS VEGAS INVITATIONAL. US PGA TOUR

TPC at Summerlin, California   20-24 October, 1993
Winner Davis Love III, fresh from his fine display at the Ryder Cup, destroyed the rest of the field with a five-round total of 331, eight ahead of his nearest challenger, Craig Stadler.
Results:

D. Love III	67	66	67	65	66	331
C. Stadler	67	66	69	72	65	339
P. Azinger	66	67	72	68	67	340
D. Edwards	72	66	68	67	67	340
B. Estes	68	68	68	67	69	340

WOMEN'S WORLD CHAMPIONSHIP. US WOMEN'S TOUR

Naples, Florida   14-17 October, 1993
Winner: Dottie Mochrie
Results:

D. Mochrie	72	71	68	72	283
D. Andrews	72	74	70	69	285
M. McGann	69	74	73	69	285
S. Steinhauer	78	69	67	71	285
M. Mallon	67	74	73	71	285

RALEY'S SENIORS GOLD RUSH. US SENIOR TOUR

Rancho Murieta, California   15-17 October, 1993
Winner: George Archer
Results:

G. Archer	68	66	68	202
B. Charles	66	69	68	203
C. C. Rodriguez	65	71	67	203

ALFRED DUNHILL CUP

Old Course, St Andrews, Scotland   14-17 October, 1993
Winners: United States
Results:
FINAL: USA 2, England 1
    Payne Stewart, 74, lost to Mark James, 70
    Fred Couples, 68, beat Nick Faldo, 69
    John Daly, 70, beat Peter Baker, 73

TRANSAMERICA SENIORS. US SENIOR TOUR

Napa, California   8-10 October, 1993
Winner: Dave Stockton
Result:

D. Stockton	68	71	64	203
L. Trevino	68	70	66	204
S. Hobday	71	66	67	203

ZURICH LEXUS TROPHY. EUROPEAN SENIORS TOUR

Breitenloo, Zurich, Switzerland   7-9 October, 1993
Winner: Tommy Horton (after a three way tie on 216 with David Jiminez
and John Fourie, Horton winning at the first extra hole)
Results:

T. Horton	74	67	75	216
D. Jiminez	73	73	70	216
J. Fourie	73	70	73	216

ALFRED DUNHILL OPEN. VOLVO EUROPEAN TOUR
Royal Zoute, Knokke-le-Zoute, Belgium   7-10 October, 1993
Winner: Darren Clarke
Results:

D. Clarke	68	68	66	68	270
V. Singh	68	69	71	64	272
N. Faldo	68	68	69	67	272
B. Langer	72	64	72	65	273
R. Davis	74	67	64	68	273
G. Brand Jnr	66	71	68	68	273
S. Ballesteros	67	65	71	70	273

WALT DISNEY WORLD OLDSMOBILE CLASSIC. US PGA TOUR
Lake Buena Vista, Orlando, Florida   7-10 October, 1993
Winner: Jeff Maggert
Results:

J. Maggert	66	65	66	68	265
G. Kraft	69	69	64	66	268
C. Stadler	68	67	68	67	270
K. Green	70	68	63	69	270
L. Roberts	66	68	67	71	270
T. Tryba	64	68	67	71	270

MERCEDES GERMAN MASTERS. VOLVO EUROPEAN TOUR
Stuttgarter-Solitude, Monsheim, Germany
                              30 September- 3 October, 1993
Winner: Steve Richardson
Results:

S. Richardson	67	66	70	68	271
R. Karlsson	68	69	70	66	273
C. Beck	72	63	69	70	274
J. Parnevik	70	72	68	66	276
B. Langer	73	64	70	69	276
J-M. Olazabal	69	69	72	67	277

THE GRAND MATCH
Brockett Hall, Herts   29 Sept, 1993
Ex-Ryder Cup players 7   Ex-Walker Cup players 5

THE 30th RYDER CUP
The Belfry, England   24-26 September, 1993
Result: United States 15 Europe 13

SEE CHAPTER ON RYDER CUP PREVIEW 1995 FOR FULL RESULTS.

BMW ITALIAN LADIES OPEN. WOMEN'S EUROPEAN TOUR

Golf Club Lignano, Lignano Sabbiadoro   16-19 September, 1993
Winner: Amaya Arruti
Results:

A. Arruti	67	65	68	70	270
A. Sorenstam	67	70	68	67	272
K. Parker	69	66	68	71	274
C. Dibnah	69	68	76	65	278
A. Jones	71	63	76	68	278

TROPHEE LANCOME. VOLVO EUROPEAN TOUR

Saint-Nom-la-Breteche, Paris   16-19 September, 1993
Winner Ian Woosnam gave his Ryder cup captain Bernard Gallacher a boost when he scorched around the final round with a 65 to win by two shots. Another boost for Gallacher was the form of Torrance, Lane, James and Faldo, who all finished in the top six.
Results:

I. Woosnam	64	70	68	65	267
S. Torrance	69	65	68	67	269
B. Lane	71	66	66	67	270
M. James	65	66	72	67	270
D. Feherty	69	63	69	69	270
N. Faldo	69	67	69	66	271
F. Couples	70	65	65	71	271

CANADIAN OPEN. US PGA TOUR

Glen Abbey, Ontario   9-12 September, 1993
Winner: David Frost
Results:

D. Frost	72	70	69	68	279
F. Couples	70	71	70	69	280
B. Bryant	68	60	70	74	282

GA EUROPEAN OPEN. VOLVO EUROPEAN TOUR

East Course, East Sussex National, Uckfield   9-12 September, 1993
Winner: Gordon Brand Jnr
Results:

G. Brand Jnr	65	68	71	71	275
P. Price	70	68	71	73	282
R. Rafferty	69	73	68	72	282
O. Karlsson	68	73	67	75	283
F. Nobilo	73	69	69	72	283
I. Woosnam	70	75	69	70	284

COLLINGTREE SENIORS CLASSIC.
EUROPEAN SENIORS TOUR

Collingtree Park, Northampton   3-5 September, 1993
Winner: Tommy Horton
Results:

T. Horton	69	72	71		212
R. Fidler	72	69	74		215
B. Huggett	74	72	69		215

PGA EUROPEAN QUALIFYING SCHOOL

Montpellier, France   11-16 November, 1993

TOP SIX QUALIFIERS

Brian Nelson	67	70	69	69	75	74	424
Ross McFarlane	68	72	73	70	73	70	426
Scott Watson	70	73	72	68	70	73	426
Manuel Zerman	74	73	72	67	70	72	428
Lee Westwood	67	69	73	70	77	74	428
Ruben Alvarez	66	71	72	70	76	73	428

OTHER SCORES:

Peter Linhart	430
Phil Golding	430
Steven Bottomley	430
Andrew Coltart	431
Alexander Cejka	431
C. M Stromberg	431
Robert Lee	432
Gabriel Hjertstedt	432
M. Gronberg	432
Ralf Berhorst	432
Jeff Hall	433
Diego Borrego	434
Paul Mooney	434
Carl Suneson	434
Stephen Hamill	434
Colin Brooks	435
Marcus Wills	435
H. Selby-Green	435
Ian Spencer	436
Adam Mednick	436
Paul Affleck	436
Chris Williams	436
Mikael Piltz	436
Mark Nichols	436
Andrew Collison	436
M. Besanceney	436
Patrick Bates	437

Martin Poxon   437
Massimo Scarpa   437
Peter Hedblom   438
Nic Henning   438
Ignacio Gervas   438
Steve Van Vuuren 438
Terry Price   438
Jesus Maria Arruti and Miles Tunnicliff missed out in a playoff.

USPGA QUALIFYING SCHOOL

LaQuinta, California
The players below all earned their 1994 Tour cards:

TOP SIX QUALIFIERS:

T. Armstrong	71	70	68	71	67	68	415
D. Stockton Jnr	68	72	66	68	70	71	415
R. Freeman	70	68	68	68	70	71	415
J. Parnevik	65	66	79	67	67	72	416
J. Woodland	68	69	71	69	68	71	416
P. Jordan	71	65	69	72	68	71	416

OTHER SCORES:

J. Rassett	417
C. Dennis	419
M. Hatalsky	419
D. Paulson	420
G. Day	421
D. Feherty	421
Y. Mizumaki	421
T. Barranger	421
S. Rintoul	421
B. Burns	421
S. Gotsche	421
T. Simpson	422
G. Boros	422
P. Goydos	422
J. Wilson	422
T. Levet	422
S. Stricker	422
M. Wurtz	423
D. Pride	423
E. Toledo	423
P. Stankowski	424
S. Brodie	424
R. Walcher	424
D.A. Russell	424
M. Heinen	424
D. Reese	425

E. Kirby	425
S. Lamontagne	425
B. Britton	425
B. Kratzert	425
C. Paulerson	426
R. Boldt	426
S. Micheel	426
M. Brisky	426
C. Kite	426
B. Larndon	426
P. Tataurangi	426
J. Furyk	426
B. King	426
T. Garner	426

SELECTED AMATEUR RESULTS
1993/94

SUNDAY EXPRESS NATIONAL UNDER 14 CHAMPIONSHIP

West Course, Wentworth   July, 1994

The competition, launched in October, 1993, attracted 5000 competitors, from over 500 clubs. Daniel Braggins and Kamilla Lawton were presented with their awards at the Wentworth ballroom by Eve Pollard and organiser Fred Moghadam hopes to attract entries for more than 1000 clubs for the 1995 championship.

Results

BOYS:

D. Braggins	74	77	151
J. Rose	75	70	152
A Frayne	76	81	157
P. Heppenstall	80	77	157
O. Wilson	78	80	158

GIRLS:

K. Lawton	90	81	171*
E. Galland	85	86	171
B. McCormack	88	87	175
S. Heath	100	92	192
C. Forryan	96	92	198

*Decided on a better back nine score.

ST ANDREWS TROPHY

Chantilly, France   24-25 June, 1994

Great Britain & Ireland retained the trophy, jumping off to a 4-0 lead in the opening foursomes. The lead was held and the final margin 14-10.
Results: Great Britain & Ireland 14, Continent of Europe 10

FOURSOMES:
(GB&I first)
 L. James & B. Dredge lost to K. Brink & L. Westberg 3&2
 W. Bennett & G. Wolstenholme beat F. Valera & C. Hanell one hole
 B. Howard & G. Sherry lost to D. Dupin & N.Van Hootgem 5&4
 P. Harrington & R. Johnson halved with M. Backhausen & N. Zitny

SINGLES:
 W. Bennett beat M. Backhausen one hole
 L. James beat L. Westerberg 2&1
 G. Sherry beat N. Van Hootgem 5&4
 D. Fisher l;ost to F. Valera 3&2
 R. Johnson beat K. Brink one hole
 B. Howard lost to D. Dupin 2&1
 P. Harrington lost to N. Zitny 4&2
 G. Wolstenholme lost to C. Hanell 5&40

ST. ANDREWS LINKS TROPHY

St. Andrews   21 - 22May, 1994

Results:
Barclay Howard	294
Warren Bennett	295
Gary Houston	295

BRITISH AMATEUR CHAMPIONSHIP

Nairn   30 May-4 June, 1994

Results:
 L. James (Broadstone) beat G. Sheery (Kilmarnock Barassie) by 2 &1 over 36 holes.

ENGLISH WOMEN'S CHAMPIONSHIP

The Berkshire   17-21 May, 1994

Results:
Semi-Finals: J. Hall (Felixstowe Ferry) beat K. Tebbet (East Devon) 5 &4
    S. Sharpe (Peterborough Milton) beat A. Murray (Lancaster) one hole
Final: Hall beat Sharpe one hole.

WELSH WOMEN'S CHAMPIONSHIP

Portthcawl, Mid-Glamorgan   15-17 May, 1994
Results: V. Thomas (Pennard) beat L. Dermott (Royal Liverpool) at 19th.

SCOTTISH WOMEN'S CHAMPIONSHIP

Gullane, East Lothian   17-21 May, 1994
Results:
C. Matthew (North Berwick) beat V. Melvin (Stirling U.) one hole.

IRISH WOMEN'S CHAMPIONSHIP

Rosses Point, Sligo   17-21 May, 1994
Results:
L. Webb (Cairndhu) beat H. Cavanagh (Grange) at 20th hole.

ENGLISH OPEN SENIORS CHAMPIONSHIP

Broadstone   15 May, 1994
Winner: Graham Steel (Moor Park), Frank Jones (Ellesborough)
Results:

Graham Steel	72
Frank Jones	72
Gordon Edwards	73

Winner 55-59 Age Group: Nick Allen (Ellesborough)
Winner 60-64 Age Group: Gordon Edwards (Bromborough)
Winner 65-69 Age Group: Harvey Deane (Royal Ashdown Forest)

BRABAZON TROPHY.
ENGLISH AMATEUR STROKEPLAY CHAMPIONSHIP

11-15 May, 1994

The prestigious event turned into a one-man show as Gary Harris, an 18-year old from Broome Manor, Swindon, won the Brabazon by six strokes from Warren Bennett, an earlier winner of the Lytham Trophy. He also broke the course record with a third round 64. At one stage on the last day he was 12 under par and ten ahead of Bennett, both records, but a lapse of concentration cost him dearly. He also won the George Henriques Salver by a massive 11 strokes, the Philip Scrutton Jug by 8 strokes and received a memento from Little Aston for his course record. Harris is making a habit of winning by wide margins. He won the 1994 Wiltshire Boy's Title by six shots from Richard Collins of Wootton Bassett
Results:

Gary Harris	72	70	64	74	280
Warren Bennett	69	74	64	74	286
S. Burnell	74	75	69	70	288
F. Valera	71	76	71	70	288
R. Bland	73	72	71	72	288

GEORGE HENRIQUES SALVER
(Best Player under 20)

Winner: Gary Harris

Results:

G. Harris	72	70	64	76	280
M. B. Foster	70	77	68	76	291
S. P. Webster	72	77	68	76	296

SCRUTTON JUG
(Combined scores of Berkshire and Brabazon Trophies)

Winner: Gary Harris

Results:

G. Harris	279	280	559
L. James	277	290	567
S. Burnell	280	288	568
D. Fisher	284	293	577

BERKSHIRE TROPHY

The Berkshire   30 April - 1 May, 1994

Drama of the highest order as James Knight, 20, from Sandford Springs, led by two strokes after nine holes on the final day. He finished with 68 and it was just enough to earn a tie with the charging Andrew Marshall, also 20, from Dereham. Marshall had a 64, including four under par for the last four holes. Knight and Marshall share the trophy.

Results:

James Knight	68	72	66	68	274
Andrew Marshall	67	69	74	64	274
Ben Sandry	70	71	66	69	276
L. James	70	68	67	72	276
G. Harris	70	71	71	67	279

LYTHAM TROPHY

Royal Lytham   30 April - 1 May, 1994

Warren Bennett of Ruislip must have thought he'd blown his chance with a third round 77, having led at the halfway stage by five strokes. At the start of the last day, Scott Drummond from Shrewsbury, led by three, but took a six at the par five 11th while Bennett gained ground with an eagle. He grabbed the trophy with a gutsy 71, while Drummond could only manage a 75, to lose by the narrowest margin. Bennett's display in June, playing for Great Britain and Irekand in the St Andrews Trophy against Europe, prompted Michael Bonallack to tip him as an Open winner in the next ten years.

Results:

Warren Bennett	70	67	77	71	285
Scott Drummond	72	70	69	75	268
A. Emery	70	73	72	73	288
C. Downie	73	72	72	72	289

BRITISH WOMEN'S SENIOR OPEN

Ashburnham, Dyfed, Wales   28-29 September, 1993
Winner: Jill Thornhill   75   80   155
Joint 2nd: Angela Uzielli   77   81   158
           Hilary Kaye   75   83   158

US AMATEUR CHAMPIONSHIP

Champions, Houston, Texas   24-30 August, 1993
Final (36 holes): J. Harris beat S. Ellis 5 &3.

34th WALKER CUP

Interlachen, Edina, Minnesota   18-19 August 1993
Winners: United States
Result: USA 19 - Great Britain & Ireland 5

AMATEUR STANDINGS

GOLF WEEKLY AMATEUR ORDER OF MERIT
After 19-6-94

1.	Bradley Dredge (Bryn Meadows)	949 points
2.	Lee James (Broadstone)	820
3.	Warren Bennett (Ruislip)	778
4.	David Downie (Ladybank)	724
5.	Barclay Howard (Cochrane Castle)	683
6.	David Fisher (Stoke Poges)	583
7.	Craig Watson (East Renfrew)	569
7.	Matthew Ellis (Wrexham)	569
9.	Craig Evans (West Monmouth)	518
10.	Gordon Sherry (Barassie)	518

Awards Nomination 1996

The International Golf Almanack 1996 intends to make awards in the following categories:

1. Lifetime Achievement

2. New Golf Course of the Year..Europe

3. New Golf Course of the Year..USA

4. Golf Instructor of the Year

5. Golf Enthusiast of the Year

6. New Golf Product of the Year

If you would like to nominate any person, course or product for any of the awards above, please write, stating your reasons to:

Awards 1996
International Golf Almanack 1996
Blandford Press
Villiers House
41-47 Strand
London WC2N 5IE

CORRESPONDENTS WANTED

To widen the appeal of the International Golf Almanack in 1996, we would like to hear from writers and journalists in other countries, especially the USA, Canada and Australasia. Please write to the Editor at the address above.